REACHING
TOWARD *the*
HEIGHTS

DAILY MEDITATIONS ON
GOD'S WORD & HIS LOVE

RICHARD
WURMBRAND

Living Sacrifice Book Company
Bartlesville, OK 74005

Reaching Toward the Heights

Living Sacrifice Book Company,
A division of The Voice of the Martyrs
P.O. Box 2273
Bartlesville, OK 74005-2273

Cover, design, and production by Genesis Group
Printed in the United States of America

Unless otherwise indicated, Scripture references are from the New King James version, © 1979, 1980, 1982 by Thomas Nelson Inc., Publishers, Nashville, Tennessee.

Scripture references marked KJV are from the King James version.

Library of Congress Cataloging in Publication Data

Wurmbrand, Richard.
    Reaching toward the heights.

1. Devotional calendars.   I. Title
BV481 1.W87   242.2   77-4488

ISBN 978-0-88264-048-8

To Mihai and Judith
and their little
Amalia and Alex

JANUARY 1

"Teach us to number our days."
PSALM 90:12

*A*n American urged a friend of his who had just arrived in this country from Thailand, "Quick, let's run to catch this bus!" Once inside, the happy American said, "We have gained three minutes." The Thai asked, "What do you intend to do with them?"

Men in advanced Western countries have no answer to this question. Our generation has forgotten how to walk. It knows only how to run and to drive.

Jesus never ran; He only walked. There were chariots, horses, and camels in His day but we don't read that He used them. It is recorded only once that He rode, and then on an animal that advances at an even slower pace than a human's walk.

We do well to save minutes. Every minute is a jewel, but we often realize its value too late. The story is told about a man who walked in the dark along the shore of a river. He stumbled on a small bag containing stones, which he picked up. As a pastime, he amused himself by throwing a stone in the river every once in awhile. He liked to hear the *plitch-plitch* in the water. When he arrived home, only two stones were left in the bag. He saw that they were diamonds.

We run to save minutes and squander what we have saved in unworthy activities, conversation, and amusements. A cashier is answerable for every cent that has passed through his hands. A man who has lived seventy years will answer before God for thirty-seven million minutes.

JANUARY 2

"God is love."

1 JOHN 4:8

A Soviet Christian released from prison wrote the following in a letter:

> My outward appearance is not attractive. In the slave labor camp, I worked beneath the earth. I had an accident that made me a hunchback. Once a boy stared at me and then asked, "Uncle, what do you have on your back?" I was sure that some mockery would follow, but still I answered, "A hunchback."
>
> "No," said the child. "God is love and gives no one deformities. You do not have a hunchback but a box below your shoulders. In this box, angel wings are hidden. One day the box will open and you will fly to heaven with these wings." I began to cry for joy. Even now, I write and cry.

Every man has some kind of "hunchback," some physical, mental, or spiritual handicap, something that makes him different from everyone else. Things appear this way only if we look at them from the perspective of our limited earthly life. Here we "know in part" (1 Corinthians 13:12). And because of this, our lives and sufferings often seem meaningless.

God has allowed one person to have a hunchback, another sickness, or poverty, or a prison term, or bereavement, or some other sorrow. But we will not accept human standards that categorize such things as catastrophes. We will apply to them the standard of this Spirit-filled Soviet child and see in our sorrows boxes that hide angel wings, with which we are meant to fly to heaven.

JANUARY 3

*"But the LORD is in His holy temple. Let all
the earth keep silence before Him."*
HABAKKUK 2:20

*T*wo thousand years ago an Athenian statesman named Phocion waited wearily while his barber gave to the customer he was shaving a summary of the current Athenian political situation. At last the barber turned to Phocion and said, "How would you like to have your beard trimmed?" Phocion replied, "In silence." This simple answer often is quoted in the great literature of the world.

We are victims of a plot against silence, without which no spiritual life is possible. We are subjected daily to the noise of cars, trains, planes, radio, TV, vacuum cleaners, dishwashers, fans—not to mention the chatter and clatter of children and much useless speech of adults.

I have known Christians who have spent years in solitary confinement in complete silence. When they once again heard humans speak, they wondered that so much of their speech lacked content.

If you wish to reach God, create some silence around you. Switch off the many intruders on silence. Enter your closet, or teach your loved ones to be quiet at certain hours.

But silence is not altogether silent. All the screams of men in pain, all the weeping of sufferers, all the cries of real joy, the most earnest discussions, a multitude of sermons, and scientific truth are embedded in the silence that surrounds you. Above these you will hear the voice of God. You will become illuminated if you will listen, as did Jesus when He spent whole nights in prayer on silent mountains.

*"The angel said to [Mary], 'Rejoice, highly favored one,
the Lord is with you; blessed are you among women!'"*
LUKE 1:28

*I*n a Communist country, a young prisoner was taken from his cell to court. When he returned, his face shone. The other prisoners asked how it went in court. He answered, "As on the day of Mary's annunciation. What a beautiful day! A pure virgin alone in meditation. At once a radiant angel appeared before her. He tells her that she, a creature, will have the Creator as a babe in her arms; that she, a creature, will wash her Creator. She will wash the One who later will cleanse millions of men of their sins. She, a creature, will teach her Creator to walk. She will teach the eternal Word of God to speak. He will be the sun and joy of her house.

"There will be a few difficult moments. She will have to stand weeping at the foot of a cross where her Son—God's Son—will die for our salvation, but this will pass. He will be resurrected and will go to heaven, and surely He will take His mother to be with Him. And it will be joy again, without end."

The prisoners thanked him for the nice little sermon, but they insisted, "We asked you something else. How was it in court?"

He repeated, "I told you already. It was like the day of Mary's annunciation. The judges told me that I am sentenced to death. Is it not beautiful? Gates of pearl, streets of gold, angels glorifying God, the communion of saints, and above all, rest on Jesus' bosom."

Every year of our life is a new step toward death. Let us make this step joyfully and hopefully. Jesus was resurrected. Those who believe in Him will be resurrected too.

J A N U A R Y   5

"The LORD opened the mouth of the donkey."
NUMBERS 22:28

*B*elieve the Bible. Some of its stories can be accepted by our reason only with difficulty, but there is no alternative. If we don't accept the difficult parts of the Bible, the only choice that remains is to accept the absurd.

Atheists scorn: the Bible says that a donkey could speak. But the Bible does not say this. Rather, it states, "The LORD opened the mouth of the donkey." Where there is an almighty God, He can cause a donkey to speak at any time.

Set aside belief in God for a moment. What remains? Unbelief says man evolved from the ape. This means that at a certain moment an animal, the ape, started to speak without the aid of a higher, more intelligent being than himself. No child learns to speak without being taught by an adult. How did the ape achieve what a child cannot?

You have to accept the fact that an animal spoke—either an animal unaided by anyone, as Darwinism teaches, or an animal whose mouth a wise and almighty God opened. It obviously is easier for reason to accept the latter alternative.

Think also about the inner truth of the first words an animal ever spoke: "What have I done to you, that you have struck me?" (Numbers 22:28). One day all those whom we have wronged will ask this question of us. What will we answer? Even if those we have struck were guilty, was it absolutely necessary to strike them three times as the false prophet Balaam struck the donkey? Would less than that not have been sufficient? Don't listen to those who quibble about the Bible, but rather ponder its words carefully.

J A N U A R Y   6

*"If we sin willfully after we have received the knowledge of
the truth, there no longer remains a sacrifice for sins."*
HEBREWS 10:26

*A*n old Christian legend says that when God announced to
His angels His purpose in creating man in His image,
Lucifer, who had not yet fallen from heaven, cried, "Surely He will
give them no power to disobey Him." The Son answered him, "Power
to fall is power to rise." The devil then willfully decided to fall, taking others with him. His expectation that he would rise again was
never fulfilled because he had fallen purposely.

In the story where the sinful woman washed Jesus' feet with her
tears, Lucifer began to understand how power to fall is connected
with power to rise. He understood the profoundness of the words
of the Lord, "To whom little is forgiven, the same loves little," and,
"Her sins, which are many, are forgiven, for she loved much" (Luke
7:47).

So the devil thought that if he could check the power to fall, he
might check the power to rise. Therefore he tried to impose the
Mosaic law upon the first Christians. Through this teaching he
fooled the Galatians (Galatians 3:1) and many others. He also tries
to subject today's Christians to ordinances such as "Do not touch,
do not taste, do not handle" (Colossians 2:21), and plays upon our
fears.

But we have the word, "Stand fast therefore in the liberty by
which Christ has made us free" (Galatians 5:1). We will not continue
in sin that grace may abound (Romans 6:1). Sin will never again be
the content of our lives. But neither will we despair if we do sin.
Peter could strengthen his brethren because he was converted after
having fallen into grievous sin (Luke 22:32).

"The sons of God saw the daughters of men,
that they were beautiful."
GENESIS 6:2

A Jewish book of old, *Sepher Ierahmeel*, tells the following story about the Old Testament Joseph. A multitude of high-ranking Egyptian women went to the house of Potiphar, to see the handsomeness of his Hebrew servant. Lady Potiphar offered every guest an apple and a knife with which to peel it. When Joseph entered to serve them, they were all so captivated by his appearance that they accidentally cut themselves. Then Lady Potiphar told them, "You have seen him for a minute and you are charmed. Now you understand why I, who see him continually, burn with passion."

Lady Potiphar might have been beautiful, too, but Joseph was holy and refused to sin. And we are to follow his example. But if anyone sins in this regard, let us not condemn him or her too harshly. Instead, let us be charitable toward those who yield to human weakness, understanding that sex is the most powerful drive in our nature. It is written, "These things I write to you, so that you may not sin. And if anyone sins, we have an Advocate with the Father, Jesus Christ the righteous" (1 John 2:1).

And let us not despair ourselves when we are tempted, but let us look to God for strength to resist. For the Bible tells us, "No temptation has overtaken you except such as is common to man; but God is faithful, who will not allow you to be tempted beyond what you are able, but with the temptation will also make the way of escape, that you may be able to bear it" (1 Corinthians 10:13). Indeed, "the Lord knows how to deliver the godly out of temptations" (2 Peter 2:9).

Because this temptation is powerful, victory over it and refusal to sin in sexual matters is glorious.

JANUARY 8

"Some seed fell by the wayside; and the birds came and devoured them."

MATTHEW 13:4

*H*ow is it that some men hear the Word of God gladly, while others allow the birds—that is, wicked spirits—to devour this good seed?

The Old Testament Joseph was told a dream by Pharaoh's baker with whom he was in prison: "There were three white baskets on my head. In the uppermost basket were all kinds of baked goods for Pharaoh, and the birds ate them out of the basket on my head" (Genesis 40:16,17). Joseph interpreted the dream to mean that the baker would be hanged on a tree.

The renowned rabbi of Dubna was asked how Joseph could have known this. He answered, "A painter once painted a man with a basket of bread on his head. Birds came to eat from the picture, believing that it was real bread. A man said, 'What a good painter! How natural he made the bread look!' He was not a good painter. He did not make the man look natural enough to frighten the birds, or they would not have come. Likewise, Joseph understood that if the birds dared come to the baker, then he must be a dead man."

The wicked spirits cannot take away the seeds of the Word of God from a living Christian, but only from one who looks rather like a scarecrow. Scarecrows don't scare spirits. Be sure your faith is a living faith.

J A N U A R Y   9

*"Ask for the old paths, where the good way is,
and walk in it."*
JEREMIAH 6:16

A hunter shouted to his dog, "Nero, seek!" Nero lifted his eyes toward his master and answered, "I lost nothing."

What have Christians lost that they must seek so much? Some seek new cults and delve into the occult. But the old way waits for them. The religion that saved righteous Abel, King David, Mary Magdalene, and Peter will hold good for us, too. It is not true that Christianity has been practiced and found insufficient. We did not practice it. We will never find a better means of salvation than the blood of Christ, which was shed for us, nor will we find a better teaching than His teaching of love.

A bored tourist walking through the art galleries of the Louvre told a guard, "I find nothing exceptional in these pictures." The guard answered, "These paintings are not judged by us. We are judged by them."

Christianity has long since been proven true and stands independent of human opinions. The cross, reaching from earth to heaven, is its standard and is the criterion by which all religions, all isms, all philosophies and philosophers, all purveyors of truth are measured. Whether we see the beauty of Christianity and follow its precepts and its Founder, or stray after the foolish inventions of corrupt men—as the founders of strange cults are referred to in the Bible (Deuteronomy 13:13)—we cannot escape being measured and judged.

Let us choose wisely—for eternity.

J A N U A R Y   1 0

*T*here are two ways of looking at a tomb. Peter and John came on Easter morning to the tomb of their Master, found it empty, and saw in it the linen in which Jesus had been wrapped. Mary Magdalene also looked into the empty tomb, but she saw angels where the body of Jesus had lain. Some today see only the crumbling of Christian civilization, while others look beyond the dreadful headlines and see angels at work preparing the blessed kingdom of God.

How does a man get to see angels, to sense their presence? The apostles had been very active in the service of the Lord. Mary had sat quietly at the feet of Jesus and heard His word (Luke 10:39), which no doubt began with Moses and all the prophets. She probably heard from His lips the stories of many saints and martyrs for the faith and had become familiar with them.

A church that excludes from its teaching the example of saints and martyrs misses a vital dimension. Read "Moses and all the prophets" (Luke 24:27), remembering that "all these things... were written for our admonition, on whom the ends of the ages have come" (1 Corinthians 10:11). And then keep in touch with the living sufferers for Christ. Your eyes will be opened.

JANUARY 11

"Judge not, and you shall not be judged."
LUKE 6:37

*T*wo friends took a stroll along the shore of a river. One slipped and fell into the water. He began to cry, "Help! help! I can't swim." His friend answered, "You don't have to shout like that. I don't know how to swim either, but I don't make as much noise about it as you do."

We sometimes judge men harshly for their ill temper, their incivility. We behave otherwise, but can it be that we do not pass through their deep waters?

The Lord called certain men fools (Luke 11:40). A Pharisee had invited Him to dine with him. It is not recorded that the Pharisee had uttered one provocative word; he had only marveled silently that Jesus did not wash His hands before the meal. We would have wondered, too. Without any apparent provocation, Jesus insults the host and all his friends, calling them "fools." A lawyer who also was a guest at this dinner tried to quiet Jesus. The Lord then turned on him and all his companions saying, "Woe to you also, lawyers!" (Luke 11:37–52). Few hosts would tolerate such behavior today.

We judge harshly our unmannered acquaintances. We might have criticized Jesus, too. Have we passed through His deep sorrow to see the essential message of salvation rejected by His own people because of blind leaders who led them astray? Until you have walked a mile in another's shoes, don't judge him.

J A N U A R Y   1 2

"[Christ Jesus] made Himself of no reputation."
PHILIPPIANS 2:7

A king sought God and could not find Him. One night he heard someone walking with heavy boots on the roof of the palace. Going up to see who it was, he found his most intimate friend, who shared his spiritual concern. The king asked him, "What are you doing on the roof?"

"I seek camels."

"What foolishness to seek camels on the roof of a palace," exclaimed the king, to which the friend answered, "What foolishness to seek God while sitting on a throne."

God gives to everyone a task, whether one be a king, or wealthy business manager, or middle-class housewife, or low-paid worker. We should fulfill this task humbly, with joy and love, but without becoming attached to any outward situation. Positions of fame, of honor, and of riches often bind us, making every search for God fruitless. A Christian can be a king only on the condition that he consider himself a servant of his people.

Social prestige and material possessions are easily lost. The Lord long ago warned, "Do not lay up for yourselves treasures on earth, where moth and rust destroy and where thieves break in and steal; but lay up for yourselves treasures in heaven, where neither moth nor rust destroys and where thieves do not break in and steal. For where your treasure is, there your heart will be also" (Matthew 6:19–21).

Jesus, who had the highest position, "made Himself of no reputation, taking the form of a servant...He humbled Himself" (Philippians 2:7,8). Let us follow in His footsteps. Otherwise all our endeavors to come nearer to God will be in vain.

J A N U A R Y   1 3

*"In the beginning God created the
heavens and the earth."*

GENESIS 1:1

*A*n atheist shoemaker told his son that nature exists by itself, to which his son replied, "Then it is easier to have the whole of nature than a pair of shoes. For these you have to work hard." If the whole of nature is the random result of the evolution of matter, why don't atheists leave to nature the production of godless books? Why do they work with great diligence to create them? Even an atheistic book is proof that behind every organized thing there exists an intelligent design.

Acknowledge the Creator, adore Him, and don't waste time in useless speculations. Luther, when asked what God did before He created the world, answered, "He sat in the forest and cut rods with which to beat those who asked foolish questions."

There exists a better answer than this witty one. The Lord tells what the Father did before creation. Before the foundation of the world, He loved the Son (see John 17:24). To love Jesus is a full-time job. This job can fill God's eternity. The Father also did something else. Before the foundation of the world, He prepared the kingdom for those who feed the hungry, who satisfy the thirsty, who take in strangers, who clothe the naked, and who visit the sick as well as the prisoners (see Matthew 25:34–36). Acknowledge God as Creator, and do these things, just as Jesus "went about doing good" (Acts 10:38).

*"The L*ORD *gave, and the L*ORD *has taken away;*
*blessed be the name of the L*ORD*."*
JOB 1:21

*T*he story is told of an angel who appeared to a mother watching at the cradle of her babe and then asked for her child. She cried, "Death, I won't give him!" The angel smiled and said, "My name is not death, but life. I offer you someone else in exchange." He showed her a fair boy. She refused. He showed her a powerful young man. She refused again. He showed a grown-up industrious man. She repeated, "No, no!" to all the proposals. "I exchange him for no one. I wish to keep my little child."

The angel departed. Time passed, and she had to lose the child. He was exchanged for a boy. She lost the boy. He was exchanged for a young man, and so on.

Why be afraid of death? We don't lose at death what we don't lose every day. Day by day our loved ones change from one stage of life to another. What we call death is one of these many changes. The bud is no more. It has become a flower. The caterpillar is no more. It has become a butterfly. The sun may have set for you, but it gives its light somewhere else.

Whenever the angel has taken your beloved, acquiesce with humility to God's doings.

JANUARY 15

"Your enemies...shall...flee before you."
DEUTERONOMY 28:7

A Christian teacher took a walk with one of his disciples through the forest. The disciple walked a few steps ahead of the master on a narrow trail. A hare fled from him. The master asked, "Why did the hare flee?"

"Because he feared me," the disciple said.

"No," replied the master, "but because you have murderous instincts in you."

Every warrior is happy when his enemies flee before him, but much more blessed is the man to whom his fiercest enemies can come with confidence, knowing beforehand that they will be received with love.

At the end of World War II, the Soviet army occupied Romania. Much of the German army was taken prisoner. Every German soldier could be shot at sight by anyone. One evening while a group of prisoners was being transported from one place to another, two of them profited from darkness and escaped. With their uniforms on, their lives were in danger. Seeing a building with an inscription "Evangelical Lutheran Chapel," they recalled that Lutherans of Romania were mostly of German background, so they entered the precinct.

The pastor who encountered them extended a welcome, saying, "I am Jewish and Christian. My family has been killed by Germans. I have learned from Christ love and forgiveness. I don't hold you accountable for what the German troops have done to the Jews. You men are in deadly danger. You have taken refuge in our church. You are our honored guests."

One of the Germans said, "If you are a believer, we know we are safe." They had found a haven of refuge.

"When we were enemies we were reconciled to God by the death of His Son" (Romans 5:10). Let us now be men from whom enemies should have no reason to flee.

19

JANUARY 16

"We love Him because He first loved us."
1 JOHN 4:19

I was told the following story:

When the Soviet army invaded Eastern Europe, a Russian officer was lodged in the house of a painter who liked his expressive face and used him as his model for a painting. While sitting for the artist, the model looked at a picture of the crucified Jesus and asked what it was. The painter answered briefly, but the Russian officer insisted: "If He was good and wished the salvation of all for eternity, men would surely have taken Him down from the cross in time and cured His wounds."

"Please, don't disturb me in my painting," came the reply. "No, He was not freed. He died on the cross. This is what He was meant to do. He paid the price for our sins. But let us continue our business."

The Russian officer would not be quieted. "How aglow you must be in your love for someone who made such a sacrifice for you." The painter put down his brush. He had many times painted Jesus crucified, but he realized now that it had been done without love aglow. The unbeliever who was his model taught him how he must love Christ.

"On the likeness of the throne was a likeness with the appearance of a man high above it."
EZEKIEL 1:26

*T*he verse that follows the above is, "From the appearance of His waist and upward I saw, as it were, the color of amber with the appearance of fire all around within it; and from the appearance of His waist and downward I saw, as it were, the appearance of fire with brightness all around."

Rashi, the most authoritative rabbinic commentator of the Scriptures, observes, "One is not allowed to reflect on this verse." Why not? We can easily guess. It is because the description indicates clearly that the God whom Ezekiel saw in his vision had the body of a glorified man. It confirms the Christian doctrine of the incarnation of God's Son in the man Jesus.

Commenting on Zechariah's words, "They will look on Me whom they have pierced" (Zechariah 12:10), Rashi writes, "Though the verse applies to the king Messiah, we should rather apply it to king Ezechiah, so as not to allow the Christians to gain."

We can understand the Jewish revulsion against nominal Christianity guilty of the blood of millions of innocents, but still the Christian teaching about the Messiah is true and fulfills the ancient Jewish prophecies. Let us present these prophecies to the Jews and call them lovingly to Christ.

JANUARY 18

*"When he saw that the wind was boisterous,
he was afraid."*
MATTHEW 14:30

A miracle had taken place. At the Lord's command, Peter was able to walk on the water, which is contrary to the laws of nature. But while Peter walked on the water, why was he afraid of the wind because it was boisterous? Could Christ perform such a miracle only when the weather was calm?

On another occasion the disciples were fearful in a great storm, when the waves beat into their ship, so "that it was already filling" (Mark 4:37). Heeding their cries of distress, Jesus made the winds cease and calmed the sea. Now the disciples were happy. But if a ship is full of water, it sinks whether the sea is calm or is agitated by tempest.

The miracle was not that the Lord rebuked the sea. The wonder is that the ship of Jesus has navigated for two thousand years, in good times and bad, though it is full of heresies, schisms, and sins. It still navigates though full of water, when it should have sunk long since according to the laws of hydrodynamics.

You may have passed through many crushing difficulties in life. Don't be afraid when one more is added. It is through a miracle that you have made it until now.

The stone that covered the tomb of Jesus was rolled away by an angel, "for it was very great" (Mark 16:4, KJV). Even though your burden has become greater than ever before, God might send an angel to help you.

The admonition "Do not fear" occurs in the Bible 366 times, once for every day of the year—and an extra for leap year.

"One of the criminals who were hanged... said to Jesus, 'Lord, remember me when You come into Your kingdom.' And Jesus said to him, 'Assuredly, I say to you, today you will be with Me in Paradise.'"
LUKE 23:39,42,43

*B*efore his death, Lenin told a priest, "I have erred. No doubt many oppressed had to be freed, but our method has provoked other oppressions and horrible massacres. My mortal grief is to be immersed in an ocean of blood from innumerable victims. It is too late to turn back, but to save Russia we would have needed ten St. Francis of Assisi."

Lenin had come under Christian influence. He had met the Orthodox priest Gapon, later hanged by the Communists. *Nauka I Religia,* the atheist magazine of the Soviet Union, published the following in December 1973:

> Lenin showed great interest in the writings of Christian sectarians which a fellow-Communist had gathered, especially in the old manuscripts. He studied them thoroughly ...He was especially interested in their philosophical writings. Once after thoroughly reading their manuscripts he said, "How interesting! This was created by simple people. Whole books!"

The Communist magazine says this much. Who knows how much more is behind the story? Perhaps a deathbed conversion. Heaven is a place of surprises. We might be surprised to find there the converted mass-slaughterer of Christians—Vladimir Lenin.

You may be a wicked person. You may be reading this at the end of your life. You can yet go to paradise.

JANUARY 20

"A righteous man regards the life of his animal."
PROVERBS 12:10

We often see horses jumping in races and in circuses, in pictures if not in reality. Now, the foot bones of the horse are weak. This domesticated animal is not made for jumping. He is taught to perform only by being beaten severely. More recently, horses are being subjected to electric shock treatments: circus trainers have mini-electrical batteries in their whips. Horses also are struck on the legs with iron bars to teach them to jump over fences. The pain makes them raise their legs high.

Don't support or cheer such exploitation; rather, pity the animal.

I do not personally admire the pyramids. Moses did not find them worth even a brief mention. He thought about the misery of the slaves who erected them.

In Communist jails, prisoners are very hungry. One slice of bread a week is a longed-for luxury. Yet Christians there often save some to feed the pigeons and swallows that come confidently to the sills of windows with iron bars. They know how to distinguish the windows of cells containing Christians. Here they are not disappointed.

The Bible has much to say regarding the care of animals and forbids cruelty and indifference to helpless beasts (Deuteronomy 22:4). Jesus spoke about His love for the birds and His concern about animals (Luke 14:5). He did not find it degrading to be compared to a lamb, or a lion, or a hen with chicks.

Let us emulate Him in all things. As we show loving concern for our fellow men, let us not forget to be kind to animals, too.

JANUARY 21

"Bless and do not curse."
ROMANS 12:14

*M*rs. Gerda Forster, while baby-sitting for a neighbor, suffered the misfortune of having the baby fall out of her hands. The infant was injured on the edge of a large vase, with resultant brain damage. It was paralyzed for life.

The mother cursed Mrs. Forster that her fingers might rot. Mr. Forster offered to pay large compensatory damages. The mother refused and repeated the curse: may her fingers rot.

Mrs. Forster suddenly started to have great pain in her fingers. The fingertips became first white, then blue. It was a case of necrosis, the malady known as "morbus Raynaud." Psychic trauma can produce it, usually in women already possessing a precarious nervous constitution. The fingers had to be amputated.

When I was in solitary confinement, a neighbor tapped out his story in Morse code through the wall: "When I was six, I beat a schoolmate only because he was Jewish. He cursed me that my mother should not be able to see me when she was on her deathbed. Fifty years have passed since. I had just received the news that my mother was dying and intended to go to her deathbed when I was arrested." A curse had been accomplished. I know of other such cases.

I believe some curses are fulfilled. But so are blessings. So bless, don't curse.

> *"The living know that they will die…"*
> ECCLESIASTES 9:5

*T*he surest business is that of the mortuary, while other trades may come and go. You might never enter a jeweler's shop or a theater, but you will have to die. How will you meet death?

Julius Caesar died a disillusioned man. His foster son was among his murderers. The great Caesar's last words were, "Brutus, you too?"

Goethe said, "More light, more light!" He had not sought it before.

Oscar Wilde's last request was, "Please, champagne," and he added, "I die as I lived, above my means."

Napoleon died in delirium with the cry, "*Mon Dieu*, the French nation, at the head of the army!"

The renowned arithmetician Lagny passed thirty-six hours in silence on his deathbed. He did not react when his beloved spoke to him. But when an acquaintance asked, "Do you still know how much sixty-seven to the second power is?" the mathematician answered smiling, "Four thousand four hundred eighty-nine" and died.

Carlyle said, "So this is death? It is good."

The German poet Heine's last words were, "Flowers, flowers. How beautiful is nature!" He had no thought about the Creator.

The French writer Rabelais said before dying, "Let the curtain fall. The comedy is finished."

Jesus' last words were, "Father, into Your hands I commit My spirit" (Luke 23:46). When in prison, I decided that if I were conscious in the moment of my death my last words would be "Jesus and Binzea" (the name by which I call my wife). Christians know the reason for death and have the assurance that love waits for them on the other side.

"Be doers of the word, and not hearers only."
JAMES 1:22

A taxidermist once caught a bird. When he lifted his knife to kill her, she begged, "Spare my life. I have little ones. In exchange I will give you three pieces of advice, very simple, but very useful." The taxidermist wondered at a bird that could speak human language and promised her freedom if the advice was good.

The bird gave the following counsel: "First, never believe anything stupid, no matter who it is who speaks to you. Second, never regret a good thing you have done. Third, never reach for something unattainable."

The taxidermist saw the wisdom of this advice and let the bird go. The bird flew to the first branch and mocked him, "You idiot, why did you let me go? I have in my belly a diamond. Had you ripped me open, you would have been rich the rest of your life."

The taxidermist, hearing this, regretted having released her and began to climb the tree to retrieve her. But when he reached the first branch, she was already on the second, and when he was on the second, she was on the third. In the end, he lost his footing, fell from the tree, and broke both his legs.

While he lay groaning under the tree, the bird told him, "You had accepted my three pieces of advice and praised them for being wise. Why did you not regard them for at least five minutes? I told you not to believe anything stupid, no matter who said it. How come you believed that a bird had a diamond in her belly? I told you never to regret a good deed. Why did you regret having freed me? I told you not to reach for the unattainable. Did you not know that you cannot catch a bird with your bare hands? You men have invented the radio and can hear in one country speeches from another, but you have not yet discovered an apparatus to enable you to hear with your ears what your own mouths speak, or to believe in your heart what your mind acknowledges as just."

You accept the Bible as the Word of God. Don't be only a hearer or a reader, but also a doer and a fulfiller.

JANUARY 24

"The LORD God took the man and put him in the garden of Eden."
GENESIS 2:15

*I*t is more pleasant to know that our forefathers lived in a paradise than in a zoo, as Darwin asserts.

"The LORD God formed man of the dust of the ground" (Genesis 2:7). Science confirms the fact that our bodies are made of the same elements of which the earth is constituted.

Sepher Ierahmeel, an ancient Jewish book, embellishes the biblical account: "God sent the archangel Gabriel to bring Him clay out of which He would make man, but the earth refused to give it up, knowing that it would be cursed because of man's disobedience." There was good reason for the refusal. Think only of the ravaging of the earth from bombing, or from defoliation, or from pollution. But in the end, Gabriel succeeded in convincing the earth. Man was made.

"God created man in His own image" (Genesis 1:27). Modern technology recreates man in the image of machines, artificial, standardized, materialistic, programmed, always in haste. Modern mass media recreate him after their image, reducing him to a low level, filling him with thoughts of violence and lust. Modern universities induce man to repeat the sin of the first couple and to prefer the tree of knowledge to the tree of life. Abstract theories and ideologies take the place of life.

George Fox, founder of the Quakers, wished to return to the image of God, to "experience God, . . . pass beyond the flaming sword, re-enter paradise and seek the state of Adam before his fall."

Christ calls us all to this adventure. He, being God, took the nature of man that we might come back to the image of God.

J A N U A R Y   2 5

"A servant of the Lord must not quarrel..."
2 TIMOTHY 2:24

Soshi walked along the shores of a river with a friend. Soshi said, "How well fish feel in water."

The friend replied, "You are not a fish. How do you know that fish feel well?"

Soshi said, "You are not me. How do you know that I do not know that fish feel well in water?"

We fall out with one another through questioning or contesting someone else's experiences which are outside our control.

Two friends, both peasants, sat on a log one evening and chatted. The one said, "I would like to have a meadow as big as the sky above our heads."

The other said, "I would like to have as many sheep as the stars that we see."

The first one asked, "Where would you pasture such a multitude of sheep?"

"No problem," replied the other. "They will graze on your huge pasture."

The first one protested, "I will not allow your sheep on my field."

The one had no pasture, the other no sheep, but they quarreled about what they did not have. Don't we quarrel often about things we don't know?

Having the same love, let us be of one accord and of one mind. The other's opinion or attitude might be more worthy of esteem than yours. His experience of today which you consider strange might be yours tomorrow.

The Lord wished us to be one, as He and the Father are one.

*"Your servant Joab commanded me, and he put all
these words in the mouth of your maidservant."*
2 SAMUEL 14:19

I dreamed one night that I attended a party at which Solzhenitsyn, the renowned Russian writer and Nobel prize winner, read
aloud from his book, *Gulag Archipelago*. I wept bitterly about all the
suffering he described.

Solzhenitsyn asked me, "Do you know any remedy against
these atrocities?"

I answered, "I have known many criminals. Everyone had a
weak point. Some passionately loved a wife, a child; others had
great tenderness for a dog."

Svetlana, Stalin's daughter, tells how she obtained from her father
the release of a prisoner. She could have obtained more than that.
Kings of old took a rival's son as hostage, knowing the rival would
not attack as long as the beloved was held captive. There are offenders who would not commit a felony if you threatened to kill
their dog. Hardened murderers in prison gave up their only slice of
bread to feed the swallows.

The woman who has stolen your husband might dearly love
her mother, through whom you might influence her to give up your
husband.

Joab, David's general, knew that the king wished clemency to
rule in the country. He appealed to this through a woman whom he
used to tell David an invented story about a son of hers, a murderer
who should be pardoned. When David granted the petition as expected, she appealed to his desire for consistency and asked clemency for Absalom his son, who had offended greatly.

Make the man who wrongs you or society an object of your
loving study. Seek an avenue of access to his heart. The natural love
of children for parents can be used to influence them toward believing. Proceed in the same manner with other men. The emperor
Constantine was influenced by his Christian mother, St. Helen, to
favor the persecuted church of the Roman Empire and eventually to
give the Christians liberty.

> *"If you forgive men their trespasses, your heavenly Father will also forgive you."*
> MATTHEW 6:14

I received the following letter from Latin America:

> I write from a guerrilla camp in Peru. I lie awake. Sleep has fled from me. Recently I looked for some radio program to cheer me up, being sad and afraid. The programs of my comrades had become empty to me. They were repetitious and filled with hate. Then I came across your program called "The Gospel in Marxist Language." In it we were told that Jesus, the great teacher, spoke of pardoning one's enemies. That passage drove itself into the deepest part of my being. Suddenly, I experienced peace and I wept as a child. I don't understand what has happened. I had hated the rich. My parents had been victims of an exploiting landowner, but for some reason, I don't hate any more. I can't explain it. Is it possible for me not to hate?
>
> That was the only time I heard your program. How happy I have become, Don Ricardo. Now I shall not miss a single one of your programs. I want to read the Book of books.

This man left the guerillas and joined a church. Two years later he returned to the former comrades, hoping to tell them about Christ. We have not heard from him since. It is probable that he was martyred by the Communists.

Jesus healed this soul at once of the most poisonous sentiment —hatred. Has someone wronged you? Forgive. Receive forgiveness from God. Only then will you have inner freedom.

> *"Therefore do not worry about tomorrow, for*
> *tomorrow will worry about its own things."*
> MATTHEW 6:34

A Scotsman, traveling on a slow train from Glasgow to London, bought a ticket only to the first station; there he bought a ticket to the second, and so forth. He was asked why. His answer was, "I might have a heart attack while traveling and never reach London. In that case, I would have saved on my fare."

What about saving on worry and apprehension? Why worry about things far away? Perhaps those fears will prove unfounded. Perhaps you will die before arriving at that critical moment. Buy a ticket for one station at a time.

Jesus is the head of His church. Being the head, He has the monopoly on headaches. For you to have a headache because of worry is a sin. You thereby usurp the role of the head, which belongs to Jesus alone.

Luther had a habit of going to the window in the evening and saying, "God, is it my world or Yours? Is it my church or Yours? If they are Your world and Your church, please take care of them. I am tired. I am going to bed. Good night, my God."

Take this attitude. The Talmud says, "When the sun has set, the day is clean." When the evening comes, leave all the past day's problems and failures with Jesus. Take no thought of tomorrow. Sleep well. Tomorrow's worries might never reach you. They may even vanish overnight. Have a good day and a good night without worrying.

JANUARY 29

*I*n *Gulistan* (the Garden of Roses), by the renowned mystic Persian writer Muslih al-Din Saadi, there exists the story about Madshnun and his beloved girlfriend Leila. It was an unhappy love, because the father of Leila had given the daughter to another man. Madshnun, mad with love (his very name means "madman"), fled to the wilderness to live with the beasts, without purpose, without hope.

The king of the country had him brought to his palace and reproached him for his folly, to which Madshnun answered, "Should you know how beautiful Leila is, you would understand me." The king gave the order that Leila be brought before him.

She was a Bedouin woman like anyone else, even uglier, burned by the sun, frail because of poverty. The meanest slave in his harem was surely more beautiful than she. He could not understand why she should be so much beloved. Madshnun guessed the king's thought and said to him, "You cannot see Leila's beauty, nor can anyone else. This beauty is revealed only to those who look through the window of Madshnun's eyes. Love and beauty are two riddles in one. Only the one who has divined the first, can understand the second."

God so loved the sinning soul that He gave His Son. "Because He first loved us," we love Him (1 John 4:19). His love makes Him see beauty and value in men whom no one else would esteem. Let us believe in the good taste of love. He knows why He has chosen us. We rejoice in His love.

JANUARY 30

"The LORD had said to Abram:
'Get out of your country.'"
GENESIS 12:1

*I*n Hebrew the word given by God to Abram is *Leh leha*, which means, literally translated, "Go for your own benefit" or "for thyself."

Rabbi Nachum Chernobler Zatzal explained the verse as follows: Abram, our forefather in faith, was a wellspring of loving-kindness and hospitality. We read in Genesis 18:1 that, though he had just undergone a painful operation, "he was sitting in the tent door in the heat of the day" that, God forbid, no traveler should pass by without being his guest.

But his hospitality had not been flawless in the beginning because he had never been a wanderer himself. Abram had to have firsthand experience of a traveler's hardship to become perfect in hospitality.

Peter had to pass through the experience of denying Christ. The Lord had told him, "When you have returned to Me [after such a falling into sin], strengthen your brethren" (Luke 22:32). You will be able to do so because you will have passed through the bitterness of cowardice yourself.

Godhead had known the whole of human life as seen from the perspective of deity. But the Father told the Son *Leh leha*—"Go for Your own benefit as future judge of mankind and participate in their sorrows and joys. Lead a human life Yourself. Godhead will thus be enriched by human experience. You will know human life as it looks to humans." So He became a high priest "in all points tempted as we are, yet without sin." Now He can "sympathize with our weaknesses" (Hebrews 4:15).

Accept your experiences of life, the sweet and the bitter. They all prepare you to become more helpful to your fellow man.

JANUARY 31

"You shall love your neighbor."
MATTHEW 22:39

*T*hose who bring sunshine to the lives of others cannot keep it from themselves.

Jesus "went about doing good" (Acts 10:38). Therefore He could sing on the night He was betrayed (see Matthew 26:30).

Don't require a smile of people. If you see someone without a smile, give him yours. Multitudes followed Jesus. It was because He did not expect from them sympathy for His great sorrows. He comforted them in theirs.

Don't get angry at the man who acts in a manner that displeases you. He might have heard a different drummer. Everyone walks to the music he hears. Let him hear from you a more beautiful melody. It might change his pace.

At a party in my home Christians were discussing their friends. Some they considered good believers, others weak, still others unbelievers. An old missionary from India intervened: "Don't classify people. Our judgments might be wrong. As often as we speak, let us better propagate the love of Christ. This will gladden the strong believer, strengthen the weak one, and convert the unbeliever. So we will have done something positive. By categorizing men we are not helping them."

Spread sunshine among others instead of judging how much sunshine another has in his or her life.

FEBRUARY 1

"[Love] bears all things."
1 CORINTHIANS 13:7

*T*he Jewish people have a legend about Abraham, the father of the faithful.

One evening while in deep meditation, the patriarch was disturbed by a knock at the door. It was a drunkard who asked for hospitality. Abraham's first impulse was to drive him away and to continue his sweet communion with God. But then the thought occurred to him: "What would be the purpose of so much more meditation? I know already that God bears with sinners and that He makes the sun to shine over this drunkard and provides him with daily bread. Why should I refuse a man whom God accepts? I can bear with him. God bears with my sins, too." So the patriarch washed, served the drunkard some food, and prepared a bed for him.

Abraham had less spiritual light than we. Can we not follow his example?

Christians learned that a brother was in the act of committing adultery. They called Bishop Ammona to come with them and to convict the sinner on the spot, so the church would not be contaminated by his membership. However, when they arrived at the house, the adulterer quickly hid the woman in a big empty case in the room. The bishop was the only one who observed it. He sat on the upturned case and said to the brethren, "Seek." They did and found no one. Ammona told them, "May God forgive you for your suspicions and unseemly behavior." When they had left, he told the brother ensnared in sin, "Beware of the devil!" Then he left. Bishop Ammona could sympathize with his brother in his sin, remembering that he, too, belonged to the same category. He had tried to win him through kindness and understanding.

When Jesus was brought as a lamb to the slaughter, "He opened not His mouth" (Isaiah 53:7) to say that the sins for which He suffered were not His own. He bore our sins. Let us not only be saved from hell through this, but saved also from judging others. Let us bear everything, and above all, human failures and weaknesses.

36

FEBRUARY 2

*"The fruit of the Spirit is love . . .
Against such there is no law."*
GALATIANS 5:22,23

*S*t. Mechtild of Magdeburg once said, "Love has no virtues." Love has no fixed rules, no immutable principles of action. Augustine's renowned injunction was, "Love God and do as you please." Normally, the lover will fulfill the commandments of Scripture, but he is free in exceptional circumstances.

In the Nazi concentration camp of Auschwitz pregnant women were killed. A Christian woman doctor, herself a prisoner, performed primitive abortions on hundreds of other prisoners. Thus she saved their lives. It is true she killed the embryos, but without her intervention both the children and their mothers would have died.

A German lady had been taken prisoner by the Soviet army and sent to a slave labor camp in Siberia. Women were allowed to come back from there only if they were gravely sick or pregnant. She had left behind three children who had no one to care for them. Her husband was in British captivity. She asked a guard to impregnate her. Thus she was able to return to care for her children. When her husband returned, she explained to him what she had done. He agreed that it was the only recourse under the circumstances.

Missions to Communist and Muslim countries smuggle in Christian literature, using all kinds of strange tricks. Against love there is no law, though in normal circumstances love walks according to law.

"Go therefore and make disciples of all the nations."
MATTHEW 28:19

*M*ohammed's son-in-law Ali, who should have been his successor, was killed, as was Ali's son Husain. The Shiite Muslims, who are the closest to Christianity in their theology, have the following text in their sacred writings: "To weep for Husain is the sense of our life and of our soul. Otherwise we would be the most ungrateful beings. Even in Paradise we will mourn for Husain. It is impossible for a Shiite not to weep . . . The death of Husain prepared a way to paradise."

The Kerbela book considered holy by them says, "The death of Husain is our entrance into life. The love toward Ali consumes all sins, as fire consumes the dry wood." They also venerate Ali's wife, Fatima. They believe that she is "the incarnation of everything divine in female nature, the most noble ideal attained by human reason, the queen of paradise." They believe that the "unseen Iman," their religious leader in every generation, is an incarnation of Godhead.

The twelfth descendant of Ali, Mohamed ibn al-Hasan, who disappeared at the age of four, is considered to have been raptured to heaven, from which he will return at the end of time as Mahdi, universal Savior.

We find in Islam, as in many other erroneous religions, tenets which are vaguely akin to our Christian faith. Souls grope after the truth of which they have only a foreboding. But they don't have the light of Christ. Almost all Muslim states forbid Christian missionary work. Let us pray for the conversion of the Islamic world.

FEBRUARY 4

The American cancer specialist Eugene Pendergrass was the first to observe that in most cases cancer appears six to eighteen months after some tragedy in life, be it a bereavement, the disloyalty of a marriage partner, loss in business, etc. But if sorrow of soul can produce this sickness, then peace and hope of soul must be able to contribute greatly to the recovery of health. The cancerous cells can multiply, but the white blood cells can attack and destroy them. This depends much on our faith and determination.

Sometimes we are sick because subconsciously we wish to be sick in order to gain attention and the lovingkindness we miss. But it is wrong to wish only to be the object of love. Be its subject; love others. Those who harbor hatred, those who cannot forgive, are much more prone to cancer and other illnesses than those who forgive easily.

I was sick at one time with generalized tuberculosis of both lungs, backbone and bone tuberculosis, intestinal tuberculosis, jaundice, diabetes, and heart disease. I was in prison where the "medicine" consisted of hunger, lack of air, lack of sun, and beatings. But I was determined to live because I felt that I had a calling to fulfill. I prayed, and many others prayed for me. A general confession of all my past sins unburdened my soul. Thus God gave me the energy to overcome the sickness.

Some day you must die. It may be that your present sickness is God's means to take you home. Miraculous healings are the exception; otherwise they would not be miraculous. Still, believe in the miraculous. It is in the realm of the possible. And concur with it by having peaceful faith.

FEBRUARY 5

"Let every soul be subject to the governing authorities."
ROMANS 13:1

Of twenty-nine members of the Central Committee of the Communist Party which created the revolution in Russia, three were killed by their enemies, two committed suicide, and fifteen were executed by their own comrades. Stalin was disowned after his death. If these revolutionists who wanted to overthrow tyranny had known that the result of their rebellion would be death at the hand of their own comrades and the establishment of a tyranny directed not only against the enemies of the revolution but also against those who made it succeed, would they have started on their career as rebels against the existing powers?

Would Trotsky have become a revolutionist had he known beforehand that this revolution would finally bring Stalin to power? Stalin killed two of Trotsky's children plus many relatives, all his adherents, and in the end sent a henchman to finish Trotsky himself with an axe.

The Czarist regime, which had many injustices, would never have committed such crimes against revolutionists or the people.

Most revolutions have not been worth the fight. Revolutions are the worst of solutions. The Jewish state would not have been destroyed by the Romans in A.D. 71 if the people had listened to Jesus' advice: "I tell you not to resist an evil person. But whoever slaps you on your right cheek, turn the other to him also" (Matthew 5:39).

Let us make revolutionists and terrorists a matter of prayerful concern, asking that they may use their energies in the service of peaceful reforms.

FEBRUARY 6

"The serpent said to the woman, '...God knows that in the day you eat of it your eyes will be opened."
GENESIS 3:5

*I*t seems as if the purposes of God and those of Satan are the same. The Lord Jesus said to Saul of Tarsus, "I now send you [to the Gentiles] to open their eyes" (Acts 26:17,18). The devil promises the same thing. Still, the difference is great.

If the serpent opens your eyes, they will always be wide open. Those whose eyes God opens can close them as often as they like. They can close them to the sins of their brother, just as Shem and Japheth covered the nakedness of their father. This is what Christians do for every man.

On the other hand, those whose eyes the serpent has opened are wide open to all future dangers and troubles. They are open to the distractions of biblical intricacies and to all the problems that faith leaves unsolved.

Those who allow God to control what they see can close their eyes in faith in the midst of perils. Why should I worry? "He who keeps Israel shall neither slumber nor sleep" (Psalm 121:4).

The day is coming when we shall see "face to face" (1 Corinthians 13:12).

Refuse the devil as your eye doctor. Allow only God to take care of your vision.

> *"Not one of [the sparrows] falls to the ground
> apart from your Father's will."*
> MATTHEW 10:29

*T*he Chinese pastor Wang-Min-tao had risked his life under the Japanese occupation to maintain the purity of the gospel. Among other things, he refused to allow a picture of the Japanese emperor to hang in his church. He also refused this honor to a picture of Mao Tse-tung. His excuse was that he did not have a picture of Jesus Christ either.

In 1955 he was arrested for his refusal to compromise with the Communists. For two years he was subjected to extreme brainwashing techniques. Maddened by torture, he signed a confession enumerating his "imperialist" sins. He was released.

In freedom he had no peace. He went around muttering continually, "I am Peter; I am Judas," until one day he went to the Communists and told them that he recanted his former confession. For this, he and his wife were put in prison. From jail he wrote the biblical words: "Do not be anxious about me; I am of more value than many sparrows." He died in prison.

Once a prominent leader in Christianity, he had denied his faith. He had fallen. Sparrows don't fall from the tree without the Father's leave. Neither do Christians fall without His awareness.

Why should God allow us to fall in sin? Daniel says, "Some of those of understanding shall fall, to refine them, purify them, and make them white" (Daniel 11:35). Falls from which we return to the Lord are sources of humility, of light, of strength, and of comfort to others.

"All things work together for good to those who love God" (Romans 8:28). Augustine adds, "even their sins."

FEBRUARY 8

"It is easier for a camel to go through the eye of a needle than for a rich man to enter the kingdom of God."

LUKE 18:25

*C*ommunist China's former minister of foreign affairs, Chou En-Lai, once declared that he was much impressed by this verse, but the Communists criticize Jesus for allowing the rich young ruler to depart in peace. He should have arrested him and confiscated all his property.

The Communists believe that the expropriation of capitalist property creates an immediate paradise. Even some leftist clergymen in the West as well as the East have embraced this conviction.

Why should Jesus have taken riches from the young ruler? A man of means and a mean man sometimes are the same person. Whoever takes a rich man's means might also take his meanness, without which he might not have remained so rich in a starving world.

Taking the ruler's riches, Jesus also would have taken away the restlessness of his soul which made him to go from rabbi to rabbi asking for the way to life eternal.

Rich men must part with their riches at death if not before.

"My kingdom is not of this world," said Jesus (John 18:36). We are to gather our treasures in heaven, "where neither moth nor rust destroys and where thieves do not break in and steal" (Matthew 6:20).

FEBRUARY 9

*"The Lord God called to Adam and said to him,
'Where are you?'"*
GENESIS 3:9

A professor of homiletics (preaching) at a seminary asked his students to read this verse of Scripture. Most read the question as would a policeman who had just caught a robber about to break into a house. But a good preacher reads these words as if they were uttered by a brokenhearted father. The world would be less mysterious to us if we could realize that Adam was created by a sad God, sad because of the fall of Lucifer.

And now the new disappointment. Adam fell too. God lost a fellowship in which He had placed great hope.

Later God asked an even more tragic question of Cain: "Where is Abel your brother?" (Genesis 4:9).

Where is the good preacher who can read these words as expressing all of God's sadness?

These questions must be read so that the listener can overcome the fear that made Adam hide himself, naked and sinful, among the bushes. The questions come from a God who already decided to send the Savior, the seed of the woman, to be bruised for the sins of mankind; they come from a God who put even a criminal like Cain under His special protection. The blood of Christ can cleanse him, too. "Where sin abounded, grace abounded much more" (Romans 5:20).

Have confidence in God for the whole of your life and trust His lovingkindness.

44

FEBRUARY 10

*"Do not be drunk with wine, in which is dissipation;
but be filled with the Spirit."*
EPHESIANS 5:18

*Y*ou might commit excesses in drinking. You might suffer because a loved one commits this sin. Don't chide alcoholics. Don't chide yourself if you are one. But remind yourself how much money you have lost because of alcohol, how many smiles of your wife or mother, how much laughter of your children, and how much happiness have disappeared from your home because of the criminal plotters of the alcohol industry, whose victim you are.

Visit a prison and a mental asylum. You will be amazed to find out how many are there because of alcohol. No one goes to jail because he is temperate or a teetotaler.

Do you like it when you vomit? Do you like it when your children despise you? Would you like to be forsaken by your sweetheart? What kind of business sense makes you enrich the bar owners and impoverish yourself? Does alcohol help you to avoid car accidents? Do you think better when drunk than when sober?

"Wine is a mocker, strong drink is a brawler, and whoever is led astray by it is not wise" (Proverbs 20:1).

If you have succumbed and feel helpless or despairing, consider the fact that God's eyes "flow with tears night and day" because of your sin (Jeremiah 14:17). He cares. He has the remedy.

You don't need wine. The fullness of the Holy Spirit is available. Unlike alcohol, it gives a euphoria, a sense of exhilaration that is not transitory. The apostles gave the impression of being drunk at Pentecost when they received the Spirit (Acts 2:13), but this was a jubilation that enabled them to accomplish great things for God.

"Blessed are the poor in spirit, for theirs is the kingdom of heaven."
MATTHEW 5:3

*I*n a theater in Moscow at the premier of a new play, *Christ in a Fur*, the hall was overcrowded.

The actor Alexander Rostovtsev had to play the main role. He belonged to the high circles of Soviet life and was a convinced Marxist.

On the stage was a mockery of an altar. The cross on it was made of bottles of wine and beer. Full glasses surrounded it. Fat "clergymen" said a drunken "liturgy" consisting of blasphemous formulas. In this sham church, "nuns" played cards, drank, and made ugly jokes while the "religious service" went on.

Then Rostovtsev appeared as Christ, dressed in a robe. He had the New Testament in his hands. He was supposed to read two verses from the Sermon on the Mount, then throw away the book in disgust and shout, "Give me my fur and my hat! I prefer a simple proletarian life." But something unexpected happened. The actor read not only two verses, but continued, "Blessed are the meek, for they shall inherit the earth" (Matthew 5:5), and so on to the end of the sermon. It was in vain that the prompter made desperate signs for him to stop.

When Rostovtsev came to the last words of Jesus, he made the sign of the cross in the Orthodox manner, said, "Lord, remember me when You come into Your kingdom" (Luke 23:42), and left the stage. He was never seen again. The Communists disposed of him.

Let us, like this actor, forget the ugly roles imposed upon us by the world and allow ourselves to be enraptured by the beauties of the Savior's words.

FEBRUARY 12

"They overcame him by the blood of the Lamb and by the word of their testimony, and they did not love their lives to the death."
REVELATION 12:11

*G*reat forces persecute the church, such as communism and Islamism. Old tribal religions have revived in Africa. Christians often suffer persecution in their homes and at their work in other countries.

How can the dragon of persecution be killed? Martyrdom is one weapon.

Thomas à Becket, archbishop of Canterbury in the twelfth century, showed the tyrannical King Henry II of England that the church has powers superior to those of this world, and that the divine and permanent cannot be subject to the human and transient. He fought for the noninterference of the state in church matters. For this he was killed. His last words were, "I die willingly, for the name of Jesus and for the defense of the church." The news of his murder so horrified Europe that the movement against the church's liberty was stopped. All recognized him as a martyr.

His blood still showed red on the cathedral stones when, in 1174, King Henry II walked barefoot to Canterbury to suffer a flogging, accepted willingly as penance for his crime, and to keep vigil by the tomb of the man he killed. The blood of the martyr converted the murderer. Could it not happen again?

The first Christians were persecuted by the Roman emperors, but in the end, Roman emperors became Christians.

Cross near cross, grave near grave—this is how the church conquers. Patient suffering will make you, too, a victor.

"If anyone comes to you and does not bring this doctrine, do not receive him into your house."

2 JOHN 10

*A*ll the great teachers of the Christian church were what one would call today narrow-minded. They knew only one way to heaven. Astronauts, returning to earth from the moon, are also very narrow-minded. The spaceship must follow a certain limited path that permits little deviation. If they were to miss their entry "slot" by one degree, they could end up lost in space or burned up completely.

We must stay on the path and stick to what we have learned from Christ. Luther differed from Zwingli, the Swiss reformer, in the meaning of Holy Communion. Therefore Luther taught: "He who knows that his pastor teaches in the Zwinglian manner should shun him and remain without the sacrament his whole life rather than receive it from him. He should prefer to die and suffer everything...It is horrible for me to hear that in one and the same church, and at the same altar, men receive the same sacrament, some of whom believe that they receive only bread and wine while others that they receive the body and blood of Christ."

If we start by calling heretics "separated brethren," we might eventually call devils "separated angels."

Be careful with whom you align yourself. Be wary of schemes to unite the churches. When you tie two birds together, though they might have a total of four wings, they don't fly better. They will not fly at all.

Remain faithful to what you have learned from God's holy Word.

FEBRUARY 14

"Our Father in heaven..."
MATTHEW 6:9

A document making the rounds secretly in the Soviet Union tells the story of a large group of nuns in a labor camp who had refused to work for their captors. They had been manacled and reduced to hunger. All was to no avail. Common prisoners were converted under their influence, and they now had a real convent in the camp. When Irene, the daughter of the prison camp's director, fell gravely ill, he had no choice. He asked for the nuns' prayers. The girl was healed.

The wife of the Communist officer Tcherednitchenko was having a difficult time giving birth. Her life and the life of the child were in danger. Someone suggested to him, "Promise that if everything goes well, you will have the child baptized."

"I can lose everything by this act."

"Well, choose between what you call 'everything' on the one hand and your wife and child on the other." The birth went well. He had the child baptized.

The Communists wished to compel the nuns to abandon their religious habit and to wear the uniform of prisoners. They answered, "We will not wear the badge of the antichrist." Because of this they were compelled to walk naked through the snow in freezing temperatures. They walked singing "Our Father." Not one of them fell ill. When a Communist inquired of the camp's doctor, Mrs. Bravermann, herself an atheist, how this was possible from a medical point of view, she replied, "Did you not hear them singing about a Father in heaven? Well, this is the scientific explanation."

He is your Father, too.

FEBRUARY 15

*"Look at the birds of the air... Consider the
lilies of the field."*
MATTHEW 6:26,28

*A*n anthropologist asked an aborigine in Australia: "Tuplin, is the earth round like a ball [holding up a ball of crochet cotton] or square like the box I am sitting on?"

"Round like a ball," the girl promptly replied.

"How do you know?" she asked.

"Oh, Missus, just look all around you; see sky touching the earth all round. Wherever you stand and look, it is all round; put baby down to walk he soon run around, not always straight like a fence; see sheep get lost they run round and round. See younger kangaroo run straight very little, then run round and round...All trees are round, all bushes grow round...Oh, Missus, why do you ask us?" Here in the mind of a primitive native the problem of the roundness of the earth was solved in the simplest manner.

Without genial minds, education, telescopes, and complicated calculations, aborigines have discovered the shape of the earth.

We rely too much on the sayings of scientific, religious, and philosophic authorities. We look into books to discover reality and truth, though the "eternal power and Godhead" can be seen in His creation even by simple people. "His invisible attributes are clearly seen, being understood by the things that are made" (Romans 1:20).

Exercise your own powers of observation, Jesus says, so that you will be better able to judge men, things, and events.

FEBRUARY 16

"The tax collector... beat his breast, saying,
'God be merciful to me a sinner!'"
LUKE 18:13

*I*n Russia, a Christian asked his pastor, "How must I say the words, 'Lord, have mercy'?" The pastor answered, "You do well to ask. It is a short but important prayer and is not easily said. When you say the words, evoke the image of the crucified Lord. Look at Him with nails driven into His body and remember His words, 'Come unto me, all ye that labor and are heavy laden, and I will give you rest.' If you say the simple prayer like this, you will glorify God, serve men, and grow in grace yourself."

Say your prayers without worrying about the fact that either others don't pray or they pray in a pharisaical manner.

A religion takes in believers and unbelievers, saints and hypocrites, those who love God and those who only fear Him. It includes persons who yield absolute surrender and others who obey only up to a point. It embraces elaborate rituals and humble prayers of penitent sinners. A religion without all of these is hardly imaginable.

Let others play the role allotted to them. You say again and again the simple prayer given for you, "God, have mercy." He will be merciful to you.

"If we live, we live to the Lord; and if we die,
we die to the Lord."
ROMANS 14:8

When Paulinus, the Christian missionary, came to the Anglo-Saxons asking them to embrace his faith, an old warrior told the king in the national assembly, "On a dark night, when the tempest was abroad and snow was falling without, when you were seated by the fire in the lighted hall, a sparrow entered through a window open for a moment, fluttered through the room, and then left by that same window. We have never seen it again. So we come from somewhere, we enjoy light and heat for a moment, and afterwards we go. If this stranger can tell us whence we come and where we go, we should accept his religion."

Christians have the answers to these questions. All the stars, the planets, the earth, and everything upon it are not as valuable as one single soul—your soul—because your soul knows both itself and them, whereas they know nothing. Our souls came from God but have gone astray, attracted by the things of this world. Therefore Jesus, the Son of God, came to this earth, pleasing the Father by His life of perfect obedience and His sacrificial death on the cross. He did not need to earn these "credits," since the heavenly Father loves Him for His divine nature, but the credits acquired on earth are imparted to His believers, who thus may inherit a beautiful paradise forever.

"He who has the Son has life [the only life really worth the name]; he who does not have the Son of God does not have life" (1 John 5:12).

It is amazing how many intellectuals call themselves "agnostics," not realizing that this is the Greek word for "ignorant." To be ignorant is a shame when one has the possibility of acquiring knowledge.

The Christian religion gives satisfactory answers to the ultimate problems of life.

A letter smuggled out of Russia by the Baptist church in Barnaui tells how the Secret Police infiltrated their ranks six years ago in the person of a lady named Z. Polushina. She pretended to be a teacher. She wept and prayed and declared herself converted. She soon became a hero. She refused to renounce her faith, lost her job, and was fired by one factory after another because of her Christian testimony. Her husband, a Communist, mistreated her and deprived her of her son. He destroyed her radio because she listened to sermons from abroad.

All the members of the church saw her courage in suffering. So she became highly regarded and appreciated. It was she who unmasked a new member of the church as being an agent of the Secret Police. Held in high esteem, she knew all the secrets of the church, especially since her prayers were always accompanied by tears. After six years, it was discovered that she had been an informer for the Communists, that she had had no husband, no child, and no teacher's job to lose. Everything had been staged.

Don't be bitter nor even surprised if you have been betrayed in friendship or love, or if your trust in a person has proved unfounded. The fault may be yours for not heeding Jesus' commandment, "Beware of men" (Matthew 10:17). The number of French, Dutch, and Norwegians who betrayed their fatherland under German occupation was large, as was the number of American soldiers who cooperated with the enemy as prisoners of war in Korea and Vietnam.

Instead of asking fidelity from others, whenever you hear about a treason ask yourself, as did the apostles, "Lord, is it I?" We are all potential Judases, and it is only the grace of God that can keep us loyal to God and to our fellow men.

FEBRUARY 19

"He who tills his land will be satisfied with bread."
PROVERBS 12:11

*M*ankind has three times the weapons necessary to kill every living being and only half the food it needs. Every second man is undernourished or starving. Strikes, riots, and revolutions do not increase the output of food. Furthermore, they do harm to our fellow men.

Try the means shown by God for such circumstances:

1) Pray regularly, in the words taught by our Lord, "Give us this day our daily bread."

2) Be obedient to God. It is written, "If you walk in My statutes and keep My commandments, and perform them...you shall eat your bread to the full" (Leviticus 26:3,5).

3) Be careful how you eat. "God created [meats] to be received with thanksgiving" (1 Timothy 4:3). "Eat your bread with joy" (Ecclesiastes 9:7). The first Christians "ate their food with gladness and simplicity of heart" (Acts 2:46).

4) "'Bring all the tithes into the storehouse...and try Me now in this,' says the LORD of hosts, 'if I will not...pour out for you such blessing'" (Malachi 3:10).

5) Change your attitude, if necessary, to suit the promise, "He who walks righteously and speaks uprightly, he who despises the gain of oppressions, who gestures with his hands, refusing bribes, who stops his ears from hearing of bloodshed, and shuts his eyes from seeing evil:...bread will be given him" (Isaiah 33:15,16).

We, on the contrary, spend "money for what is not bread" (Isaiah 55:2). We all squander. We give little thought to the needs of others.

Knowing that hunger stalks the earth, let us change our ways today for the sake of our own spiritual health and for the sake of those who starve.

A woman in tears entered the police station.
"Find my husband. I can't live without him. He has disappeared."

"Please, lady, let us get the facts in order. When did your husband disappear?"

"A week ago."

"Why did you wait until today to let us know?"

"Today he gets his paycheck."

Many of us seek the Lord when we need His help, when we pass through some crisis, not simply because we love Him.

Would you have loved a Savior who hung on a cross and declared Himself to be forsaken by God? Would you have spent your love and sweet spices on a Savior who was a corpse and could be of no help to anyone? Mary Magdalene did.

She sat loving and weeping near His tomb. Though buried on Friday evening, He was alive again on Sunday morning. His Spirit saw Mary weeping at the tomb and He could not bear her tears.

Show God and your fellow men a disinterested love that is not altered by circumstances.

*"Be strong and of good courage, do not fear
nor be afraid of them."*
DEUTERONOMY 31:6

I have before me a letter smuggled out from a Northern Siberian prison. Dated December 21, 1966, it is written by a Christian who was sentenced for a May 1966 demonstration before a building of the Central Committee of the Communist Party in Moscow. In the letter the writer tells about the trial before the tribunal of those arrested for the demonstration. When the judge scorned the Bible, our brother said, "Mr. Judge, may I ask you a question? How is it that the manure of rabbits has the form of a pellet, the manure of a horse the form of an apple, and the manure of a cow that of a pancake, and so on?" The judge said, "I could not answer such a question." And then our brother said, "You know nothing about manure and you dare laugh about the Word of God." The same judge laughed about the fact that in the Russian Bible the expression is used, "Abraham gave birth to Isaac." To this our brother answered that the great Russian writer Gogol, in his renowned novel *Taras Bulba*, uses the same expression when he says to his son, "I have given you birth and I will kill you." In this manner our brother dispensed with the stupid remarks of the Communist judge.

The brother made such an impression upon generals, members of government, and Soviet leaders, who came to prison to speak with him, that his interrogator said to the brethren of Moscow who inquired after him, "David Davidovici is a true Christian." The interrogator's conscience was most disturbed about the role he had to play. In our brother's beautiful letter, he states that now there are dark clouds over the people of God, yet the Word of God tells us that when the clouds are full they give rain. Noah and his family had no need to fear the clouds of the flood. The more so we, who are in a better ship than theirs, have no need to fear.

FEBRUARY 22

"The fool has said in his heart, 'There is no God.'"
PSALM 14:1

*I*n the psalmist's day, people lived close to nature and only isolated fools could deny the existence of God, however they conceived Him. This is no longer true. Modern atheism is an urban phenomenon conceived by men who live in crowded cities, walk and ride on concrete, and are out of touch with nature. Inhabitants of cities have polluted the air and the water. Now they ask where God is. Those who live where the skies are blue, the air clean, and the water sparkling know. There are very few, if any, atheist farmers.

The early crocus, the first robin of spring, the rhythm of the seasons, the dark woods and the fields of ripening grain, the work of insects, the migration of birds, the intricate design of the snowflake all speak of their Creator. "Day unto day utters speech, and night unto night reveals knowledge" (Psalm 19:2).

Chief Seattle of the Squamish indians in Washington said in 1854, "The white man's dead forget the country of their birth when they go to walk among the stars. Our dead never forget this beautiful earth, for it is part of us. The perfumed flowers are our sisters; the deer, the horse, the great eagle, these are our brothers. The rock crests, the juices in the meadows, the body heat of the pony, and man all belong to the same family."

But this Indian's reproaches against white men were unjust, as far as the Christians are concerned. We look upon the earth as God's footstool. Jesus walked on it and was buried in it. His body was formed of its elements. He took this body with Him to heaven. He loved the earthly elements, which sing of God's glory.

There is no atheism among those brought up in nature. May this assurance confirm your faith in God.

FEBRUARY 23

"The water in the skin was used up . . . Then God
opened [Hagar's] eyes, and she saw a well of water."
GENESIS 21:15,19

*H*agar was sent away by Abraham into the wilderness. After traveling a long way with her son, Ishmael, she found that the contents of her only bottle of water were depleted.

She was in a desert place. There was no hope. She sat the child under a shrub and then sat down across from him "at a distance" and wept. It seemed that the child was lost. A thirsty child, an empty bottle, a scorching sun. She expected him to die.

But there was one factor she had forgotten to take into account. We also tend to forget this when we pass through difficulties. There is a God. He revealed a well of water to the woman who went about with an empty bottle. God may have deprived you of small possibilities in order to give you great ones.

We carry bottles; God has wells.

Let us draw water from the wells of salvation.

FEBRUARY 24

"It is appointed for men to die once."
HEBREWS 9:27

Fourteen of the Japanese war criminals sentenced to death were converted. The last letter of one of them, Nishizawa, says, "I am living thankful days, believing that I may receive salvation... Saved by the grace of God, to live in Christ and to die is gain." An atheist said on his deathbed, "There is one thing that mars all the pleasure of my life. I'm afraid the Bible is true. If I could only know for a certainty that death is an eternal sleep, I should be happy. But here is what pierces my soul: if the Bible is true, I am lost forever."

The dying advice of Louis IX, King of France, to his daughter was: "I conjure you to love our Lord with all your might, for this is the foundation of all goodness. I wish you could comprehend what the Son of God has done for our redemption. Never be guilty of any deliberate sin, though it were to save your life." Philip Melanchthon, Luther's closest co-worker in the Reformation, said, "I want nothing but heaven; therefore trouble me no more."

Francis Spira, after having been an evangelical preacher for years, recanted in the presence of a multitude for fear of persecution. His last words were: "I have denied Christ voluntarily and against my convictions. I feel that He hardens me and will allow no hope. It is a fearful thing to fall into the hands of the living God."

A dying minister said, "I call heaven and earth to witness, that if I were to recover, I would labor for holiness. As for riches and pleasure and the applause of men, I count them as dross. But now the best resolutions are insignificant, because it is too late."

Remember that you too will die. Repent while you have time.

FEBRUARY 25

"Being justified freely by His grace through the redemption that is in Christ Jesus."
ROMANS 3:24

A poor beggar prayed to God that he might be fed. A divine voice came to him in his sleep and directed him to go to a certain location, place an arrow in his bow while facing east, and wherever the arrow fell dig for treasure. The beggar shot many arrows and dug in every direction, but all in vain. Then a voice from heaven came to him saying, "You were directed to fix an arrow in your bow, but not to draw the bow with all your might, as you have been doing. Shoot as gently as possible that the arrow may fall close to you, for the hidden treasure is near."

Don't make arduous efforts in religion. When my son was small, he asked me how he should examine himself to see if he was in the faith, as enjoined in 1 Corinthians 11:28. I told him that at train stations he must have observed a mechanic proving the wheels with a hammer to see if they had the right vibrations. Then, beating my breast powerfully, I said, "So you must beat your breast, too, asking again and again, 'Heart, do you love Jesus?'"

"Father," he replied, "you are wrong. I once asked the mechanic in the station to allow me to handle the hammer. I discovered that it is very light. We have to beat our breasts very softly. If I hear from inside only a low whisper 'I love Jesus,' this should be enough."

There are some who would rather impose upon themselves great hardships in religion instead of simply believing that the blood of Jesus Christ saves to the uttermost. The Beloved is right here. Just embrace Him.

FEBRUARY 26

*"[Beware of] useless wranglings of
men of corrupt minds."*
1 TIMOTHY 6:5

*T*wo men disputed over the meaning of the word "glass." The one said, "It is a cylinder, and cursed be he who says otherwise." The second says, "A glass is a vessel of any shape for drinking and accursed is the one who says otherwise."

A glass can also be defined in other ways. It has many relationships and utilitarian possibilities. For instance, it can be a projectile thrown at someone else's head in anger. Ultimately, however, a glass is a glass. Its reality has nothing to do with its name "glass," which it bears only in English. In French it is called *verre* and in Russian *stakan*. Definitions are subjective, incomplete, and are given from a certain point of view.

Let us never forget that every point of view is a point of blindness because it eliminates other points of views which may be equally valid. If I look up, I cease to see the floor of the room. If I look down, I don't see the ceiling. I arrive at truth only through an intuition of the whole of reality with all its intricacies. But reality is not only material, it is spiritual. It knows itself. Christ is the expression of this self-knowledge of the whole reality. Therefore He says, "I am ... the truth" (John 14:6).

Observe that He never said "*He is*" the truth. He said, "I am the truth." We are not allowed to change the pronoun. If Jesus is for you a "He," you cannot have the truth; He must become your "I." He wishes to live in your heart as truly as He lived in the Virgin Mary's womb. Then, as you identify with Him, your doubts will disappear. You, too, will become a personification of truth. Imperfect? Yes. But with "Christ in you" you have "the hope of glory" (Colossians 1:27).

FEBRUARY 27

"Let both grow together."
MATTHEW 13:30

A gardener in the United States once wrote to the Department of Agriculture: "I've tried everything I've ever heard about or read, including all your bulletins, on how to get rid of dandelions—and I've still got them." By return mail, he received the last word on the subject: "Dear Sir: If you have tried everything and you still have dandelions, there is only one thing left for you to do. Learn to love them."

Whatever means you employ, you will never get rid of false friends, enemies, rivals, opponents, or annoyances with your marriage partner or other relatives. But you can rid yourself once and for all of the burden they present to you, by declaring them the objects of your love. There exists no alternative to loving your enemies unless you wish to kill yourself slowly by nurturing hatred.

Don't judge your enemies by the attitudes they take toward you, but by the circumstances of their own lives. They may never have been beloved. You might be the scapegoat for their resentment against other persons they do not dare attack. A man who has a nasty employer in the office may sometimes say bitter words to his wife. He has to be silent when the boss rebukes him. His wife becomes the target.

You can't always change the stream of life. Love it with whatever it brings. Jesus said, "I am the life"—the life in all its aspects. Consider it sacred—and handle it with care.

FEBRUARY 28

"Come out from among them and be separate."
2 CORINTHIANS 6:17

A peasant, hearing a proclamation issued by the prince of Tirmid that a large reward would be given to whoever would take a message to Samarkand in the space of four days, hurried to Tirmid as fast as he could. The city became alarmed, thinking that his extreme haste announced the approach of some calamity. When admitted to the presence of the prince, all he had to say was that he had hurried to inform the prince that he could not go to Samarkand that fast.

I often think about this story when I hear many prayers in churches in which men, who had driven to the service at great speed, excuse themselves before God for the fact that, being sinners, they will not be able to fulfill His commandments. What was the good of coming to tell God this?

You are a weak believer. God does not ask much from you, but that you should not yoke yourself together with an unbeliever, or else you too might receive the same damnation.

A mouse developed a great affection for a frog. That he might be able to communicate with his friend at all times, he fastened a string to the frog's leg, and the other end of it to its own. Shortly afterward a raven swooped down on the mouse and carried him off, and the frog, being fastened to the mouse, was dragged off and destroyed with it. If it would not have been attached to the mouse, it would have been safe. The raven could not have entered into water.

Instead of telling God again and again that you can't fulfill His commandments, however weak you might be, separate yourself from the world and at once you will be in new surroundings favorable to the keeping of God's will.

63

"Christ may dwell in your hearts through faith."
EPHESIANS 3:17

When Michelangelo used a stonemason as his model for a statue of Christ, he was criticized by his teacher, Ghirlandaio. Michelangelo defended himself: "But Christ was also a workingman, a carpenter."

The master replied, "Florence won't accept a working-class Christ. They are used to thinking of Him as a nobleman."

Some are accustomed only to a historical Savior. They will not accept an inner Christ, though to be real Christ must dwell within the heart.

In a renowned French novel, we are told about a British lord who loved to play the fool over a prima donna in the opera. He would go night after night to listen to her. He would send her flowers and jewels. She became interested in him and made an arrangement that they should meet at a party, but she was not introduced under her real name. He did not pay any attention to her then, or at later encounters. He loved her only in her roles on the stage. He did not even recognize the real person.

Many of us bow before Jesus as portrayed in the pages of the Bible; we bow before Him as represented in communion or in a statue. But when He passes near us in the person of a hungry man, when He suffers in a jail or in a hospital, we do not give Him reverence or take His side. Let us invite Jesus to dwell in our hearts and recognize Him in the shape of the needy who surround us! Let us also recognize His presence in our life and in the lives of others.

"The flesh is weak."
MATTHEW 26:41

*U*nder Lenin and Stalin, eighty thousand Orthodox priests had been killed. Father Mikhail was among the few who had not yet been arrested, but he lost his faith. He had just said during the liturgy, "Blessed be God," when a voice whispered, "There is no God." He looked at the images of saints hanging on the wall. What did their friendship with God mean? Does such a mighty Friend allow believers to be thrown to wild beasts, burned at the stake, tortured? He tried to repress the thought, repeating, "The fool hath said in his heart, There is no God." It did not help.

He continued to act as a priest out of duty, but he no longer believed. The sorrow around him had been too great. He had to restrain himself to keep from crying out to the peasants who filled the church, "Go home, poor people. There is no God. God would not have permitted this bloody chaos."

Drunk Communists arrested him on an Easter eve, telling the priest, "We have decided to kill you. What have you to say?"

Life was worthless for Father Mikhail. He answered, "As you like." But he was given a chance. "If you renounce Christ and trample on a cross, you will be freed." He thought, *I don't believe. What does a cross mean to me? Let me save my life.* But when he opened his mouth, he said, to his own astonishment, "I believe in one God."

It was Good Friday. In remembrance of the crown of thorns, they put his fur cap on his head, with the linen on the outside; they put a sack on his shoulders as a royal garment, and knelt saying, "Hail, king of the Jews," and they all beat him. He prayed to the One in whom he did not believe anymore, "If You exist, save me." With a loud voice, he repeated, "I believe in one God."

This made such an impression on the drunk murderers that they freed him. He went home, prostrated himself on the earth in his prayer corner, and said with tears, "I believe."

When assailed by doubts, don't seek an intellectual solution. Take some burden upon yourself for Jesus' sake. Where reason fails, faith will conquer.

MARCH 2

"He was wounded for our transgressions."
ISAIAH 53:5

*J*esus took our sins upon Himself and suffered for them. Should I not do the same for my guilty fellow man?

An unmarried girl became pregnant. To save her lover from her father's wrath, she told him, "It is my pastor who did it." The father nursed his grudge against the pastor. When the child was born, he brought the baby on Sunday morning into the church, and in front of the congregation he threw it into the pastor's arms shouting, "Take it, the fruit of your whoredom with my daughter!" Swearing and shouting insults, the father left the church.

The astonished congregation expected a word of explanation from the pastor, but he only caressed the baby and said, "So you are mine? You will surely be my darling." It goes without saying that he lost all his following. Despised by men, he brought up the child in utter poverty.

After a few years, the girl was overcome by remorse and confessed the truth to her father. Stunned by the news, he rushed to the pastor and begged his forgiveness; then he told the truth to the entire church. The congregation waited again, expecting now that their former pastor would explain his strange behavior. But the pastor said only these words: "Do you wish to tell me he is not mine? He surely is my darling." Now he had a congregation bigger than ever before. He had not justified himself when accused unjustly; nor did he boast of his innocence when it was proven.

The Lord has said, "If anyone desires to come after Me, let him deny himself" (Luke 9:23). If one denies himself, everyone's self becomes his own; and he realizes that every man is co-responsible for everyone's sins. He never rejects any accusation as not applying to him, but is happy to take it upon himself to ease his brother's burden. This means to have the mind of Christ.

> *"[They] became valiant in battle."*
> HEBREWS 11:34

*L*isten to the story of a hero of the faith.

His name was Florea. He died in the prison of Gherla (Romania). He had been beaten until both arms and both legs were paralyzed because he refused to do slave labor on the Lord's Day. He could only move his neck. It is bad enough to be in such a situation in a nursing home or with one's family, but he was in a prison cell where fellow inmates had no water, no sheets—nothing with which to help him.

We had to spoon-feed him, but where did we get a spoon? Yet he was the most serene and joyful among us. His face shone. When we prisoners sometimes sat around his bed brooding about our sorrows, moaning that our outlook was bad, he would reply, "If the outlook is bad, try the uplook. Stephen, surrounded by men who threw stones at him, abandoned by the other members of the church who did not stay with him in his moment of trial, nevertheless looked up and saw Jesus standing at the right hand of the Father. This comforted his heart; it will comfort yours also. Look up!"

After my release from prison, I spoke to his son, age nine, and told him the story of his father's faithfulness. I added, "I hope that you will become a good man like him." He replied, "Brother, I would like to become a sufferer for Christ as my father has been."

There is no law that obliges Christians to be dull, lukewarm, half-hearted. Christianity can be heroic. The right spelling of the word "love" is s-a-c-r-i-f-i-c-e.

[Jesus said,] "This is My body which is given for you."
LUKE 22:19

When the pastor repeats the word of consecration at communion, "This is my body," which body does he mean?

Jesus has two natures in one body, a divine nature and a human nature. He also has two bodies: the glorified human body with which He ascended to heaven, and the church, which is His body too. At communion we commemorate the body that suffered on Golgotha, but we remember also His mystical body, the church universal, which in every century has given martyrs whose blood was shed for the glory of God.

To the glorified body of Christ we can bring adoration. We adore His pierced heart which bled for us. For His mystical body, the church universal, we can do much. We can share the cross of the martyrs of today and alleviate their suffering.

At every communion remember both bodies.

MARCH 5

"All sins will be forgiven the sons of men, and whatever blasphemies they may utter."
MARK 3:28

Once a traveler was sitting in a railroad coach next to a young man who appeared to be depressed. Finally the latter revealed that he was a convict who had just gotten out of prison. He also admitted that his imprisonment had brought shame on his family and that they had neither visited him nor written much. He tried to convince himself that their negligence was only because they were too poor to travel, too uneducated to write. Despite his misgivings, he hoped they had forgiven him.

To make it as easy as possible for them, he had written suggesting that if his family had forgiven him they should put up a white ribbon in the big apple tree near the tracks as a signal. If they didn't want him back they were to do nothing; he would understand, stay on the train, and head West.

As the train neared his hometown, the suspense became so great he couldn't bear to look out the window. The older man changed places with him and said he would watch for the apple tree. In a few minutes he put his hand on the young convict's arm. "There it is," he whispered, his voice suddenly unsteady. "It's all right. The whole tree is white with ribbons."

The Hebrews don't even have a singular word for God's compassion. It is *rahamim*—compassions. Every Hebrew word with the "*m*" ending is plural. Whatever you have done, there is enough forgiveness in Jesus' blood.

> *"The multitude being very great and having nothing*
> *to eat . . . They ate and were filled."*
> MARK 8:1,8

$\mathcal{A}$ bout fifty million people die a year, more than a third of them as the result of malnutrition or starvation.

Remember every morning when you awake that you awake in a hungry world. To use food recklessly and wastefully is a grave sin. When grain is fed to livestock to turn it into meat, three quarters of the food value is lost. Americans consume nearly a ton of grain annually per person, whereas an Asian consumes only a fifth as much. If you give up your meat consumption three times a week, you allow agricultural products that now feed livestock to be diverted to the poor and hungry.

The food situation will grow worse. Many Indian children are given the name *Dashkal*, which means hunger. It is easier to multiply men than the means of existence. Morocco, Kenya, Iraq, and India, for example, will double their population in twenty-five years. This trend virtually guarantees utter catastrophe.

The fact that I cannot solve the global problem does not free me from the responsibility of doing the little I can, through some bona fide institution, to help at least one hungry child survive.

Jesus had been poor as a child. When He saw hungry multitudes He did not dismiss them or turn His back on them. He gave them bread and fish. Do the same. Share what you have with those in need.

"They found a man of Cyrene, Simon by name.
Him they compelled to bear His cross."
MATTHEW 27:32

*Y*ou could put into Africa the entire territory of the United States, all of Europe, China, India, and Japan and still have much space left over. This is how large Africa is. So large also must be every Christian's concern for Africa.

In order that this continent might belong to Christ, St. Perpetua and her husband were willing to be hacked to pieces in the year A.D. 201, on this day, March 7. They had refused to burn some incense before the statue of Caesar. That Africa might belong to Christ, the great missionary Livingstone died on his knees at his bedside in Chitambo, in what is today Tanzania. The French missionary Francois Coillard died in Bulawayo (Rhodesia). In one of his last letters he wrote, "The old tent is wearing out, but my heart is still young. My heart belongs to Africa. There is work waiting for me, and there my grave shall be. My great desire is not to live a day longer than I can work."

Africa was a piece of hell on earth when Robert Laws went there along with five other missionaries. The natives were killing each other indiscriminately in tribal wars. Livingstone had cried, "Blood, blood, blood everywhere!" Dr. Laws and his companions worked six years before winning the first convert, but not before four of the missionaries had died from fever.

Dan Crawford, a Scotsman, was the first missionary who decided that "we must think and speak black" in order to win the blacks. He became one of them, and as such he was subject to the cruel King Mushidi of Katanga. The king had five hundred wives, was growing rich and fat on the sale of slaves, rubber, and ivory, and each day was putting to death as many human victims as he liked.

Almost all African countries are dictatorships even now. Islam and heathenism, as well as modern secularism, prevail. Communism has taken over many countries.

Jesus, while carrying the cross, was helped by an African. Help Africa come to Christ.

MARCH 8

"[David] pretended madness."
1 SAMUEL 21:13

*C*ardinal Trochta of Czechoslovakia, when he was a priest, was a prisoner of the Nazis. During a mass execution, he was only wounded. He pretended to be dead, was carried away with the corpses, and managed in this way to escape. Thus Trochta deceived the Nazis. A simulated death is the enacting of a lie.

According to strong moralists, he should have been obedient to the authorities who had decided to kill innocents. He should have cried out, "I am not dead yet. Please, another bullet."

Every righteous rule pushed to an extreme becomes ridiculous. We surely have the duty to tell the truth. We as surely have the duty to defend ourselves against murderers; we have to defend our families, our church, and our nation.

The supreme Christian rule is neither love, nor sternness, nor truth, nor wisdom, nor seeking of pleasure, nor asceticism, nor generosity, nor economy, nor self-sacrifice, nor self-defense. It is, in the words of St. Anthony the Great, "to have in all things the right measure."

Our conscience illuminated by the Holy Spirit as we search the Scriptures will show us in every circumstance the right way.

> *"Behold, henceforth all generations will call me blessed."*
> LUKE 1:48

*T*he renowned Jewish novelist Sholem Asch, who had become a Christian, wrote, "The tread of your feet, Mary, is dear to me as the beat of my heart, and the air I breathe in your presence purifies my being, for you, Mary, lend sanctity to all that come near."

As often as we look to Jesus crucified, we see His mother watching the body of her son convulsing with pain. She had tended that same body when He was a babe. She had bathed and fed Him. How often it had been her delight to kiss Him. Now she gazed at the red welts where the soldiers' whips had struck. She heard the singing leather of the whip snap loud against His skin, which she, stricken by awe, had scarcely dared to touch.

What should we admire most in her who was so highly favored of God?

I will extol her virginity. She, the virgin who conceived without knowing a man, she it was who gave birth to the highest being—the God-man.

"Forgive us our debts, as we forgive our debtors."
MATTHEW 6:12

During World War II, Simon Wiesenthal, the renowned Jewish hunter of war criminals, wrote that, while doing slave labor in a concentration camp in Lvov (Ukraine), he was called by a nurse to the deathbed of a Nazi officer. This officer told him that his mother was a Christian who had been much grieved when he joined Hitler's youth and afterward his army. He was in a unit that occupied the Soviet town of Dnepropetrovsk. There, two hundred Jews—among them women, children, and babes—were locked in a small house, into which Karl's unit tossed grenades. The house burned. Some Jews, with children in their arms, tried to jump through the window, but Karl shot them.

A few days later, in a battle, Karl's unit was ordered to attack. In this battle he was completely blinded and badly injured. The last thing he remembered to have seen was a Jew in flames with a burning child in his arms coming toward him. Now he waited for death, tortured constantly by the vision of the martyred Jewish women and children. Karl wished to be absolved by a Jew. However, Wiesenthal did not pronounce the longed-for word of forgiveness.

We can sympathize with this man who lost almost his entire family because of the cruelty of the Nazis. Criminals have to be defeated and punished. But the man Wiesenthal had before him no longer represented danger. He was suffering the pangs of death. Here a word of forgiveness should have been spoken. But one has to realize first his own sinfulness in the light of Christ's forgiveness. Only then will he be able to absolve others.

*T*he Lord Jesus said to Peter, "I will give you the keys of the kingdom of heaven" (Matthew 16:19). Every child of God can open the kingdom to anyone, even to the worst of men, by proclaiming to him Christ's forgiveness. But the same Jesus says, "I have the keys of Hades and of Death" (Revelation 1:18). These He gave to no one. He reserved them for Himself. Otherwise some of us would have thrown ourselves into hell through our foolishness, and we would have doomed to hell those who don't believe like us. A mother gives her child a toy, not a knife with which to cut himself. Therefore, we are given the keys of heaven, but not of hell.

Luther said about Erasmus, his philosophical adversary, "He died without light, without a cross, and without God," which means he doomed him to hell. Erasmus' last words were, "Beloved God."

Only one key has been entrusted to you. Open the gates of heaven to others. Don't condemn anyone. Don't damn yourself either.

MARCH 12

"Jesus said to him, 'I am . . . the life.'"
JOHN 14:6

Why did God give us His Word? Why not a picture instead? The atom is not picturable. Neither is reality; even less so is God. A range of fragrances or tastes could also not have instructed us as does His Word.

But is the word a perfect means of communication? Some words have many meanings. In Hebrew *barach* means both "blessing" and "curse"; *kedeshah*, "prostitute" and "saint"; *hesed*, "grace" and "abomination." In Greek *afes* means "to forgive" and "to leave." Bible verses can be interpreted variously. We need assurance. Our eternal life depends upon knowing clearly the will of God.

A pastor told a Jewish boy of twelve, "If Jesus is really the Messiah sent by God and you don't believe in Him, you will be lost eternally." The boy answered, "If Jesus is really the blasphemer our court declared Him to be, you as a preacher who clings to Him will pass your eternity in hell." There can be no joking in religion. If Christ has not risen and we have given up so many earthly pleasures hoping for the resurrection, "we are of all men the most pitiable" (1 Corinthians 15:19). If there is a resurrection and we have spent our life in vain pleasures, we are fools.

Don't confine yourself only to the words of the Bible but accept the total revelation of God. He reveals Himself through all His actions. The Hebrews through whom the Word of God was given have no word for " word." They use for it the expression *davar*, which means "thing, something real." The whole of outward and inward reality is God's sure revelation—the entire happening at Golgotha, your whole life with its sins and repentance, its falls and recoveries, its sorrows and joys. Believe in life, His life. Accept Him in *your* life. Then you will have the assurance of *eternal* life.

MARCH 13

"The scripture cannot be broken."
JOHN 10:35

A Zionist named Shifrin was jailed in Russia. While in prison he met the Baptist Solodiankin, age seventy-two. "The goodness and transparent purity of that man made a deep impression. Even the soldiers who guarded us became better when he was there." He was almost blind. His glasses had been broken by the interrogator. "Everything he earned as a slave laborer he used like this: half for his sick daughter and 25 percent for his church. From the rest (7.8 rubles) he bought for himself a little sugar and bread; the rest he gave to the sick prisoners in the camp."

Shifrin told him that he had a Bible and was ready to read it to him. In the evening, Solodiankin came. He had changed his shirt and combed himself with great care. "To read the eternal book is a feast." The Jew read to the Christian from Isaiah. At a certain moment, he was interrupted: "You made a mistake in reading."

It was true. "But do you know the text by heart?"

"Of course."

"Then why should I read it to you?"

"Because it is a joy for me to hear the Scriptures. One gets new ideas."

We recognize the value of a thing only when we don't have it. Let us learn from those who are deprived the real value of the Scriptures, and let us search them diligently.

"...aimless conduct received by tradition from your fathers."
1 PETER 1:18

We don't belong to a church because of the plausibility of its tenets. We measure their plausibility by the conviction already formed of its veracity.

The majority of mankind adhere to the religion of their parents. If a Catholic man is married to a Catholic woman, the child born of this union will hear from the beginning things that will incline him toward Catholicism. As an adult he will tend to accept all its arguments, just as someone born of Jewish or Baptist parents will have a bias toward these beliefs.

It is not otherwise with conversions. When an individual passes through a crisis or has his early beliefs shattered, a devotee of some other religion may show him what he conceives to be the way to God. Accepting the comfort, the new sense of life needed at that moment, the individual finds it easy to swallow uncritically a multitude of other dogmas, beliefs, or rituals held by the person who brought him to faith.

It is difficult to find the truth. Start by examining and questioning ancestral religion, the process by which hundreds of millions of men are made to call themselves Christians, Hindus, Muslims, or Jews.

Real religion begins with a readiness to acknowledge that all your beliefs, including the most cherished, may be wrong, that your own religion may be a variety of prejudice just as you conceive others to be. None but the finest spirits ever rose above a hazy group consciousness.

Pass with a broom through your heart, sweeping away everything that does not come from a personal experience with God. This is what I did. In the emptied heart—the heart of the man who denies not only his belief, but himself, his own person—God, the source and aim of all religion, shines.

Acknowledge that you have acquired prejudices of both birth and education. Then "test all things" by the Word of God and "hold fast what is good" (1 Thessalonians 5:21).

> *"[God said to Abraham] 'Take now your son, your only son*
> *Isaac...and offer him [on mount Moriah] as a burnt offering.'"*
> GENESIS 22:2

A girl named Mary tells the story of the court trial in the Soviet Union in which her mother was deprived of parental rights. They shouted at her, "You are a mother. Deny God! What did He give you? Whom do you love more, your own children or your idol? How can you?" And her mother sat with her scarf covering her eyes, repeating, "God sees everything. He will reward accordingly." When the children, including Mary, cried to her, "Mother, do not leave us," she did not even turn to them.

It is a scene exactly like those we read about in the history of the early martyrs who went into the circus arena to be devoured by wild beasts. They refused to listen to the pleading of their loved ones when asked to recant and save their lives for their children's sake.

With God, it was the mystery of preferring the death of His Son to permitting the eternal death of sinners; with saints, the mystery of preferring to lose their children rather than deny God. Such is our God; so are we. We can do nothing but sing His praise whatever the consequences.

Where choices are to be made, don't hesitate. Sacrifice even what or whom you love most for God. He sacrificed all for you.

> *"If you have faith as a mustard seed, you will say to this mountain, 'Move from here to there,' and it will move."*
> MATTHEW 17:20

I tried to move mountains and did not succeed. Nor do I know any child of God able to perform such a deed.

I asked the Lord how it was that His words did not correspond to reality. A disciple of Christ should not deliver monologues in prayer, but should expect to receive answers to his questions. I received an answer to mine:

"You, my beloved, cannot move mountains because your faith is not the size of a grain. You have bushels full of faith. Nobody uses a one-thousand-ton hammer, such as those employed by heavy industry, to crack open a nut. Such a hammer can only perform great works. By the same token, you are called to do greater things than amuse yourself by moving mountains. You can move God. Remember how God decided to destroy the Jewish people after they had worshiped a golden calf, and Moses through his prayer made God change His mind? To produce changes in heavenly decrees is much more important than moving mountains."

Since then, I have stopped trying to move mountains. We are seated with Christ in heavenly places. We participate in things happening there. And when in our earthly life mountains hinder us, we don't need to command them to move. We can follow the example of Christ, about whom His bride says, "My beloved . . . comes leaping upon the mountains, skipping upon the hills" (Song of Solomon 2:8).

Don't try to remove mountains of difficulty in your own life. Jump over them. Do your Christian duty in spite of them.

MARCH 17

"Do good to those who hate you."
MATTHEW 5:44

*T*he following episode took place in a prison cell in a Communist country:

One day the guards pushed a new prisoner into a cell where only Christians were detained. He was shorn, dirty, and thin. First no one recognized him. But after a few minutes one exclaimed, "This is Captain X." He was one of the worst torturers of Christians. He had arrested and beaten many of those with whom he now shared the prison cell. They surrounded him and asked how he came to be in prison. With tears rolling down his cheek, he told his story.

A couple of months before, while he was sitting in his office, a boy of twelve entered, holding in his hand a flower for the captain's wife. The boy told him, "Captain, you are the one who put my father and mother in prison. Today is my mother's birthday. I always buy her a flower on this day. Because of you I have no mother to gladden today, but she is a Christian and taught me to love my enemies and reward evil with good. So I thought I would bring a flower to the mother of your children. Please, take it to your wife and tell her about my love and about the love of Christ."

It was too much even for a Communist captain. He also is a creature of God, enlightened with "the true Light, which gives light to every man who comes into the world" (John 1:9). He embraced the child. He could not torture anymore, nor could he retain his position. He now considered it a privilege to sit in prison with those he had himself imprisoned.

Forgiving love is the key to a victorious Christian life.

"God has chosen the weak things of the world."
1 CORINTHIANS 1:27

Nelson achieved all his triumphs by overcoming great handicaps.

Frail and weak, he fell victim to yellow fever in India. He contracted some other unidentified sickness in the West Indies. He, a navy commander, suffered all his life from seasickness. He lost an eye in Corsica. Later his right hand was amputated. In another fight he was heavily wounded in the chest.

But he had learned to overcome pain. And it was he who defeated the naval forces of France and Spain at Trafalgar.

The hero Nelson also had a weak point. He became the subject of a huge scandal in London and Naples through his involvement with Lady Hamilton, another man's wife. It is not the physical handicaps that are apt to wreck a man's life, but rather his weaknesses of character. "He who rules his spirit [is better] than he who takes a city" (Proverbs 16:32).

As a human being, Jesus entered life with many handicaps. His birth was rumored to have been irregular. He belonged to a poor family in an oppressed nation. He never had a rabbinical education. But He showed that by faith one can conquer obstacles and be the right kind of person. Jesus is the Son of God. Those who believe in Him become children of God. He said, "Everything is possible to the one who believes."

Don't worry about your physical handicaps or any other kind of handicap. They can be the best stimulants to great achievement.

Find out your specific weakness, and through Christ strengthen the wall of the fortress that is most exposed to the enemy.

> *"You have given Him authority over all flesh,*
> *that He should give eternal life."*
> JOHN 17:2

*G*iacomo Puccini was a great success in life. His operas *Manon Lescaut* and *Madame Butterfly* made him world-renowned. He had money and fame. Women were after him. It seemed that he had everything needed to make him a happy man. He was anything but happy.

He wrote when he was at the peak of glory, "Success? What is it worth, if in any case old age comes and death. I would like to create new operas, write more musical pieces, but alas, I have no more power."

At the age of eighty-two Mao Tse-tung received the president of Western Germany and told him about his grandiose plans for Red China. The president answered that with persistence he might achieve them, quoting the proverb, "Persistent rivulets of waters pierce the stone," to which Mao replied, "Yes, but I don't have enough water anymore."

Kirov, one of the top leaders of Russian Bolshevism, was killed by Stalin. He had finished his last speech with the words, "I would like to live, to live and to live."

If everything ends with death, even the grandest life is like a banquet given to someone sentenced to death. You enjoy a meal and then you are hanged.

Do you wish lasting achievements and endless energy to create valuable things? Then your first priority must be to assure yourself of life eternal. Jesus said, "Whoever lives and believes in Me shall never die" (John 11:26).

> *"Whatever they know naturally, like brute beasts,*
> *in these things they corrupt themselves."*
> JUDE 10

*I*t is out of the question that man should have descended from a monkey. Monkeys are faithful to their wives; they don't perform abortions. Monkeys have no bombs with which to exterminate their own species. Crime, alcoholism, drug addiction, prostitution are unknown among them. They neither make nor view immoral movies.

The monkey, a creature of God which has remained as God made it, never claims mankind for progeny. The Darwinist theory is an insult to the ape. No ape ever conceived a book as unsubstantiated as *The Origin of Species*.

Man has a much higher provenance. He was created by God in His image. The higher the first position, the more catastrophic the fall. Man shows in his intelligence traces of his first state, but too often he bears greater resemblance to the wolf, the fox, the snake, the pig. When man becomes beast, he becomes the beastliest beast. And his descent is all due to the sin of the first human parents, perpetuated and aggravated by their progeny.

It is true that "the ox knows its owner and the donkey its master's crib; but Israel does not know" (Isaiah 1:3). What man needs is not to be told he is a relative of the beast. The animal kingdom is distinctly separate from humanity. It has suffered degradation because of the Fall but is closer to its original state than mankind. The urgent need of man is to return to his primary privilege, to regain the innocence Adam lost.

Jesus, through His shed blood, washes us from all sins in this world and will restore us to our forfeited state in the world to come, when "this corruptible has put on incorruption" (1 Corinthians 15:54).

MARCH 21

"All things work together for good to those who love God."
ROMANS 8:28

The story is told of a lone survivor of a shipwreck who was thrown upon an uninhabited island. After awhile he managed to build for himself a crude hut in which he placed the "little all" that he had saved from the sinking ship. He prayed to God for deliverance and anxiously scanned the horizon each day to hail any ship that might be passing that way.

One day, upon returning from a hunt for food, he was horrified to find his hut in flames! All that he had salvaged was now going up in smoke! The worst had happened, so it appeared. But what at first seemed so great a tragedy was, in reality, for the best, though to the man's limited vision it seemed a devastating loss.

In God's infinite wisdom, his loss was actually an answer to his most earnest prayer. The same day a ship arrived. "We saw your smoke signal," the captain said.

Can we not take our seeming calamities and look for God's best in them?

Even the calamity death worked for the glory of God in the case of Lazarus. And John the beloved was given his great visions of the future of the world and of heaven itself while in exile on the Isle of Patmos.

> *"When [David] was in need and hungry, ... he went into the house of God ... and ate the showbread, which is not lawful to eat, except for the priests."*
> MARK 2:25,26

*P*owerful needs and strong urges sometimes put a human being in a position that obliges him to break the normal rules set up by God, or his culture. Never rationalize as to what you should do in those circumstances. Be aware of the law; be aware of your special condition, and your psychological complexes, which are as real as metal. Regret the state of fallen man who sometimes cannot even satisfy a legitimate hunger without trespassing against a rule. Say like the apostle, "It is no longer I who do [the unlawful thing], but sin that dwells in me" (Romans 7:17). Separate your "I" decidedly from the forbidden bread that hunger obliges you to eat.

The much-persecuted Russian Orthodox priest Dudko tells about a Soviet girl who had come to confess. She said, "I believe, but they force me to wear the red neckscarf which is the badge of the pioneers, the atheistic Communist children's organization. I am powerless." If she refused, she would be beaten and expelled from school, and her parents might go to prison. So she sprinkled the red neckscarf with holy water, over which special prayers are said by the priest and which is used in Orthodox rituals. "I put the neckscarf on," she confessed, "only after having sprinkled it."

In the free world, we also are compelled at times to do things that normally should not be done. But then face the facts as they are; don't try to find excuses, but do them in Christ's name. You are only human. And everything is sanctified by prayer (1 Timothy 4:5). "Happy is he who does not condemn himself in what he approves" (Romans 14:22).

> *"My house is a house of prayer, but you have
> made it a den of thieves."*
>
> LUKE 19:46

*M*any Christians are dissatisfied with their churches. This is to be expected in view of the work of self-demolition that faithless bishops and pastors have done in the church. Would Jesus call the modern churches "dens of thieves"? This pronouncement on the part of Jesus was a broad generalization in His time as well.

How many "thieves" were in the house of prayer? Some of the top leaders of the temple were dishonest, and they brought the temple into ill-repute. But the rank-and-file priest and worshiper could have been very devout. Zacharias, a priest, and his wife Elizabeth, parents of John the Baptist, "were both righteous before God" (Luke 1:5,6). They were righteous in a den of thieves. "[Simeon] came by the Spirit into the temple" (into the den of thieves). "This man was just and devout...and the Holy Spirit was upon him" (Luke 2:27,25). So the Holy Spirit works in temples even when they have become dens of thieves.

A publican stood in the temple, in the den of thieves, and found there no encouragement to continue in his sinful life. On the contrary, he "beat his breast, saying, 'God be merciful to me a sinner'... This man went down to his house justified" (Luke 18:13,14). So a man can find salvation even in a temple which has deteriorated to the point of becoming a den of thieves.

The Jewish temple was not a dead or apostate church. It was a den of thieves which the Messiah had not forsaken, in which He worshiped, in which the rituals prescribed by God were fulfilled, in which the law was taught, and in which there were many saints.

Look for the saints in your church, too. Don't forsake a church lightly or casually. Better still, *be* a saint.

"The King will say to those on His right hand, 'Come'... He will also say to those on the left hand, 'Depart from me.'"
MATTHEW 25:34,41

*T*he existence of an objectively real right and left, with some men separated for eternal life on the right while their fellow men are set apart on the left for everlasting destruction, once was considered only a metaphor of speech. But that is not so. It is a fact.

Certain molecules exist in two forms, one being the mirror image of the other, which means they are related like a left hand and a right hand. If I hold my left hand to a mirror, what I appear to see in the mirror is a right hand. So it is with these molecules called isomers. Proteins are exclusively composed of L- (left-handed) amino acids. This is regarded as a unique characteristic of life—that is, life as we know it, in a fallen creation. The whole purpose of life is to pass from the left, the sinful state to which we belong by nature, to the right, the place of grace. D- amino acids (those of the right hand) are never found in proteins, but in antibiotics which save endangered life.

There exists a right and a left not only in living matter. In 1957, the particle physicists discovered a basic asymmetry in the matter out of which our part of the universe is composed. Electrons emitted during the beta decay of radioactive nuclei such as cobalt 60 are predominantly left-handed. Their particle spin is coupled to their momentum like a left-handed screw. The positron is right-handed.

Nature makes an absolute distinction between right and left, just as there is an absolute distinction between the sons of light and those of darkness. Through repentance the latter can change to the former during their short life span on earth. Those remaining on the left will go to the lake of fire. Time is running out. Hurry!

> *"There was a certain beggar named Lazarus...*
> *who was laid at [the rich man's] gate."*
> LUKE 16:20

*L*azarus begged without ever protesting against social injustice. Today this is not the case. The poor have become vocal. No sermon telling them to hold their peace would be effective. In her "Magnificat," the virgin Mary foretold a time when the hungry would be filled with good things and the rich would be sent away empty (Luke 1:53). We live in this time of total world revolution.

Marie Antoinette, on hearing that the Parisian mob was rioting because it had no bread, suggested, "Let them eat cake." The French monarchy, so completely out of touch with popular feeling, was thus doomed. By the same token, Czar Nicholas II never read Lenin.

The world's richest one billion people have an average income of $3,200 a year. The world's poorest one billion have an income of $120 a year. Many starve in shanty towns. Their days are lived in poverty and illiteracy. Sixty percent of mankind cannot read.

Nevertheless in the eyes of God people are most precious. The Lord tells us, "Sell what you have and give alms" (Luke 12:33). Don't give simply castoffs, but give what is needed. Hungry people are more important than houses, cars, chocolates, or operas.

In thirty years the world population will have doubled, along with its demands and hopes. Be understanding and generous about anticipating their material and spiritual needs. Otherwise you may find yourself among the rich who will be sent away empty.

MARCH 26

> *"[The Pharisees said about Jesus,] This Man is a sinner."*
> JOHN 9:24

*T*hese Pharisees had never met Jesus personally. They had drawn rash conclusions about who He was from hearsay regarding a single event. Jesus warned against attitudes rashly taken. "[Those] who, when they hear the word, immediately receive it with gladness . . . have no root in themselves, and so endure only for a time" (Mark 4:16,17). Don't accept Jesus hurriedly under the impulse of an urgent evangelistic appeal. Don't reject Him hastily without having listened attentively to the arguments for His case.

Geologists, men of science, were asked to look at this picture for seven seconds:

It contains a fault with concave cleavage lines at the synform and convex cleavage lines at the antiform. No more than 20 percent of those tested, including experienced geologists, reproduced it. This drawing, with both sets of cleavages convex, was a common response.

No quick look at a man or an event can give you the truth. Mary sat an entire evening at Jesus' feet, listened to His words attentively, and pondered them. So she became a faithful disciple. Thomas asked for proofs of Jesus' resurrection, received them, and later became a successful missionary to India.

I don't ask you to come to Jesus immediately if you lack sufficient motivation. Jesus said that you should rather "search the Scriptures" (John 5:39), an operation that takes quite a while. But do not reject Jesus without checking His claims carefully. Christians do not ask anyone to believe blindly. Only thorough inquiry and careful decision produce true Christians.

> *"The Son of Man did not come to be served,*
> *but... to give His life a ransom..."*
> MATTHEW 20:28

Let us pray for China. One-fourth of the world today is Chinese. On the mainland of China Christianity is completely forbidden, but God's Spirit has strange ways of penetrating dark places.

In a hut in a commune, a family gathered around the grandfather who entertained them with stories from the rich Chinese folklore. This time it was the story of Tso-Po-Tao, the man who had been a symbol of goodness. He had traveled once with his friend, Yang-Chiao-Ai. They had to reach Tsu Yuan Wang, but after a few days' journey, they found the snow to be too deep and their food and clothing insufficient. Both could not survive. Tso-Po-Tao urged, "I am a servant. Take the garments of us both and all the food and reach your goal. Why should we both die?"

Yang was reluctant to accept this offer, but Tso had already removed his clothes and laid down on the snow with hands outstretched as though wishing to embrace all mankind with his love. In a few minutes he was frozen to death. Then Yang dressed himself in his garments and had food enough to reach the destination. He always remembered with gratitude what Tso had done for him.

A child asked, "Is this a real story or a story-story? Do such good men like Tso exist? I never met that kind of man. Most around us are brutal."

The grandfather replied, "I guess you will not meet many Tsos. I heard once a white man saying that something just like this had happened long ago in a country far away. A man gave His life meekly like a lamb to save many others. The white man said this is why our Chinese character for 'righteousness' is the 'I' covered by 'a lamb.' We have been saved by this good being, but I am illiterate and did not understand much of his talk. In any case, child, you would do well to take Tso as an example for life."

"God... at various times and in various ways spoke in time past to the fathers" (Hebrews 1:1).

> *"Be faithful until death, and I will give you the crown of life."*
> REVELATION 2:10

C. T. Studd saw a strangely worded notice in Liverpool in 1908. It caught his attention and his sense of humor. "Cannibals want missionaries." He entered the meeting hall where Karl Kumm told the story of his walking through Africa and of all the tribes who had never heard the story of Jesus Christ. Explorers had been to those regions, even though they knew they were inhabited by cannibals. Big-game hunters, Muslim missionaries, traders of weapons and liquor, European officials, and scientists had risked their lives, but no Christian had ever gone there to tell of Jesus.

Studd asked himself why Christians did not go. God replied, "Why don't you go?" Studd already had long terms of missionary work in China and India behind him. He was sick. He went, notwithstanding, and won cannibals for Christ.

There are still individuals, tribes, and countries that take pleasure in torturing and murdering Christians. Today you can give your life among primitive peoples in Latin America, in the Philippines, in Papua New Guinea. Muslim fanatics are always ready to kill Christians. They have killed great numbers in the last century in Turkey and Lebanon. Communists are ready to jail anyone who dares to bring Bibles into Communist countries. There are still backward and unreached tribes in Africa. Go there even if you are old and sick. If you cannot go, help with your prayers, your home work, and your contributions to those who do go.

Let us all pray for the Christians who do missionary work in places of great danger, at the risk of their own lives.

> *"They were stoned, they were sawn in two."*
> HEBREWS 11:37

*I*t was in 1964. Kingese, the mad ruler of Stanleyville, and other Sambi leaders had vowed to end religious teaching in their country and wipe the name of God from the Congo.

In one hamlet every man who wore trousers instead of a loin-cloth was killed. In Kindu, the rebels burned so many bodies before the monument of Lumumba that the sidewalk cracked under the constant heat. At Paulis, observers placed the toll at four thousand. Some died by dismemberment, some by being forced to drink gasoline and then having fire touched to their bodies.

Twenty members of the Unevangelized Field Mission and nine from other societies died as martyrs. Seventy among the Catholic missions lost their lives in this world. They all died for Christ. They also died because of the foolishness of granting independence to peoples who were still at an infantile stage.

The missionaries had the consolation of knowing that many Congolese stood firm in their commitment to Christ in spite of the terror.

The grains of wheat had fallen into the ground and died. Their example brought forth a harvest of new souls for Christ. Not everyone of us is called upon to be a martyr, but everyone has to be a co-martyr. We should love Christ wholeheartedly as they did and vicariously share their sorrows, trials, and triumphs in prayer. Let us intercede regularly for Africa.

> *"Greater love has no one than this, than to
> lay down one's life for his friends."*
> JOHN 15:13

Nate Saint, one of the five missionaries martyred in the jungles of Ecuador in 1956, before leaving Quito had delivered a premonitory sermon on the subject of expendability. He said: "During the last war we were taught that, in order to obtain our objective, we had to be willing to be expendable, and many lives were spent paying the price of our redemption from the bonds of political slavery... We know that there is only one answer when our country demands that we share in the price of freedom—yet when the Lord Jesus asks us to pay the price for world evangelization, we often answer without a word. We cannot go. We say it costs too much... Missionaries constantly face expendability."

Then he was sent to the Auca Indians. The missionaries knew them to be savages, so they used "Jacob's tactics." They dropped gifts while flying over their territories. They received gifts in return. On the last flight, the natives put a beautiful parrot in the bag let down from the plane with a rope.

Then five missionaries landed among the Aucas. Saint was one of them. First they had a happy encounter. The next day they were killed. Betty Elliot, one of the wives of the martyred, wrote that same evening, "Nothing was more burning in Jim's heart than that Christ should be named among the Aucas."

Choose one nation, one tribe, one social category to the service of which, for Christ, you would dedicate your heart. You might not be called to go as a missionary to them, but you can be a co-missionary through your prayers, spreading the news about the mission, and helping financially from your earnings.

> *"I have become all things to all men, that I
> might by all means save some."*
> 1 CORINTHIANS 9:22

*D*id you ever think about the immortal souls of Somalia, at the northwest tip of Africa? In Somalia's sands there is a simple gravestone with the inscription "Merlin R. Grove, Feb. 9, 1929–July 16, 1962. Jesus said, . . . 'No man cometh unto the Father but by Me' (John 14:6)."

Grove was a Mennonite missionary. A Muslim priest, aroused to anger against him, stabbed him twelve times. Grove's wife Dorothy heard something happening, and when she rushed outdoors, her husband was already dying. The murderer turned on her and stabbed her in the abdomen.

Dorothy had questioned before if she were in the right place as a missionary, not feeling sure that she could love Somalians, whom she considered lazy, fierce, prone to kill. Now that she lay bleeding on the floor, the love of Calvary for Somalians filled her heart. She recovered. She no longer doubted her calling.

The quickest way to have the assurance of salvation is to take upon yourself some suffering for the fact that you are saved. The quickest way to be sure about a certain calling is to take upon yourself a specific cross connected with this calling. You have chosen the right wife or husband or boyfriend if you can bear some heavy burden for him or her.

Today Somalia is almost entirely Muslim. Is there anyone willing to do his best that Somalians might be saved?

"A bishop then must be blameless, . . . not greedy for money."
1 TIMOTHY 3:3

*T*he Reformation and the irreparable split in Christianity might never have happened if it were not for some of the clergy's love of money and the many personal sins of those involved on all sides. I still wonder if the reformation of the church was necessary.

The church is a continuation of the incarnation of Christ. Christ, its head, sees to it that it should function well, so the church cannot die. Even the gates of hell cannot prevail against it.

However, there exist human institutions called churches, full of men and women who have not been born again. And they do not need to be reformed, but transformed. New birth can change every man into a child of God.

On the human level, scandalous things have happened through the years. Indulgences, and with them the eternal destinies of souls, were offered for sale. The bastard children of King James of Scotland were appointed to some of the wealthiest abbacies in the kingdom while they were still infants. Acts like these produce public revulsion. Certainly they made it easy for a Henry VIII, angry with the Pope because he could not get a divorce from his wife, to take his nation away from Rome. Both sides later made it a crime punishable by death not to agree with the Vatican, guilty of greed, or with the king, guilty of lust. Similar things happened in other countries.

We must take a look at our clergy and denominational leaders today. Are their priorities in life obvious? Use your dedicated Christian influence to keep them holy in thought and action. Transform your church after the pattern given by Christ, but above all be sure to belong not only to a human institution.

Through new birth become a member of the "glorious church, not having spot or wrinkle or any such thing" (Ephesians 5:27).

APRIL 2

"God also has...given Him the name which is above every name."
PHILIPPIANS 2:9

*S*ome men are given names that foreshadow their destiny. Vladimir, in Russian, means "the ruler of the world." Russian history has known two influential men who bore this name. In A.D. 998 Prince Vladimir of Kiev became a Christian. Having to choose between Roman Catholicism and Eastern Orthodoxy, he sent envoys to Europe to find out which of the two religions would be more suitable. These emissaries were impressed with the beautiful music of the Orthodox service and inclined the prince to embrace this form of Christianity. As a result, he ordered all his subjects to be baptized.

About nine hundred years later another Vladimir was born in Russia. At the age of sixteen he became an atheist, all because of a stupid incident. A sin of a Christian can make a God-hater out of a man who was previously a worshiper. Like many young men, Vladimir Lenin had neglected going to church for some time. The lad overheard his father asking a priest what he should do about it. The priest answered, "Beat him and beat him." Indignant, Lenin tore the cross from his neck, resolving never to have anything more to do with religion. He hated it now. As a result of the revolution he fomented, millions of Christians have been killed. Perhaps this never would have happened if the priest had given a wiser and more loving answer.

It is sobering to realize that one word of ours can elevate a soul. One wrong word can destroy it.

Vladimir the prince could not make all his people disciples of Christ. Lenin could not make all the people atheists. In any case, neither of them was truly a "Vladimir"—a ruler over the world. Only one is such a ruler—Jesus Christ. He will reign, and before Him every knee will bow.

"Present your bodies a living sacrifice."
ROMANS 12:1

*D*uring the Vietnam war, Buddhist priests who saw their religion endangered by the politics of the Catholic Thieu set fire to themselves. Two monks would pour gasoline on a priest, and then he would commit ritual suicide while thousands watched, kneeling. The Czech Christian Jan Pollach and the East German evangelical pastor Brüscwitz self-immolated themselves as a protest against Communist injustice.

Christians might learn something from this. Suicide in the usual sense of the word is normally forbidden by our religion, but we all have to give ourselves as a living sacrifice to the only cause that really counts.

Jesus' death could be called a sophisticated suicide. He said, "I lay down My life . . . No one takes it from Me, but I lay it down of Myself" (John 10:17,18). He seemed to do His utmost to provoke His enemies to utter anger. He took issue with all the impulses by which men live. Don't even look at a woman with lust! Let your speech be yes, yes, or no, no, which makes all advertising and all promotion impossible! Christ did some of His miracles on the Sabbath, even though He knew that this would irritate His enemies. He wished to be crucified, because He knew His death was the only means of salvation for mankind.

Christians also go against the standards of this world, because they too wish to be sacrificed through bearing their cross daily.

"I have been crucified with Christ; it is no longer I who live, but Christ lives in me" (Galatians 2:20).

[Jesus said,] "He who is faithful in what is least is faithful also in much."
LUKE 16:10

We deceive ourselves if we believe that payment of the tithe discharges our financial obligation to God. Imprisoned Christians under persecution, who received one slice of bread a week plus soup containing dirty potato peels, would tithe. Every tenth week they would give their piece of bread to someone who was sick or weaker than they. But this was not all. They knew that man's responsibility encompasses 100 percent of what he has. Many Christians gave their bread every third or every fifth week. Some never ate bread, but gave it always, being content themselves with the dirty soup.

Not simply 10 percent, but all our money belongs to the Lord. It is not true that after giving 10 percent we can do with the rest as we like. Rather, we have been given an expense account by the Lord and we will have to answer for every cent we spend. A traveling salesman cannot buy a fur coat for his wife from his expense account. Neither are we allowed any luxury.

Is your conscience clear? Can you justify before God all that you spend for yourself on food and clothing in a hungry and naked world? Can you justify the luxurious church buildings, choir robes, upholstered pews, when missions lack a dollar to give a Bible in a heathen country? Can you justify your expenses on cosmetics, on entertainment? Will you be able to look in the face of Jesus in the Day of Judgment and tell Him, "I did well to spend my money like this"? Will He say to you, "Well done, good and faithful steward"?

*"Moses said to the LORD, '...I am slow of speech
and slow of tongue.'"*
EXODUS 4:10

*R*ichard Hext was born with crippled hands and feet. His hands hung normally following an operation, but he had not the slightest power in them.

This did not keep him from attaining his ambition to become a painter. He attended the school of arts for seven years. Then he earned his living as a painter—wielding a brush with his teeth. Some of his paintings are so beautiful that they hang in Buckingham Palace.

Moses became a great preacher, though he was a stutterer. Rahab became a saint and an ancestor of the Lord, though she was first a prostitute in a heathen nation. Peter became a martyr, though he was a coward by nature. We first see him trembling before a servant maid who could do him no harm. After the Resurrection the same man stood in a marketplace in Jerusalem defying the rulers of the nation and the mob. History tells us he eventually died for his Lord—by his own request, crucified head down.

A Christian convicted of both adultery and murder probably would give up hope of ever again being useful to the Lord. But David repented and wrote beautiful psalms that are our spiritual nourishment. Solomon fell into idolatry and promiscuity but became the author of three books of the Bible.

No physical, intellectual, or moral handicap is unconquerable. If you have no hands, paint by using your teeth, but make pictures for the Lord.

> *"This is My commandment, that you love*
> *one another as I have loved you."*
> JOHN 15:12

*H*uman sin has marred the history of Christendom, which could have been beautiful if those bearing the name of Christ had followed their Master's precepts. Everyone knows of the Catholic Inquisition, but Protestants could be cruel as well.

Her Majesty the Gracious Sovereign of Britain, Elizabeth I, condemned Bishop Plunkett for his Catholic beliefs, ordered him to be partly hanged, then lowered, then ripped off, then his bowels burned (he being still alive), then quartered. Catholics in Piedmont apprehended the Protestant Giovanni Michialin with four of his children. As three of the children were hacked to pieces before Michialin's eyes, the soldiers asked at the death of each child if he would recant; he constantly refused. When the same answer was given the fourth time, a soldier grabbed the child by the legs and dashed out its brains.

Catholics killed thousands of Orthodox in Croatia during the war. Orthodox priests wickedly persecuted Evangelicals in Romania and saw to it that they were jailed. Priests led mass slaughters of Jews. Today Protestants and Catholics kill each other in Northern Ireland in the name of the One who enjoined love even for an enemy.

Let us decide once and for all that we will uproot any thought of resentment or hostility toward another for holding a religion different from ours. Let us guard against using inflammatory language against someone else's religion. It might incite an irresponsible person to rash acts and lead even to murder. Religious differences have to be discussed in love. Whenever there are seemingly irreconcilable differences, each should retain his convictions based on the Word of God. But the supreme commandment is love.

APRIL 7

*"I exhort first of all that supplications, prayers,
intercessions, and giving of thanks be made . . .
for kings and all who are in authority."*
1 TIMOTHY 2:1,2

*T*he text does not say that we should pray only for our country's rulers and government. This is what British, German, Russian, and American clergy did in World War II. Having done this, one can comfortably kill those who belong to the army of another sovereign. It is wrong to pray only for our own king or president.

Rulers and kings are a specific class of society for which we have to pray, just as we pray for the hungry or the sick. A Christian, then, prays at once for his own ruler, as well as for the ruler of the neighboring country and the chief of an aboriginal tribe.

By praying for our rulers and loving them, even though they may be wicked, we will be enabled to lead "a quiet and peaceable life," because the thought of rioting and rebelling will never occur to us.

Furthermore, with such an outlook we can be a leaven for good in society. Therefore . . . pray.

A P R I L   8

"Do not be drunk with wine, in which is dissipation;
but be filled with the Spirit."
EPHESIANS 5:18

I will take the figures of the European country least reputed for vice.

Since the end of World War II the consumption of alcohol has doubled in Switzerland. The number of alcoholics has increased from 100,000 to 130,000. Twenty percent of the court cases and 23 percent of the divorces are due to alcohol. Alcohol is responsible for one-third of the suicides. Each year 1,300 persons enter psychiatric asylums as a result of alcohol abuse. The figures for other countries are much worse.

The Bible speaks about being drunk with love, about being so filled with the Holy Spirit as to give the impression of being a drunkard. Does anyone know of any evil effects from such holy drunkenness?

Drink therefore from the miraculous wine that Jesus gave to the apostles at Cana. You will have many symptoms of drunkenness: drunkards praise their wine, you will praise yours; drunkards sing, you will have an irresistible impulse to sing to the glory of your Savior; drunkards are ready to fight, you also will be willing to fight, even if you are very weak, against much stronger foes.

I am not against drunkenness. But I consider alcohol the wrong beverage. Let us drink of the wine which Jesus freely offers to those who thirst.

"We did not yield submission even for an hour, that the truth of the gospel might continue with you."
GALATIANS 2:5

*B*eware of tolerance in matters of faith. Imagine two schools, one run by a wise man, the other by a fool. In the first, children are taught that 2 and 2 are 4; in the second, that 2 and 2 are 3. Then along comes a teacher who says that after all love is the most important thing. Why should there be differences between teachers of mathematics? Let them each agree to make a small concession so that both can teach the same way. Then children can be taught that 2 and 2 are 3½. Whoever refuses to accept such a loving, agreeable solution is a fanatic, a bigot, and is no longer worthy to be a teacher of mathematics. What would you say to this?

Christians love unity but not at the expense of truth.

The Christian church possesses definitive truth much surer than mathematics because it has been revealed by God Himself. From my wallet I can give a man as much as I like, because it is my money. From God's truth I can give nothing. There might be variations among Christians in nonessentials, just as there exist varieties of orchids. I will accept any rose of another color, but I cannot accept a thistle as a rose. Love is not sufficient reason to abandon one word, one letter of the Bible. I can love the heretic, but not the heresy.

Christ is God. He became man, was born of a virgin, died for our sins, was resurrected bodily, and ascended into heaven. Anyone is free to believe otherwise, but then I wish no unity and no dialogue with him. Professors of mathematics don't conduct dialogues with their pupils. They proclaim the truth and it must be accepted. Christians also proclaim the truth. Whoever refuses to accept it will perish.

"Oh sing to the LORD a new song!"
PSALM 96:1

*I*t is much more important to save the youth than to save the old manner of worship or the old songs to which we are accustomed. We live in a world in which minds and hearts have been revolutionized. New songs and new manners of worship have arisen. The older generation of Christians feel offended, as if God were inseparably linked only to the liturgy which they have known from childhood. They forget that what is now old was itself once new.

The *St. Matthew Passion* of Bach was not accepted in his day. After a few performances it lay forgotten for a hundred years. The *Great Organ Mass* of Haydn was declared sacrilegious by the founder of the German Cecilian order, who wrote: "It compares to pure church music like a prostitute to a queen or like a waltz to the death of Christ." This priest, Witt, wrote to the Pope that he considered this music more suitable for salons: "The military and bacchantic rhythms don't correspond to the earnestness of the church services and the sacrifice on the cross."

Missionaries to Africa tell how much more the hearts of converts are moved when the organ is replaced by their drums.

Open your heart to music and church practices which you personally may not like. They may be helpful to someone with another frame of mind. They may even help someone else praise the Lord better.

"You shall love your neighbor as yourself."
MARK 12:31

*D*on't be content simply to admire the beauty of this commandment or even to tell it to others. Rather sit down and write on a sheet of paper the names of the neighbors who are in need of your love.

Who is frustrated? Who is lonely? Who has been forsaken by his marriage partner or by his children? Who is a dropout?

Squeaky Fromm, of the infamous Manson cult, was driven out by her parents who never exhibited any love for her. When she sat helpless and forsaken in a gutter, Manson, the future killer, passed by and asked her, "Do you need love? I love. Follow me." She followed him and became a member of a satanic sect that knew how to disguise itself behind loving words. She became a drug addict and made an attempt on the life of former President Ford. Now she is serving a life sentence in prison. Think how different her life might have been if a Christian had stopped to befriend a girl weeping by the roadside and had shown her the love of Christ.

Your neighbor who needs your love might be a refugee from a foreign land, he might be one of the many who starve in Africa or India, he might be one of those who lack a knowledge of Christ on a Pacific island, in a Communist or Muslim land, or in your own reputedly Christian country. Don't stop to admire the dictum "Love your neighbor" as you would a picture in an art gallery, but begin to love in a practical way.

"What God has joined together, let not man separate."
MATTHEW 19:6

*G*od hates divorce (Malachi 2:16). There is really only one basic reason why people divorce. It is that they had no real motive for marriage. They either did not marry with the intent of sacrificing their whole life to the well-being of the spouse, or else they have abandoned this intent.

It would be unrealistic not to admit that sometimes it is best for a couple to part. Jesus cites the case of adultery, by which He does not mean one instance of falling into sin, but a permanent life style of the marriage partner. We cannot limit permission to divorce to this either. Otherwise we would be like some who might quote the Scripture, "Pay tithe of mint and anise and cummin" (Matthew 23:23), to justify not tithing other sources of income. The items mentioned in this Bible verse are only examples of different kinds of earnings.

Likewise, Jesus' mention of adultery as a motive for divorce is that there must be a motive as important as this. What can one do when the spouse is a compulsive gambler or an incurable drug addict or alcoholic, endangers the upbringing of children, deserts the family, or when overt cruelty and homosexuality persist? If the erring spouse refuses to take corrective measures, one cannot insist that the partner remain involved in his illness. I would not remain married to someone who obliged me to be an accomplice in crime.

The best prevention of divorce is earnest prayer and the willingness to open one's eyes and engage in mature reflection as well as consultation with experienced people regarding marriage and children. Girls who marry under the age of twenty have, statistically, three times as great a chance of winding up in divorce court as those who marry later.

Parents, be loving to and considerate of each other, not only for your own happiness and to prevent divorce, but also to serve as an example to your children of what marriage should be, so that theirs will not end in divorce.

A P R I L   1 3

"Search the Scriptures."
JOHN 5:39

*I*n Madagascar, during all the persecution between 1836 and 1861, Christians not only kept their faith alive by secret Bible reading, but the church increased tenfold under this experience. The Formosan hill tribes, almost untouched by Christianity before the Second World War, resisted Japanese pressure and emerged with firmly planted Christian communities based on nothing but the study of the Bible. In Kenya, under the threat of the Mau Mau, it was the Christians whose lives were most deeply rooted in the Bible who stood firm against all attempts to get them to take the heathen Kikuyu oath. The toughness of indigenous churches depends on the degree of devotion to the Bible. The organization of the church, even its ministers and priests, may be destroyed without ultimate disaster so long as the people have—and read—the Bible.

Not everywhere is there persecution, but everywhere the world is adverse to true Christianity. We have to be versed in the Scriptures if we wish our faith to survive.

In Communist China, Mao's book of "thought," the most pestilential volume ever vomited forth from the jaws of hell, is chanted in every house and on every street under compulsion. Erasmus, one of the great translators of the Bible, said, "I could wish that the husbandman might sing parts of Scripture at his plough." Speak to each other in psalms and Scriptures. In this lies the salvation of the church.

Be thankful to God that you belong to the privileged elite (only 40 percent of mankind) who know how to read. Be thankful that you belong to the much narrower circle of those who can have a Bible. (In half of the world it is not available.) You are privileged in that you are able to afford to buy a Bible. (Many desirous Christians in Latin America, Africa, and India have no money for a Bible.) Make the searching of the Scriptures your daily occupation.

"It is no longer I who live, but Christ lives in me."
GALATIANS 2:20

*A*mong all the biblical authors, I particularly love those whose names are unknown. Moses quotes "the Book of the Wars of the LORD" (Numbers 21:14). Who is its author? Joshua (10:13) mentions "the Book of Jasher," which means "the righteous." Who might have written it? Paul quotes a Greek poet who said, "We are also [God's] offspring" (Acts 17:28). His saying was of such a superlative nature that it transcended the importance of its author.

When people sing your verses they have become verses indeed, but when a poet is quoted as authority by an apostle of Christ to support his argument, there is no longer need to remember his human name.

Such is the glory of those who write the real songs of God. It is as if they were not written by mere man. A Buddhist legend says a man painted such a masterful picture of Buddha that when he finished only the painting remained. The painter was no longer there. The same is true of the real Christian author, poet, preacher, and of the layman who witnesses as a rank-and-file Christian to another person. He must cease to be himself and must unite with the soul of his listener who starts to believe. He must become one with Jesus about whom he writes or speaks.

When you write, speak, or act for Jesus, let Him infuse your heart with His sacred spirit. You might lose your name by this, but you will gain eternity. You will be quoted by God without mention of a name, because the mystical marriage will have taken place. You will have become united with Him.

APRIL 15

"The greatest of these is love."
1 CORINTHIANS 13:13

An old legend says that in the beginning there was God and two swallows. One swallow whispered into the ears of God, "Make something. We should have trees in which to make nests, and air through which to fly, and many countries so that we might migrate to and fro. Life is boresome in a nothing."

The other swallow chirped, "Don't create, my God. Once You create matter, energy, and movement, who knows which molecule will unite with which. Some rapacious birds might appear which would eat us up, there might be tempests in which we will perish, and who knows what else. Let it be as it is."

God answered, "I wish to create. I wish to have beings on whom to pour My love and who would love Me."

The swallow warned again, "Once You create beings with changing sentiments, thoughts, and moods, they may at a certain moment not love You, but come to hate You. Let us be just as we are, You and the two swallows."

The other bird insisted, "Make a world. I promise that I will chirp even if the world turns bad. I will chirp even when I know rapacious birds are stalking me and naughty children have set traps to catch me."

So God decided to make the world. He took upon Himself the risks of love, the risks everyone has to take when he begins a friendship or a marriage, the risks everyone has to take when he launches a new idea. He decided to love and, because He loves, we learn to trust and to hope and to aid.

The only alternative to love is nonexistence. If love should totally disappear in the world, the world would no longer be. Think about it.

APRIL 16

"Do all things without . . . disputing."
PHILIPPIANS 2:14

*S*ix blind men tried to ascertain what an elephant was. One felt its side and thought it a wall. One felt its ear and thought it a fan. One felt its leg and thought it a pillar. One felt its tail and believed he had touched a snake, and so on. We know in part (1 Corinthians 13:12).

The story is told how several blind men, cured by the Lord, discussed at a party how Jesus heals blindness. The one said, "I can tell it from my own experience. He simply says, 'Your faith has healed you.'"

The other objected, "This is Protestant disregard of good deeds. Faith alone does not suffice. Jesus touches the eyes of the blind man."

To which a third added, "It must be done twice. If He touches you only once, you see men walking like trees." The former insisted that he had been touched only once and notwithstanding saw perfectly.

A fourth one said, "You all have talked nonsense. Jesus makes mud by spitting on the earth. He puts the mud on your eyes. Then you have to go to wash yourself in a certain pool in Palestine. No other pool will do. What you have spoken until now are fancies."

So the four former blind men fall into a great quarrel. Each formed his own denomination. Once Jesus gathered the heads of the four denominations and asked them, "I have healed you all, each one in a different way. Would it not have been better for you to unite in thanking Me for what I have done? Am I not free to heal everyone as I see best?"

What you condemn as the error of your brother might very well be a valid personal experience of his with the Lord Jesus.

"'Not by might nor by power, but by My Spirit,'
says the LORD of hosts."
ZECHARIAH 4:6

*A*n admirer of modern art wrote in an English newspaper that "this art is democratic. Anybody can do it." You can make two strokes with the brush in yellow and three others in blue. Make a circle around them in red. The circle does not even need to be round. Paste on it a nose and one eye of a girl cut out of a newspaper. Call it "Mankind's Glorious Future" and critics may well label your painting exciting. It is really exciting. Exciting of what?

Ungifted, untalented, and untaught men produce so-called works of art. Ungifted preachers preach. The result is that many churches are being emptied. Luther made preaching the center of the worship service, rather than communion, as had been the case before. He forgot that the world does not have many good preachers.

Look at the *Pietà*, two life-sized statues combined into one. Michelangelo placed the body of a full-grown man in the lap of a maid. She looks much younger than her son. She has kept the beauty of virginity. He has been the Man of Sorrows. Her face is calm. She knows about resurrection. Such artists are not found on every street. Neither can you make preachers like John Chrysostom by passing boring speakers through theological exams.

Jesus must live within the heart before He becomes the subject of a sermon or a personal witness. "Out of the abundance of the heart the mouth speaks" (Matthew 12:34).

Preachers who are not gifted should become something else or be born again with the gift of preaching. Even an uncultured and untalented man can speak interestingly about the person he loves most. Mothers know how to tell about the good in their children. Only those who love Jesus greatly should speak about Him. Otherwise our witnessing for Him will look like modern art. Anyone can do it, but it is not beautiful. Or significant.

To be eloquent in personal witnessing or preaching depends not upon scholarship, but upon being fervent in the Spirit.

"The day of the Lord is ... a day of darkness and gloominess."
JOEL 2:1,2

The Lord taught us to say, "Thy kingdom come." He did not mean us to say it lightheartedly. If His kingdom were to come today it would mean the entering of many into everlasting fire. "He who does not believe will be condemned" (Mark 16:16). The believers in Christ are an infinitesimal minority. Where will the others pass their eternity? What will the advent of the kingdom mean for those you love?

A sifting will take place. Some will go to the right, others to the left. Your darling might be found to the left. Can you say with your whole heart, "Thy kingdom come"? Are you willing that many of your family and your nation spend eternity in hell?

The prayer "Thy kingdom come" was taught to give us a sense of urgency. Having both the knowledge of and the desire for its coming, we should spread the gospel around us to the utmost of our abilities.

We often have in us an unhealthy curiosity. When the Lord said about the buildings of Jerusalem that not one stone would be left upon another that would not be thrown down (Mark 13:2), the disciples wanted details about when these things would happen, instead of interceding like Abraham and Moses that the predicted catastrophe might not occur.

There is now much rejoicing about the pouring out of the Spirit in many places. Those who receive His gifts should not forget that the prophecy about this outpouring in Joel 2:28,29 is followed immediately by the announcement of terrible judgments upon mankind. We should not seek merely to interpret these prophecies, but having the Spirit and knowing the dangers, we should become intercessors to prevent the catastrophes from happening to others.

A P R I L   1 9

"All Scripture is given by inspiration of God."
2 TIMOTHY 3:16

*D*uring the Reformation, Thomas Müntzer mocked Luther as a scribe addicted to the dead letter of the Bible. He nicknamed Luther "a Bible-gobbler," and said, "It is of no use to have swallowed the Bible one hundred thousand times." Müntzer's religion centered on having the living Spirit. Luther retorted that he would not listen to Müntzer though he had received the Holy Spirit completely, unless he adduced Scripture.

Luther was right in this. St. Jerome had written long before, "To be ignorant of Scriptures is not to know Christ...A man who is well-grounded in the Scriptures is the bulwark of the church."

The contest between being Spirit-guided and Scripture-guided is artificial, because those who have been inwardly taught by the Spirit feel an entire acquiescence to the Scripture and perceive that "it is self-authenticated, carrying with it its own evidence" (Calvin).

A man would have to demonstrate that his attitudes or words were really inspired by the Holy Spirit. The Bible need not and ought not be made subject to demonstrations and arguments from reason. We have received it from God's mouth by the ministry of men. It is superior to any human judgment. When you read the Scriptures with faith, they give you the perception of God Himself. It is wrong to believe the Bible because arguments prove it to be true. We do not judge the Word of God; it judges us. It is the invincible truth. Christians submit to it completely. Don't allow any spirit to separate you from any part of it.

114

A P R I L   2 0

"For the Jew first."
ROMANS 1:16

*T*he sun has never shone on such a bloodthirsty and vindictive people as the Jews, who cherish the idea of murdering and strangling the heathen. No other men under the sun are more greedy than they have been and always will be, as one can see from their accursed usury."

These are the words of Martin Luther. There are other sayings like this in the writings of other great Christian divines, of popes and church fathers.

The sentiments have gone beyond mere words. The Jewish people described as being so despicable have been slaughtered over the centuries by those calling themselves Christians. Hitler received his first education in a Catholic school. He must have heard many times the story about the Jews being God-killers. No wonder that the unjustly hated Jews do not believe in Christ.

The Scriptures, on the other hand, say that the Jews gave to the world the human Son of God (Romans 9:5).

A wanderer walking in a storm drew his overcoat around him tighter and tighter. Then the sun came out with its warmth and light, and the wanderer took off his outer garment. Only warm Christian love will lead the chosen people of God, who have gone astray, to give up their prejudices against Jesus and embrace Him as their Savior. Let us as Christians allow ourselves to reflect on them the light and warmth of the Sun of righteousness.

"Remember the Sabbath day, to keep it holy."
EXODUS 20:8

*M*any businessmen spend their lives in a frantic endeavor to make money, much of which they don't even need (the best proof being that they keep it stored in banks). This accumulation of wealth enables them to buy things they can go without, in order to impress people they don't like.

What is the good of all this frenetic activity to amass wealth?

One of the most important laws of God is the law enjoining rest: Remember to keep the Sabbath. Stop running after money. Cease your constant striving for achievement. Let up on your engagements and committees. Ease the stress of living. Come apart and rest.

The Sabbath is the oldest of God's institutions. Even the heathen understand the importance—could they have had it from Adam? Relax when possible from work, even from important work. Socrates recuperated from stressful experiences by playing with children. In the Jesuit order it was formerly a rule that after two hours of study there was a relaxation period of fifteen minutes when something else had to be done. Cardinal Richelieu relaxed by doing strenuous exercises, such as competing against his manservant in the high jump.

Don't allow yourself to be consumed with the desire to earn more money. An increase in your income may not be a necessity, especially if it increases your worries. Take time to enter into a Sabbath rest. Relax. "Come to Me," Jesus said, "all you who labor and are heavy laden ... and you will find rest for your souls" (Matthew 11:28,29). And while you rest, the One who keeps Israel neither slumbers nor sleeps (Psalm 121:4).

A P R I L   2 2

*T*hose who accept the materialistic philosophy of life believe that the individual ceases to exist at death. This contradicts the principle of conservation of energy which is a cornerstone of science. The energy condensed in the atoms constituting my body doesn't disappear at death. As the body decays, these atoms form other combinations. The caloric energy I have does not disappear. It remains a part of the constant total energy of the universe. When the stove gets cold, its former warmth has been communicated to the room. So it is when my body becomes a cold corpse.

I also have spiritual energy; the power to will; sentiments; conscience. We know of no kind of energy that disappears in this universe. There is not the slightest proof to convince us that spiritual energy would be an exception. Death can only transfer it into a new dimension, but cannot destroy it.

The renowned physicist Maxwell wrote that "scientific progress ... obliges one to make a profound distinction between the visible side of the human being, which obviously perishes, and that which constitutes our 'I' and to adopt the position that human personality, by its nature and calling, lies beyond the borders of the sphere of science." The fact that we cannot comprehend how consciousness could exist when death has severed its ties with the brain—because in us, while we are living, mind and brain are connected—does not prove that after death consciousness has disappeared.

The German writer Goethe said, "My conviction that we will live eternally stems from the notion of activity. If I will be energetically active until my end, nature, when it sees that my body cannot bear anymore the burden of my spirit, will be obliged to provide me with some other form of existence."

Continue your good work diligently, not worrying about death. God, who has given you a body for the present work, will give you another one at death if your work is pleasing to Him.

A P R I L   2 3

*I*n Numbers 31, we are told how God gave the Jews a great victory over the Midianite people. The Jews took a great spoil. God told them to give to the temple a five-hundredth part of it. God is modest. There are times when He asks little.

When the Son of God became incarnate, He chose as His place of birth a stable; as His way of life, sorrow; as His manner of death, crucifixion.

He chose as disciples twelve despised men (1 Corinthians 1:28). He allows the world at times to be ruled by monsters and keeps for Himself a little flock. The wicked triumph and the Christians pass through sufferings.

If you ask "Why this modesty of God?" the answer would be, "It is a very immodest thing to question the Creator. Don't ask why, but take your modest place near your modest God."

Christ's church and real Christians never boast of great achievements. His kingdom is not of this world. Here the great achievements belong to tyrants and crooks. God's successes in this world are always modest, for His triumph is in the realm of the spirit.

Be happy about your modest achievements.

A P R I L   2 4

"I, the LORD your God, am a jealous God."
EXODUS 20:5

*T*he great painter Van Gogh, when very sick, wrote to his brother, "I promised myself to consider my illness as nonexistent. Art is jealous. She does not want us to choose illness in preference to her, so I do what she wishes. Enough time has been lost, my hands have become too white. People such as I are not allowed to be ill, so to speak. So I have set to drawing regularly from morning until night."

We have a God who is jealous, as art is. He does not want us to escape from problems, disappointments, failures, mischiefs, into nervous breakdowns or mental illness. Christians are not allowed to absent themselves from their work under the pretense of being ill. There should be no spiritual sickness.

A man watched Michelangelo shape a statue. He asked him, "What do you do if your chisel has taken away a bit too much of the nose?"

Michelangelo answered, "It does not happen."

The man insisted, "Suppose it has happened. Can you repair the fault?"

The sculptor answered again, "It does not happen."

The man could not understand. *"What if* it happens?"

Michelangelo shouted angrily at him, "Be quiet, and leave me alone! It does not happen!"

"Whoever abides in [Jesus] does not sin" (1 John 3:6), in the sense that he never allows himself the luxury of abandoning his art, his calling, for sin's sake or for trouble's sake. He continues his walk in the way of the Lord. The Lord is jealous. He does not willingly accept or allow us to wallow in sins, sorrows, or laziness.

APRIL 25

"We are surrounded by so great a cloud of witnesses."
HEBREWS 12:1

A Christian prisoner in Cuba was asked to sign a statement containing accusations against brethren, which would have led to their arrest. He said, "The chain keeps me from signing this."

The Red officer replied, "But you are not in chains."

"I am," said the Christian. "I am bound by the chains of witnesses who throughout the centuries gave their lives for Christ. I am a link in this chain. I will not break it."

Thomas Aquinas, after having called martyrdom the greatest proof of perfect love, adds: "Words pronounced by the martyrs before authorities are not human words, the simple expression of a human conviction, but words pronounced by the Holy Spirit through the confessors of Jesus."

Learn from the martyrs. You too are a link in this chain. Remain faithful!

Nijole Sadunaite, a young Christian lady, said before the court in Lithuania when she was sentenced for her faith, "This is the happiest day of my life. I am tried for the cause of truth and love toward men...I have enviable fate, a glorious destiny. My condemnation will be my triumph. I regret only to have done so little for men... Let us love each other and we will be happy. Only the one who loves not is unhappy...We must condemn evil, but we must love the man, even the one in error. This you can learn only at the school of Jesus Christ."

This is the teaching that the Holy Spirit gives you through a sufferer for Christ. Apply it in your own life.

"The fruit of the Spirit is love... Against such there is no law."
GALATIANS 5:22,23

*M*ore than one-third of the world is presently under Communist dominion. One aim of the Communists is eradication of religion. Bibles have to be smuggled into most countries of the Communist bloc. Is it right for Christians sometimes to do illegal things and things that contravene generally accepted moral standards?

The Jewish high priests had a promise from God that He would speak to them from between the two cherubim on the ark of the covenant in the temple. They felt safe. Never would the Messiah dare to come without telling them in advance. No ruler from abroad would visit a country without giving notice. Thus the Roman governor was also sure. The king of the Jews could not appear in the world without his knowledge.

One night, the Light of the world "smuggled" Himself into Palestine as a babe, after having been in the womb of a virgin, contrary to accepted moral standards and the laws of biology.

Then He was crucified and buried. A seal was put on His grave by the authorities. Now everyone knows that one is not supposed to break a government seal. But angels are not bound by earthly laws. An angel just rolled away the stone, not caring about the seal.

Would we have advised Jesus to abide by the law and remain in the grave once the authorities had sealed the tomb? Jesus "smuggled" Himself out of the grave into life again.

Some think that we should not break the laws of Communist tyrants. Jesus "broke" the law of gravity and ascended into heaven.

Augustine taught a principle valid for all spheres of life: "Love God and do as you like."

"Be angry, and do not sin."
EPHESIANS 4:26

*A*natolii Krasnov-Levitin, a Soviet writer, said, "Love and anger are sisters. Where there is no anger, there is no love. The words of the ancient prophets were full of a strong wrath because their hearts were full of a powerful love towards their own people, and love brought forth wrath not only against the oppressors of the people, but also against the people themselves because they did not follow the ways of truth. There was also a strong wrath in the words of our Saviour when he looked on the Scribes and Pharisees..." Who does not feel horror and anger against sins has no Christian or human feelings.

To be kind toward offenders is not always the wisest course. Absalom had committed a crime. He had directed his servants to kill his brother Amnon (2 Samuel 13:28). After this murder, Absalom fled from before the face of King David. Banishment is a well-deserved punishment for someone who takes the law into his own hands and kills someone who has never been sentenced to death by the only appointed judge, which was the king. Absalom should have been left in this self-imposed exile.

Instead, David listened to bad advice and forgave the murderer, though he had not shown any sign of repentance and change of life. Nor had he even humbled himself to ask for pardon. So Absalom became big again in Jerusalem and was free to organize a bloody rebellion against his father, King David. Much innocent blood flowed and there was much sorrow. It could easily have been avoided if David had shown in this case holy wrath instead of unholy meekness.

Everyone must pay for his sin, unless he has become a new person through new birth by believing that Jesus paid the penalty for his sin; as it is written, "the chastisement for our peace was upon Him" (Isaiah 53:5). Only then do we have a guarantee that goodness will not be misused.

APRIL 28

"Jesus said, 'Take away the stone.'"
JOHN 11:39

*I*n a small town, the hearse driver was an unbeliever. The pastor had tried repeatedly to bring him to God without success. One day the car of the pastor was being repaired, and on that day he had to conduct a burial service. So he sat in the hearse next to the driver. He made a new attempt to bring the driver to conversion.

"Sir, would you please do me a favor?" the pastor asked. "The Bible contains a difficult verse that speaks about your profession. Help me to understand it. Jesus said, 'Let the dead bury their dead.' Now, a dead hearse driver cannot drive a corpse to the cemetery. A dead grave digger cannot dig a grave. A dead pastor cannot deliver a funeral sermon. What then is the meaning of these words?"

The driver laughed. "Have I not always told you, pastor, that the Bible is sheer nonsense? Take these words of Jesus only and you have the proof of it."

The pastor replied, "Before discarding it, let us consider it. When the coffin with the dead man whom we have behind us was taken out of the house, you heard his wife crying, 'George, don't leave me alone! Return!' The children also begged their father to stay with them. It was in vain. The dead did not answer because he was dead.

"The same happens with you. For years Christ, the Holy Spirit, and Christians have called you to repentance and you have not answered, because you also are dead—spiritually. So a man who is dead spiritually buries a man who is bodily dead. The words of our Lord do make sense."

Every man who does not have Christ is dead spiritually. Bodily he may live in a nice home. Spiritually his abode is in a grave. Jesus would like to resurrect him from there, as He resurrected Lazarus bodily long ago. Bodily resurrections have been rare, but the Lord wishes the spiritual resurrection of all who are dead in sins. He asks us to be His coworkers in this. He is the only One who can raise the dead, but we are called to take away the stones from the graves.

APRIL 29

"The Scripture, foreseeing that God would justify the Gentiles by faith, preached the gospel to Abraham beforehand, saying, 'In you all the nations shall be blessed.'"
GALATIANS 3:8

Which Scripture preached the gospel to Abraham? The first book of the Holy Scriptures which we possess now was written centuries after Abraham's death. How then did a Scripture give him the news about his becoming a blessing to all nations?

The Scripture explained to Abraham that this promise would be fulfilled in a descendant of his, Jesus Christ. It spoke to Abraham with such power that he rejoiced thousands of years beforehand to see the day of Christ (John 8:56).

Now, which Scripture spoke to Abraham? He did not have our Scriptures. But our Bible tells us that it is based upon more ancient Scriptures, that it is an outcry in simple human words of eternal values, for whose expression we lack the adequate language. In Daniel 10:21, a being from heaven told Daniel, "I will tell you what is noted in the Scripture of Truth," and he showed him things which were not contained in any holy Scripture written for men until then. As stated earlier, in Numbers 21:14, "the Book of the Wars of the LORD" is mentioned and Joshua 10:13 mentions "the Book of Jasher" (which means in Hebrew "the righteous").

Under special circumstances men specially endowed by God are privileged to read these books. This is what Abraham did. Our Bible puts in human words, accessible to us, thoughts inspired by God. Those other books contain the same thoughts, as they are before being pressed into the narrow frame of human language.

Climb to spiritual heights. Then you will arrive at mysteries of God that can only with great difficulty be put into human words.

A P R I L   3 0

"God so loved the world that He gave
His only begotten Son."
JOHN 3:16

A minister had tried unsuccessfully to bring faith to a great railroad trade union leader. Then a strike broke out. It was prolonged. The strikers tightened their belts and held to their demands in the face of hunger and mounting debt.

The minister went to visit the trade union leader and told him, "I have a suggestion that will enable you to win the strike. You can get the full weight of public opinion behind you."

For the first time, the leader became interested in the words of the preacher and asked to learn the proposal. The minister explained, "To demonstrate the truly desperate condition of the workers, and to arouse compassion for them, tie your son to a railroad track and run over him with a locomotive. You will have the victory."

Indignant, the trade leader refused. "I would rather see the whole world starve before I would sacrifice my only son."

God could have sent an ancient saint or an angel to die for us, but instead He gave the best in heaven, Jesus Christ. Realizing the extent of the sacrifice, our hearts are moved to repentance. Jesus died for our sins on Good Friday. But death could not hold Him. Death is a low-quality phenomenon. It could not contain the best. He was resurrected. This is what we celebrate on Easter Sunday— Christ's conquering death.

God gave the best He had. We also are meant to give our best to Him.

MAY 1

"He who has two tunics, let him give to him who has none."
LUKE 3:11

*H*e commanded them to . . . wear sandals, and not put on two tunics" (Mark 6:8,9).

During the persecution of Christians under the Roman emperor Diocletian, Eustrat, a Christian, was shod in iron boots with big, sharp nails fixed inside. In these boots, beaten the entire time to run faster, he was led to martyrdom. The church honors his memory.

We are not all called to such sufferings. Martyrdom is the exception. Not all have to wear shoes with nails that would pierce the flesh.

However, God does look into our wardrobe. He taught His first disciples simplicity in clothing. Some contemporary Christians are careful to have the right doctrine, others the right ritual. What about the right number of shoes and suits and dresses?

Christians should give everything they have to the Lord, considering themselves not as owners, but as stewards of material riches. They strip themselves even of their own selves to follow the naked and barefoot Christ on His way to Golgotha.

Christians should be careful about how much clothing and food they have. Billions of souls need the gospel. The children of God will be arrayed in glory in the future.

"God has chosen... things which are not."
1 CORINTHIANS 1:28

*H*e took the seven loaves and gave thanks, broke them and gave them to His disciples to set before them . . . So they ate and were filled" (Mark 8:6,8).

Suppose the disciples would not have had seven loaves, but only three or one; what would have happened? The multitudes would have been satisfied just the same. As a matter of fact, on another occasion Jesus had only five loaves of bread instead of seven. Notwithstanding, He fed an even bigger multitude and a greater number of baskets of fragments remained behind (Mark 6:41–43). You can serve God with the little you have. His blessings do not depend upon the size or quantity of what you have, but upon the fact that you bring them to Him.

Suppose I have nothing to bring, what then? This is impossible, for a man who has nothing to bring to Jesus does not exist. Neither the word nor the symbol for "zero" occur in the Bible.

He can bring his own person, that person who says, "I possess nothing; I am nothing." He has something valuable: himself and his utter poverty. He can bring his sins to Jesus. From the sin of being a fanatic persecutor, Saul of Tarsus was made by God into a zealous apostle. From a woman indwelt by seven demons Mary Magdalene was made a saint possessing steadfast love. Bring your weakness to Christ. This you surely have. His strength will show its perfectness in your weakness.

Start with little, but instead of using this little, bring it to Jesus. And He will multiply it and greatly bless it.

MAY 3

"...cunning craftiness, by which they lie in wait to deceive."
EPHESIANS 4:14

*C*hristians should study Mao Tse-tung's works. Before he quarreled with his Russian comrades, he stated the tactics of all Communists in his book, *On Protracted War:*

> Deliberately creating misconceptions for the enemy and then springing surprise attacks upon him in one means... of achieving superiority and seizing the initiative. What are misconceptions?... Making a feint to the east but attacking in the west is a way of creating misconceptions among the enemies... There can never be too much deception in war.

Add to this the fact that for Maoists class struggles and revolutionary wars are the desirable, permanent state of things for centuries to come, and you will learn that according to them, deceitfulness must be a main feature of man's character.

Jesus teaches, "Let your 'Yes' be 'Yes,' and your 'No,' 'No'" (Matthew 5:37). We have to choose between a life of lies and a life rooted in truth.

*T*he disciples were hungry and the Lord Jesus had provided them with a meal.

In this instance He prepared it Himself. At other times He charged an angel to care for a saint. When the prophet Elijah slept under a tree, an angel touched him and said to him, "'Arise and eat.' Then he looked, and there by his head was a cake baked on coals, and a jar of water" (1 Kings 19:5,6).

It is easy to believe in these miracles after having eaten well, but in some parts of the world Christians are in jail where the food is soup made of unwashed intestines. The dung is swimming in the soup. For such food, you have to do hard slave labor.

Our imprisoned brethren do not suffer only physically. Their faith is stressed, too. Doubts arise. "The Lord is almighty. He could provide food for the first apostles or for Elijah. Why does He not provide some fried fish or cake for me? Why have I to eat unwashed intestines?"

God has provided the necessary food for the Christian prisoners. Only this time, He has not entrusted angels with it, but their fellow Christians. As He had charged an angel to feed Elijah, now He has charged the Christians of the free world to provide their imprisoned brethren with food. It is tragic that many of those who have the task of feeding martyrs steal what God has given them for this purpose and deprive the martyrs of their due.

Are you one of these thieves?

God has also provided for the freedom of Christians under different anti-Christian rulers. However, the Moseses and Joshuas of today, those to whom God has entrusted the freedom of the world and of His people, are on strike. Pharaoh has bribed them and they are now on his side.

Would you do something for the freedom of the world?

MAY 5

"An angel of the Lord appeared to [Joseph] in a dream."
MATTHEW 1:20

A Chinese poet said, "I dreamed last night that I was a butterfly and now I don't know whether I am a man who dreamed he was a butterfly or perhaps a butterfly who dreams now that he is a man."

The Bible attributes great significance to dreams. It tells thirty-six dreams and also their interpretations. Was Old Testament Joseph basically a shepherd who dreamed of being a ruler or had he the character and talents of a ruler and only dreamed while awake that he was a shepherd? Had Nebuchadnezzar been a king who dreamed at night that he was a beast or was he essentially a wild beast who fancied during daytime he was worthy of kingly honor?

Whoever wishes to know himself and others should be attentive to his dreams. If New Testament Joseph would have despised dreams as a source of knowledge, he would not have covered the unusual pregnancy of the virgin Mary. She would have been stoned under the suspicion of being an unfaithful bride.

Have paper and pen beside you when you go to bed. Date and record the dreams you have. You will find that things which you considered as incredible in the Bible are daily occurrences in your dreams. Practice will make you understand your dreams. The Talmud says, "Dreams which are not interpreted are like letters which have not been opened."

MAY 6

"Does the hawk fly by your wisdom?"
JOB 39:26

*I*n wild Alaska, where beavers have not seen men before and don't fear them, you can watch for hours as they fell trees with their sharp teeth and then transport the branches on artificial canals created by them to the sea where their humid castles emerge from the waters. What they accomplish is a miracle. No atheist could explain how it is that beavers, supposedly the result of an evolution at random, can regulate the level of water in artificial lakes made by them at the exact height necessary for them.

They have dams that open and close according to the changing affluence of waters exactly like it happens in manmade dams. So the level of the water remains equal the entire year. How do the beavers calculate their actions? To create canals and dams like those of the beavers, we would need a staff of first-class engineers. What is a recent discovery in human technique—to give dams a slight curl toward the front in order to distribute equally the pressure of the water on the waft—is a secret that the beavers have known for thousands of years. Where waters run quickly they give to the dams a concave curl, which dislocates the pressure of the water from the center to the shore.

It takes an intelligent Being to create intelligence. If the world of men does not make you believe in God, believe in the One who made the beavers and the ants.

MAY 7

"You are an epistle of Christ."
2 CORINTHIANS 3:3

O ne of the proofs of God's existence is the existence of good men. An atheist thinker said that the universe is a gigantic accident consequent upon an infinite succession of happy flukes.

Suppose that chance could have brought forth a material universe. No reasonable being will accept the fact that goodness, noble character, self-sacrifice, forgiveness, and generosity are the result of an accidental coming together of elementary particles. Throw symbols of notes into the air: they will not fall as Beethoven's *Ninth Symphony*.

Why would anyone enter the most difficult of fights—how to become a good human being—if he was an accidental aggregate of molecules that will be decomposed tomorrow and of whom no remembrance will remain? Some are good because we are designed as good and these have realized their calling.

Become good yourself, after the model of the divine Master, and your own life will become a proof of God's existence.

MAY 8

"God so loved the world that He gave His only
begotten Son, that whoever believes in Him should
not perish but have everlasting life."
JOHN 3:16

*T*his verse is the heart of the Bible. It contains its main message. Every word in it is grand:

"God"—He is the grandest source of everything good;

"so loved"—it is love at its highest peak;

"the world"—it is the widest object that love can have;

"He gave"—giving is the best expression of love;

"His only begotten Son"—the grandest gift that could be given;

"whoever"—it is the greatest number that can be comprehended;

"believes"—the simplest condition possible;

"in Him"—the One most trustworthy, faith in whom presents no problem;

"should not perish"—it is delivery from the worst fate;

"but"—the greatest alternative to perishing;

"have"—the greatest assurance—it is a possession not a hope;

"everlasting life"—life of which there can be no longer and no better.

When my son was six years old I asked him if he did not find this verse to be wonderful. He said, "Not at all. I find it normal. For a rich man it is normal to give much and for a God it is not wonderful, but normal to give no less than His Son and no other life than the everlasting one."

Why is God unseen? For the same reason that a snowflake that has fallen on a white blanket would be unseen. God is very good. "Everything that He had made . . . was very good" (Genesis 1:31). How can you distinguish very good from very good? There is not the slightest bit of goodness in Him that He would not have communicated to His creatures.

He does not stand before a mirror, like the wicked queen in Snow White, the fairy tale, to ask, "Mirror, mirror on the wall, who is fairest of us all?" He cannot be the fairest; no superlative can be attributed to Him, because there exists no fairness of His that He would not have shared with the singing birds, the brooks, the majestic mountain peaks, with children.

How much effort does it take for a girl to fall in love with a fair prince? None. So every striving to love God wholeheartedly is false. You cannot help loving Him. The angels told a prophet, "The whole earth is full of His glory" (Isaiah 6:3), of no less glory than He has on His throne.

"Blessed are the pure in heart, for they shall see God" (Matthew 5:8). God is seen in all things and in all events. What makes Him seem unseen is our impurity. Be washed in the blood of Christ, receive the Holy Spirit, and you will behold with open face, though as in a glass, the glory of the Lord, yes, you will be changed into the same image (2 Corinthians 3:18).

MAY 10

"We . . . rejoice in hope."
ROMANS 5:2

*T*he most unfounded hope is much more founded than the most founded despair. I know it from my own experience.

I was sentenced to twenty-five years of hard labor. I had been deathly sick in prison, and doctors had abandoned any hope that I would recover. Under those circumstances I had a completely unfounded hope of ever leading a worldwide mission, having as its purpose the helping of persecuted Christians in Communist countries. Despair and suicide would have been logically justified. There seemed no hope that I would see my son again. Now I have my grandchild on my lap.

Never give up hope. The Talmud says that if a man is sentenced to death, has his head on the block, the executioner has already lifted his axe, and he thinks, "Now I am lost," he is unfaithful. The axe can fall from the executioner's hand. It happened like this with the Romanian King Michael the Brave.

Euthanasia is false. Men doomed by all the doctors of the world can live. Hope for your business, for your children. Hope for your character even though, in spite of thousands of endeavors, it has not improved yet. We have as our hope a God who hung "the earth on nothing" (Job 26:7). A hope that He gives holds good even without any foundation.

> *"I am the L*ORD* your God, who brought you out of the land of Egypt, out of the house of bondage."*
> EXODUS 20:2

Some Christians think that we should not care about politics. Did Livingstone know the gospel? When he came to Africa, slave trade was going on. Should Livingstone have allowed the slaves to remain slaves? He had read in the Bible how God freed slaves. He could not remain unmoved when he saw the gangs of innocents, chained by the wrists to a long chain, being beaten with whips, exactly as it happens at the transport of prisoners in many countries today.

These terrible things made Dr. Livingstone burn with anger. Many Christians today have lost the virtue of becoming angry against slavery. Some never do get angry, except against those who fight slavery.

Livingstone never forgot to beg the British people to put down the terrible trade in human flesh and blood. He succeeded. Slavery was abolished in the British empire. Today Livingstone's body lies in Westminster Abbey.

The Jewish ark of the covenant was not only a ritual object, but also an ensign of battle. When the Jews, former slaves, passed the Jordan to fight for a land of their own in which they should be free, the ark was borne by the Levites as a flag would be borne now. It was a symbol of the fight for liberty.

Christians are fighters not only for personal righteousness, but also for righteousness in social relations.

MAY 12

"We who have believed do enter that rest."
HEBREWS 4:3

*M*en have not been created to be torturers and murderers. To be criminal is unnatural. Therefore the criminals are terribly tormented themselves. Only a tormented man torments others.

In the "White Book About the Trial Siniavski-Daniel," we find the description of how Lenin used to leave his room and go into the yard at two o'clock in the morning. Standing in the snow, he would howl at the moon. He did it every night. He howled a little bit, listened if everything was quiet, then he would howl again, until he began to freeze. Then he would re-enter his room to make plans for the future destiny of Russia.

The story has been told by Lenin's own bodyguard.

Not every man is a tormentor on such a large scale as Lenin or Hitler were, but many have the "stuff" of a Bolshevik. We torment our marriage partners, our parents, our friends, our employees. We are brutal, sadistic.

We find our joy in tormenting others, but in reality we are tormented ourselves. Only a troubled man is a troublemaker.

You could free others from your wickedness and you could be free yourself if you would only listen to Jesus' gracious invitation, "Come to Me, all you who labor and are heavy laden, and I will give you rest" (Matthew 11:28).

"You shall not murder."
DEUTERONOMY 5:17

*I*n prisons you may hear thieves condemning murderers harshly. They say, "We can repent and make restitution for what we have stolen. Even if we don't, our victim can earn other money. But you cannot give back the life you have taken from a man. You are criminals."

They have a point. Every sin destroys the relationship between man and man. It also renders man more and more insensitive to the appeal of God. But murder is an irresponsible sin. If you impoverish a man or destroy his good fame, not everything is lost. The victim still has the chance to attain a good position again. However, murder is definitive. It brings a man before his Judge and, if he is unprepared for this, to eternal hell. It is a sin apart, this "sin unto death."

Therefore clergymen who condone violence and propagate revolutions are wrong, as are also all bloody rioters.

Why should revolutions be needed?

V. Tarsis, the Soviet writer, tells in his book, *Message from an Asylum*, the story of a man who was considered to be crazy by the Communists. This man said, "I began to read the Bible daily. I must confess it is the most dangerous and seducing book. I don't wonder that the comrades observed it and forbade its distribution. Because, if you have read the wise words of the Bible, you can only roar with laughter about revolutions."

When you can have perfect peace of heart and joy even while being oppressed and poor; when you are sure of an eternal, beautiful life in paradise, it will not pass through your mind to spill blood in order to change the social order in this transitory world.

Christians do not participate in these things. They remember God's words, "You shall not murder."

> *"The master of the feast... said to [the bridegroom],*
> *'Every man at the beginning sets out the good wine,*
> *and when the guests have well drunk, then that which*
> *is inferior; but you have kept the good wine until now.'"*
> JOHN 2:9,10

*T*he devil sometimes gives good things first: beautiful promises, selfish pleasures. After much of life has been drunk, a worse wine follows these: a wrecked life, remorse, spiritual blindness, and, in the end, the worst—eternal damnation.

Love knows that the best things are yet to come. It already has the joy of obeying God's commands, fellowship with Christ, and the great communion of saints. This joy, for the present, is mingled with the bitterness of the cross. Now it is a glory in tribulation, distress, persecution, and nakedness, in that amid tears and shedding of blood, the bride of Christ never ceases to hope. She knows her Bridegroom has stored up in His banqueting house the best of wines for the age to come. She is not in a hurry as those who believe they have only this short life. Love does not hasten to obtain results. She can bear with transitory failures, sufferings, and defeats. The last victory is hers.

Not daunted by conflicts, but positively inspired by them, Christians go ahead. Our adversaries don't know the unspeakable joys reserved by Christ for those who are on His side when He is in pain. We love and believe that love will win.

The church of Christ is not endangered by the sinful world. Even the gates of hell cannot prevail against her. It is the sinful world that is rather endangered by the existence of the church, because the last victory is ours.

*"Put on the new man which was created according to
God, in righteousness and true holiness."*
EPHESIANS 4:24

Ordinarily, men confuse holiness with goodness, though these are different virtues. "God saw everything that He had made, and indeed it was very good" (Genesis 1:31). After this "very good" followed something entirely different.

"God blessed the seventh day and sanctified it" (Genesis 2:3). Sanctification belongs to another sphere than goodness.

A man can be very good, without being holy or put aside for God. There are extreme cases when men are holy without being good. Where is the goodness of Gideon, Jael, Joshua? They were fighters for the triumph of the chosen people. By this they were holy. Those who have read the lives of Athanasius, Luther, and Calvin see little trace of goodness in them. These men fought ruthlessly for a truth entrusted to them, hitting their adversaries relentlessly. The truth must be victorious.

We become holy by feeding upon the right spiritual food.

An experiment found that worms which usually live in the darkness can be conditioned to prefer the light. As often as they would withdraw into darkness, they would get electric shocks, whereas if they came out in the light, they found abundant food. With time, these beings "put on a new worm," to use the biblical expression. Contrary to the habits of their species, from that time on they preferred the light to darkness. Then these worms were cut into small pieces and added in the food given to other worms; and, lo, these worms also changed their habits. They had increased, with the addition of the flesh of the new breed of worms, their ribonucleic acid, the depository of memory. They would shun darkness and prefer light just as the beings upon which they had fed. Similar experiments have also been made with other animals.

If you wish to put on the new man, a man of righteousness and holiness, feed upon Christ. He has become flesh in order that He might become your daily food.

> *"And the Lord God prepared a plant and made it come up over Jonah, that it might be shade for his head...So Jonah was very grateful for the plant."*
> JONAH 4:6

*I*n the Bible the shadow is an image of the transitory. "Our days on earth are a shadow," says Bildad (Job 8:9). "[Man] flees like a shadow and does not continue," says Job himself (14:2). "All the days of [man's] vain life...he passes like a shadow," says Solomon (Ecclesiastes 6:12). He had inherited this thought from his father, David. "Our days on earth are as a shadow, and without hope" (1 Chronicles 29:15).

Even prophets like Jonah are sometimes "very grateful" in what is transitory.

Jonah first made himself a booth so he could sit under its shadow, forgetting that whatever a man constructs is transitory. A vehement wind overthrew the booth the next day. There is nothing we construct for ourselves that will not be destroyed. Nothing lasts forever. Not even civilizations. Neither will we last here.

Then, Jonah was glad because of the shadow given by a tree but the next day a worm damaged the tree. Every tree will die someday. The worm that has eaten it also dies. So too the prophet who sat under the tree's shadow. Nineveh to whom he preached would also pass away, although it repented in Jonah's day. Believers die as do unbelievers. There is no sense being glad because of a shadow. Tomorrow you may wish to die because you lost this joy. However, the despair will not last either. It is transitory like every sentiment. Then the earth on which the trees grew, on which men were sometimes glad and sometimes angry will also burn.

Only God is everlasting who says, "Should not I spare?" (Jonah 4:11, KJV). He will not spare Nineveh forever. He spares no one forever on this earth. Lazarus, like the others whom Jesus resurrected, had to die again later. Only God remains forever. His word, "'Shall I not spare?" remains. Shall I not spare in eternity the soul who has trusted in Me?

> *"Nor did we eat anyone's bread free of charge, but worked with labor and toil night and day..."*
> 2 THESSALONIANS 3:8

*P*aul's main subject in his epistles was the One whose countenance is like a thousand suns, releasing their splendor, whose eyes are pure and whose whole being is snowy as white jade.

Christ is his main subject, but not the only subject. Sometimes he writes about himself and his coworkers, as in the verse quoted above.

For us, too, the main preoccupation is the One whose virtues resemble the boundless great ocean and in whom infinitely wonderful jewels are amassed. When you know Him, thought expires in enjoyment.

Notwithstanding, we cannot avoid speaking about pastors. Remind your pastor that for those who live of the gospel it is demanded that:

1) They don't eat the bread of their fellow believers for nothing. A medical doctor can report at the end of the year how many patients he has treated, how many he has cured. A shoemaker can report how many pairs of shoes he has made. A pastor must be able to report about his work of spreading the gospel and about the efficiency of his work.

2) They labor day and night. The day alone is not enough. "Blessed is the man who... [in the Lord's law] meditates day and night" (Psalm 1:1,2). The fruits come when you continue to work during the night.

Christians must be pastors to their pastors.

MAY 18

"He was bruised for our iniquities."
ISAIAH 53:5

*I*n a country where persecution reigns, a police officer came to arrest a pastor. He asked the latter, "Do you consider me a monster, like everyone else does?"

The pastor answered, "Monster? No, but an unhappy man who believes that no one loves him. God loves you, yes, even in a special manner. It is for evil men that He became man. He did not come to earth because we were nice like altar boys, but because we were dirty. The dirtier we are, the more right we have to His pity."

The officer defended himself, "I am not as bad as that. I am not a thief."

"You are," answered the pastor. "You have stolen from God."

"What?"

"You have robbed Him of your sins. Our sins belong to Him. They are His property. He came to be born as Son of man to take them. All the dirt of our evil deeds are His, not yours. You are a thief, a robber, if you refuse to give them to Him, to the Lamb of God who takes away the sins of the world, who has the right to take them away because they are His property and no one else's. You keep what belongs to someone else."

On that night the pastor remained unimprisoned. The police officer confessed to him his sins.

Are you a thief? Do you declare as yours the sins you have committed, though by right they belong to Jesus?

MAY 19

"At midnight a cry was heard: 'Behold, the bridegroom is coming; go out to meet him!'"
MATTHEW 25:6

*T*he earth turns on its axis. Midnight is the moment when a part of the earth is the farthest from the sun. Spiritual midnight is the period of the greatest departure of men from God. We are approaching this midnight and its terrific events.

But midnight is not received with the same feelings by the children of God as by the world. At midnight, the firstborn of the Egyptians died, but the chosen people got their freedom.

The Lord has said, "The night is coming when no one can work" (John 9:4). But when a thing is declared impossible in the Bible, this does not refer to the faithful. About them, Jesus declared, "all things are possible to him who believes" (Mark 9:23).

The holy people can work even at midnight. It was at midnight that Samson took the gates of the city of Gaza (Judges 16:3). At midnight, Ruth received from Boaz the promise, "I will do for you all that you request" (Ruth 3:11). At midnight, Paul and Silas won the jailer of Philippi for the Lord (Acts 16:25).

At midnight, the people of God do their greatest exploits. Therefore, the psalmist says, "At midnight I will rise to give thanks to You" (Psalm 119:62).

We are not afraid of the darkness in the world. We work. The Bridegroom comes soon. We should not meet Him empty-handed.

"Behold, you despisers, marvel and perish..."
ACTS 13:41

*P*aul quotes here Habakkuk 1:5, adding to the latter's prophecy, by his authority as an apostle, the word "perish," a word of curse addressed to the adversaries of the gospel. The Lord had already pronounced a doom over Jerusalem. He had cursed the fig tree and it withered. Here Paul warns the Jewish state that it will perish—and so it did soon after. It was only recently that God showed again His pity, gathering in a new Jewish state the scattered sheep of Israel.

It sounds unusual for us that an apostle could say to adversaries, "perish." We know that God is love. This He is, but nowhere does the Bible say that He is only love. You cannot exhaust the description of God by one word, "love." You could describe no man by one word. I am a Christian, but I am also male, tall, a pastor, a sinner, a father, and so on. So, love is only one of the attributes of God. There exists also a righteousness, a wrath, a terror of the Lord. These are as clearly expressed in the Bible as His love.

Paul, after having written the hymn of love in 1 Corinthians 13, writes in the same epistle (16:22), "If anyone does not love the Lord Jesus Christ, let him be accursed."

Christians have the power to loose and to bind, to bless and to curse. They love their adversaries as individuals and do their best to bring them to salvation, but to the institutions that persecute them, they say prophetically, "Perish," and perish they will.

Remember Genghis Khan and his powerful Tartars. In the thirteenth century, without jet planes or atomic weapons, they swept from China to the middle of Europe. It took him half the time it took the Soviets to conquer this territory. But Genghis Khan passed away. We don't fear the stockpiles of bombs that enemies of the gospel have manufactured. Remember Suleiman the Magnificent and his tremendous Turks. Christians prayed and pronounced the word of doom—"perish." The enemy perished. Spiritual weapons are powerful. They are deadly. One word of Peter dealt death to Ananias and Sapphira, the unfaithful Christians.

"Keep justice."
ISAIAH 56:1

*A*natolii Krasnov-Levitin, a Hebrew Christian writer who has been in Soviet prisons for ten years, described a discussion he had with a Christian pacifist. Levitin asked him, "If a bandit attacks your family, why not wrest the axe out of his hand and hit him on the head?"

The pacifist answered, "This is forbidden by the Holy Scriptures. Jesus taught us to turn the other cheek if anyone strikes you."

Levitin replied, "But Jesus never taught to allow your children to be killed by bandits."

He explained further. "What is sensible when only you are attacked becomes foolish when other persons are involved. A man who looks on quietly while another man without defense is beaten, and does not intervene in his favor, is a coward and selfish. This cannot be justified by the doctrine of nonresistance. A man who is silent when falsehood triumphs is also a coward and selfish . . . Mildness, forgetting about insults addressed to your person, are needed to concentrate the will of man toward fighting against injustice, lies, and evil in which the world lives."

The words, "Blessed are those who hunger and thirst after righteousness," Levitin explains as a blessedness not only for those who try to make righteousness triumph in the world. Jude writes about the "common salvation." Every saved man fights to make salvation common, to make Christ's principles rule the world.

All real Christians are fighters against injustice and cruelty. Therefore they are persecuted. Don't be satisfied with personal salvation. Save others also.

> *"Charity. . . doth not behave itself unseemly."*
> 1 CORINTHIANS 13:4,5 (KJV)

These words usually are understood in the sense that a Christian does not behave impolitely. But Paul himself was sometimes terribly impolite. So was the Lord. So were the reformers and their opponents. Where the fate of the church and of the world are at stake, politeness can do much harm.

The Greek word translated "unseemly" is *aschemon*. A literal translation would be "charity does not behave without a scheme."

Christ categorizes men as does a zoologist; He frames them in a system, in a scheme. Some men are "sheep," others "wolves," others "dogs," others "foxes." Some He calls fools, hypocrites, and vipers. Others are beloved disciples. He knows about a beast, a dragon, and a chosen dove. Love does not behave unseemly, that is, without having this scheme in view.

All men must be loved, but I cannot behave toward the "sheep-type" as toward the "wolf-type." I cannot behave with hypocrites as with beloved disciples, with tyrants as with victims. Woe to the shepherd who would not make a difference and would behave the same toward his sheep, his dogs, and toward wolves. Charity does not behave the same toward a good and a bad husband, an obedient and a disobedient child. The attitude of charity depends upon the situation.

Suppose some gangsters attacked an innocent man; I might love them all, but I would try to protect the innocent man, shooting if necessary at the gangsters. Otherwise I would behave unseemly or *aschemon*, not taking into account the fact that in the scheme of the world they occupy different positions. The same holds true in our attitude toward those who benefit the church and those who harm it, those who defend their country and those who attack it.

Love does not behave unseemly. It has a diversified love according to the place that every man occupies in the scheme.

"Let Him alone; let us see..."
MATTHEW 27:49

*T*here exists an invincible indifference, insensitivity, and apathy toward suffering.

There was a multitude on Golgotha who attended the crucifixion of men, who actually heard their cries when nails were hammered into their hands and feet. They must have known that at least one of the three crucified on that Good Friday was the best of men. Otherwise He would not have prayed for His torturers. Otherwise He would not have cared to bring a robber to God, while passing Himself through unspeakable physical suffering. Now this Jesus cried, as in despair, "My God, My God, why have You forsaken Me?"

And what was the reaction of the multitude? They said to each other, "Let Him alone; let us see..." It did not enter their minds to alleviate His suffering by at least giving Him a little bit of water or a word of compassion. "Let Him alone; let us see if Elijah will come to save Him."

Elijah is not only the proper name of a prophet of old. It is in Hebrew a short sentence that means "Jehovah is my God." In this sense everyone can be an Elijah. In this sense the Lord said that John the Baptist was Elijah. Each of us must have Jehovah as his or her God. If the compassionate God Jehovah is master of our lives, we will never remain passive when we see innocent suffering.

Those who are in reality without God have the attitude, "Let Him alone; let us see." Men of this type were attending the crucifixion on Golgotha and were not moved by it. Such men will not be moved by the message of today's sufferings. They are damned. They do not care if the little brethren of Jesus are hungry or in jail. We leave these men to the judgment of God.

There is much inertia and apathy to be overcome even in God's elect. Don't remain passive wherever there is a need; if you can, help.

> *"He is kind to the unthankful and evil."*
> LUKE 6:35

One of the greatest beauties of the Bible is the fact that two verses do not exist in it. First of all, there exists in the Bible no verse in which Jesus asks anyone: "What sins did you commit? How many? Under what circumstances? With whom? Tell me if your sins were venial, small offenses, or huge crimes." Rather, the Bible tells us Jesus went from person to person saying, "Be of good cheer, son; be of good cheer, daughter; your sins are forgiven"—without inquiring what these sins had been. Neither does He ask you about your past.

Second, there is not one instance in the Bible in which someone apologized to Jesus or asked forgiveness. After the Last Supper, all apostles except John had fled; Peter had denied Him. When they met the resurrected Lord, it would have been nice if they had said, "We are sorry." They did not. This was because whoever looks into the face of Jesus sees on it so much understanding and love he can be sure beforehand that "He forgives everything." Christ wishes to save me much more than I wish to be saved. He wishes me to be in heaven much more than I wish to go there. A man must run fast to run away from God, who is after him with His blessings.

Rely on these two verses that are not in the Bible. Believe that He does not hold your sins against you when you repent and that His utmost desire is to forgive you.

"Forsake foolishness and live."
PROVERBS 9:6

King Lear said, "When we are born, we cry that we are come to this great stage of fools." He was right. He has been a fool himself entrusting prematurely all he had to children. He should have known that they were shaped in iniquity and conceived in sin (Psalm 51:5).

This is a world of fools. It spoke evil of the Best. It called Him a devil. Hamlet was right: "Be thou as chaste as ice, as pure as snow, thou shalt not escape calumny."

Othello called pure Desdemona a whore. "A beggar in his drink could not have laid such terms upon his callet."

Juliet was foolish. She had all the right to be enamored at the age of fourteen. Only she did not love wisely. She told Romeo, "Thy gracious self is the god of my idolatry." It is foolish to make an idol of the object of your love. Would she have lived one year more, she might have changed her idol.

Hamlet said to Ophelia, "Marry a fool, for wise men know well enough what monsters you make of them." How many men are wise and beware?

Iago said about Cassius, "If I can fasten but one cup upon him, he'll be as full of quarrel and offense as my young mistress' dog." Liquor producers succeed in fastening upon us many cups. The world is drunk.

How well that Jesus told us not to belong to this world. We are in it only as strangers and pilgrims. We don't partake in its foolishness.

> *"If there is any virtue and if there is anything*
> *praiseworthy—meditate on these things."*
> PHILIPPIANS 4:8

While Cleopas and a friend journeyed toward Emmaus, Jesus joined them. But He had changed. They could not recognize Him. Cleopas asked Jesus, "'Are You the only stranger in Jerusalem, and have You not known the things which happened there in these days?' And He said to them, 'What things?'" (Luke 24:18,19).

Jesus showed interest. So many things had happened in Jerusalem in the last days. Two robbers had been crucified. Would one of His disciples have gone to comfort their grief-stricken mothers? Would one have asked Pilate for the corpses of these thieves so they would not be left on the crosses to be devoured by ravens? One of these thieves had become a brother in the faith. His disciples would at least have assured him a decent burial. And what about His executioners? They needed salvation. Would one of Jesus' disciples have loved them and shown them the way to receive forgiveness?

Three days had passed. How many things had happened in Jerusalem in that time? There might have been homes broken up, injuries, bereavements, crimes. Some might have composed new hymns to the praise of Jehovah. Mothers would have cared for children. Others would have seen that their fellow men had bread. Many things happen in three days. "What things?" asks Jesus. He is interested in human life in all its aspects, virtues and sins, joys and sorrows. He wishes to share everything with us.

The disciples, while speaking about "things" that had come to pass in Jerusalem, really were obsessed with only one thing: what had happened to Jesus, the Person they loved.

Many Christians are obsessed only with their own personal relationship with the ascended Lord, who can give them peace here and in paradise hereafter. But Christ is the life, the life around them. It is He whom you can see in His brethren, in hungry, thirsty, naked, sick, and enslaved humanity. You meet Him as often as you meet a child of God.

"Some doubted."
MATTHEW 28:17

*D*oubt has a positive value. Where would science have been if Copernicus had not doubted the generally accepted theory that the earth was the center of the universe; or if Einstein had not doubted the absolute value of Euclid's geometry and of Newton's celestial mechanic? Where would religion be if Abraham had not doubted the polytheistic religion he inherited from his ancestors— or if the apostles had not doubted the judgment pronounced by the chief priests of their nation that Jesus was a blasphemer?

Doubt is legitimate and necessary. There is more wisdom in honest doubt than in some apparent certainties. Many religious people who seem so cocksure of their place in heaven will be lost. Some preachers will even say to the Lord when He returns, "Lord, Lord, have we not prophesied in Your name, cast out demons in Your name, and done many wonders in Your name?" And Jesus will reply, "I never knew you; depart from Me, you who practice lawlessness" (Matthew 7:22,23).

Instead of insisting that you know God, when you have Him only in your imagination, you should be a seeker. Seekers of God are safe. Honest doubt is nothing else than a search for truth. But then it is an agony of the spirit. "As the deer pants for the water brooks, so pants my soul for You, O God" (Psalm 42:1). The deer does not pant after sermons and books about water. It is not interested in conversations about thirst-quenching. The highest notions, the most poetic phrases about the coolness and beauty of water do not satisfy a thirsty man; neither do exact analyses of water's chemical composition. He wishes the water itself.

So is the seeker of God. People weep rivers of tears because they have lost riches or a child. How many have ever met a teardrop because they could not find God? How many can really say from their hearts the words of the psalmist: "My soul thirsts for God, for the living God . . . My tears have been my food day and night" (Psalm 42:2,3)?

MAY 28

"Be strong in the Lord and in the power of His might."
EPHESIANS 6:10

*I*n the U.S., at least ten percent of the children in elementary schools suffer from dyslexia, a perceptual disorder that blocks their ability to read, spell, or write legibly. The percentage must be approximately the same in other civilized countries. Eighty percent of the prison population in the U.S. is affected with dyslexia, a state of mind, sometimes inherited, that makes you scramble letters and numbers. A ceiling can be confused with a floor, the word "hostile" with "hospitable." "A" may change to "U"; a number series such as 1-2-3 may come out as 2-1-3.

The rage and frustration that results from continued academic failure often is expressed in delinquent and antisocial behavior.

But it must not always be so. Nelson Rockefeller, former vice president of the United States, said that he also has had this trouble all his life. "I've got reverse reading. I see numbers backwards. I even think of them backwards—that's the worst." He has never mastered spelling, but he overcame his handicap by simply learning to cope with it. Edison was dyslexic, which did not hinder him from becoming a great inventor. General Patton could not read print by the age of twelve. President Wilson also suffered from dyslexia. The same with Albert Einstein, the physicist whose name the universe admires.

Children should be nurtured with two important medicines: the vitamins M and R, lacking often in the nutrition of children today. They stand for morality and religion. Children should be taught that they have a moral duty not to be failures; to achieve something useful in life. They should be taught secondly that there is One who helps to overcome this handicap and others.

You, too, can overcome your handicaps.

"You have made [man] a little lower than the angels."
PSALM 8:5

S igmund Freud, the founder of psychoanalysis, used to boast
that he had "completed the uncrowning of man."

Man had been considered to be the crown of God's creation. Then Copernicus showed that man's habitation, the earth, was not the center of the universe as believed until then. Our sun is but one of billions of stars, most of them much larger than ours. Copernicus was a believing Christian and remained so after his discovery; but others drew the conclusion that by reducing the importance of the earth in the universe, man had lost the right to consider himself as a being of special value. Darwin is said to have shown that even on earth man is not something unique and cannot be considered the result of God's design to have a friend, a being with whom to communicate. Man, according to Darwin's hypothesis, is only one of the results of chance evolution, just as gorillas and chimpanzees are. This was a second blow to the superiority of man.

If we really are the product of chance, only matter and not spirit, mere animals, gluttons, and sexists—whence then arises the resistance to these theories? Do apes and bulls resent being considered such? Do little ants resent that they are not considered elephants? Whence man's self-assertion, his idea that he is God's beloved creature superior to and different from all animals? Whence the voice of conscience and the reaching after spiritual peaks?

"God created man in His own image" (Genesis 1:27). Nothing similar is said about any creature in the universe. God has "crowned him with glory and honor" (Psalm 8:5). Man is the crown of creation. When God wished to become incarnate, He became man on our earth. Unto men a child was born; unto men a son was given, and among his names were Mighty God and Everlasting Father (Isaiah 9:6).

Believe in your unique and great calling and fulfill it. Let God's image be seen in you. Let your light so shine that men will glorify the Father.

> *"Indeed seven years of great plenty will come*
> *throughout all the land of Egypt."*
> GENESIS 41:29

Why this exceptional blessing over Egypt? Why should it have great plenty and be warned of famine in meager years to follow? There are three reasons for this which are also the secrets of any successful Christian work:

1) The Pharaoh of that time acted as a king not only when awake. His subconscious was also filled with concern for the welfare of his people and he would dream about it at night.

Every Christian is a king. Luther said, "A Christian is a perfectly free lord of all, subject to none." But a Christian is a loving king. Therefore, Luther adds, "A Christian is a dutiful servant of all, subject to all."

A Christian does not *strive* to be a soul-winner; it is no imposition to him to place the well-being of the church first. His Christian belief has pervaded his subconscious. He simply *is* a soul-winner, a man who puts God's kingdom first.

2) Pharaoh, the dreamer of good, meets another dreamer of dreams, Joseph, and is united with him. Do the same.

3) Pharaoh was completely unprejudiced. He called to his court a foreigner with another color of skin, a man with what must have seemed to Pharaoh a strange religion, a man who worshiped only one unseen God, a prisoner with a bad reputation. The charge for which he had been jailed was attempted rape.

But to Pharaoh, every man could be used for the welfare of the country. Men who committed bad deeds yesterday could become good men this morning. And besides, who knew if the charges against Joseph were true? Slaveholders like Potiphar often jailed their slaves without a fair trial.

The fulfilling of these conditions gave Egypt great plenty and provision for themselves and their neighbors in times of famine. These qualities will make you a winner also.

MAY 31

"All is vanity."
ECCLESIASTES 1:2

When Corinth was besieged by Philip of Macedonia, everyone was involved in the defense of the city. Some repaired the walls; others threw spears and shot arrows. Diogenes, the philosopher, became active too. He rolled his barrel to and fro on a street. Asked why, he replied, "Well, I don't want to be the only lazy one among so many who work."

"But the others do something useful for the city, which is not your case," he was told.

Solemnly, Diogenes continued to roll the barrel. He considered the work of others as useless as his own. Corinth and the Macedonian empire would pass away, regardless of who won this particular battle. The soldiers of both sides would soon die, the victors as well as the vanquished. After a few centuries, who would care about the details of the battle? Is there anyone today who remembers the names of those combatants? The citizens of the city were busy with things which, in the perspective of eternity, will prove to have been as much vanity as the rolling of the barrel.

In this world, where everything passes away, there is one thing that stands: it is what Christ the eternal One did for us on Golgotha. Other works ultimately will be of no avail. The cross of Christ saves sinners, imparting to them the eternity that the Son of God possesses.

Concerning the cross of Christ, John Chrysostom said: "It is the will of the Father, the honor of the Son, the joy of the Spirit, the jewel of angels, the assurance of the faithful, the glory of Paul."

Don't scorn those who spend their time in amusements, when the earnest labor you take pride in will bring no better results for eternity. Serve Christ, the crucified and resurrected. This is the only work that is not vanity.

J U N E   1

*"The wise men, the astrologers, have been brought in
before me, that they should read this writing and make
known to me its interpretation, but they could not give
the interpretation of the thing."*
DANIEL 5:15

While King Belshazzar of Babylon feasted merrily with his lords and women, a message in Aramaic appeared on the wall. Frightened and sobered, he summoned his counselors to declare the meaning of this unusual occurrence. However, none of them could interpret what had been written. Then he called Daniel and complained to him that his counselors did not know Aramaic.

The language was spoken by the Jews. These captives from Israel had become an important national minority in Babylon, contributing to the empire a prime minister and many other political leaders. But none of the wise men of Babylon had bothered to learn the language, religion, or mentality of the Jews. The enemies of Babylon, the Medes and Persians, were secretly entering the city while the king and his lords entertained themselves. That very night King Belshazzar was slain, and his great empire fell into other hands. His "wise" men lacked wisdom. Not knowing the imminence of the danger, they could not warn the king.

We see the tragic ignorance of these ancient counselors duplicated today. Modern wise men—many who are leaders in the church—are clever enough to secure for themselves high positions and the benefits and fame that go with eminence. But they lack an understanding of the people whom they are meant to lead to Christ, nor do they recognize the destructive forces that threaten the church. Today's "wise" men, the spiritual leaders, seem unaware of the grave danger that aggressive Islamism, communism, and widespread secularism present to Christianity.

The warning to King Belshazzar had been written by a hand on the wall. The warning to the free world is written in blood, and still our wise men cannot read it.

J U N E 2

*P*aul had decided to write an instructive letter to the church in Galatia. What he wrote down was the eternal Word of God which would serve as edification of Christians to the end of the world. In such a case you don't write your own opinion. You unite with all your brethren. There exists a faith for all which was once delivered to the saints—the faith held by all brethren always and everywhere. Only in communion with all the saints does one become able to deliver everlasting truth. Therefore, Paul wrote his letter to the Galatians in fellowship with "all the brethren" who were with him.

The One on whom Paul relied most was his brother, Jesus. In Him we trust. The glorified saints also are with us.

When Jesus spoke with Moses and Elijah on the Mount of Transfiguration, He asked His disciples not to tell anyone. No one, after meeting a man would say to someone, "You know, he had a nose." To have a nose is not unnatural. We are inclined to make much of the supernatural, but Jesus wished us to consider ourselves continually in communion with the saints who have passed on.

We are against spiritualism, the evoking of the dead; we do not wish to feel their nearness. But we believe that the saints who have gone on to be with the Lord are not far away.

The Bible says, "We are surrounded by so great a cloud of witnesses" (Hebrews 12:1). It is told that when John Chrysostom wrote his sermons a Christian saw Paul and John standing near him whispering ideas in his ear. Those who have become as children can believe this story. These experiences are not spoken of often because much talk would show that we do not believe the miraculous to be the normal in the Christian life, that we do not believe the communion of saints is an everyday experience.

Let us write our letters "together with the brethren who are with us."

J U N E   3

*T*he Bible is God's revelation. "Revelation" is a word of Latin origin with two meanings. It discovers hidden things unknown before, but it also puts some things behind a veil.

From the beginning, the words of our Lord were conveyed to us in Greek, another language than that spoken by Jesus. We have His words in the veil of a translation, which can never convey the full sense of the original. Even the Hebrew of the Old Testament veils the thoughts of God, wrapping them in the poor language of men. The purpose of the Bible is to awaken in us a longing after the blessed state when we will see God and when there will be no communication among men in words unfit to express the highest thoughts—as it will be at the consummation of the ages.

Jesus spoke Aramaic, a dialect of the Hebrew language. Neither in Aramaic nor in Hebrew does the word "to have" exist. Jesus never pronounced this word. Jesus never said of anything that He "had" it. Therefore He could keep perfect joy when they undressed Him to be scourged. They took away from Him clothes, about which He had never said, "I have them." He had never said, "I have a body." The body that they tortured was not His. He owned nothing. Jesus had yielded His body to His Father as a living sacrifice before they killed Him.

He taught His first disciples to think in the same manner. "Neither did anyone say that any of the things he possessed was his own" (Acts 4:32). Everything belongs to God and we are the stewards of His possessions. He is free to take away at any time the material riches, health, a beloved child, a good name, a friend, fame. These things are only entrusted to us. If they are taken away we lose nothing. They are not ours. This constitutes one of the joys of the Christian life. All Christians are "have-nots" and do not desire to be "haves." Those who have, worry about possible losses. This is not possible for us. Our life is one of full serenity.

JUNE 4

*"You are no longer a slave but a son, and if a son,
then an heir of God."*
GALATIANS 4:7

Since genes and DNA have been discovered, we know new things about heredity. We know what irresistible forces, working good or evil, are conveyed to us by heredity from our ancestors.

There is also a heredity of the spirit. When we are born again into His family, God is truly our Father. We inherit from God not only His kingdom, but also His character. The seed of God is in us (1 John 3:9).

The children of English-speaking people speak English; the children of Romanians speak Romanian. The children of God speak the words of God. Peter says in his first epistle, "If anyone speaks, let him speak as the oracles of God" (4:11). If a man is an heir of God, his words or writings should normally also be oracles of God. If not, then he shouldn't speak or write.

We should all be able to say with Paul, "You received me as an angel of God, even as Christ Jesus" (Galatians 4:14). This is the normal manner to receive someone who speaks as the oracles of God.

A Swedish sister writes that when she completed the translation of a Christian book, an angel appeared to her and thanked her. It may make some Christians smile. But I would not waste my time in Christianity if I did not believe at least the first page of the New Testament, where we are told that angels appear. You get the approval of Christians and angels when you speak as the oracles of God.

JUNE 5

*"Go into all the world and preach the gospel
to every creature."*
MARK 16:15

*I*f a man stood by a roadside and watched the whole population of China walk past him at the rate of one individual per second, more than twenty years would elapse before the last member of the procession would go by. The most strict Leninism rules these people. Lenin has written, "Everything is moral that is necessary for the annihilation of the old exploiting order." According to Lenin, religion belongs in this category and must be annihilated.

But there are Christians in China who do not fear death. It is the way to enter into the embrace of the heavenly Bridegroom and to receive the holy kiss. A remarkable report comes from the province of Hunan. A preacher was hanged by the Communists, but they left too quickly. The brethren were able to cut him down, and he is still alive. He says that when the rope was around his neck and he was being hauled up over the branch of a tree, all he could think of was our Lord being raised upon the cross.

Pray for the great people of China and for its believers. God loves the Chinese very much. He has made so many of them—800 million.

JUNE 6

S t. Patrick begins his "Confession" with the words, "I, Patrick, a sinner, the most uncouth and the least of all the faithful." In the fourth century, he, a Britisher, was taken as a slave in a raid by the Irish. He had to herd sheep for them in hunger and nakedness. Their cruelty kindled in the young Christian lad a foolish love toward his slaveholders.

Eventually he succeeded in escaping. In England, and free, he had a dream. A man approached him with a letter and Patrick read "the voice of the Irish." Then he heard many Irish voices crying, "We beseech you, holy youth, to come over and walk once more among us."

For a runaway slave to be caught by his former slaveholder could mean death. But Patrick loved, so the danger did not count. He confessed to a cleric some gross sin he had committed. This made his sin publicly known, and the church would not send Patrick to Ireland. So he returned on his own and brought his former slaveholders to Christ.

Let us bring persecutors to the Savior. Think about the man who has wronged you the most and make it a point of honor to bring him to conversion.

JUNE 7

"Go into your room."
MATTHEW 6:6

*T*eachers of philosophy have given to men unnatural advice. Marcus Aurelius wrote, "People seek retreats in villages, on beaches, in the mountains . . . This is vulgar, because, whenever you wish, you can withdraw into yourself. Nowhere does man find a more silent and calm retreat than in his soul." You surely can find inner quietness among the noise, but it takes a huge effort.

Why not follow the better example and teaching of the Master, who went into desert places or into the mountains to pray? And when this is not possible, why not assure yourself of quietness in your room?

The noise of this technological age is part of a plot against spirituality. Radio and television, among other things, make sure that you never have a bit of quiet. Lovers, friends, have forgotten the art of sitting or walking together in silence. A good 80 percent of the words spoken or written are useless.

The Hebrews, to whom God gave His first revelation, have no word for "word." Through them the Word of God was given, but you cannot say that in Hebrew. Instead of "word," they use *davar*, which means "the real thing." Let us speak and listen to words only if they are not useless chatter, but realities.

In Hebrew, the prologue to the Gospel of John says, "In the beginning was the real thing (*davar*), and the real thing was with God, and the real thing was God."

Instead of wasting our time in idle talk about things that don't really matter, let us pass much time in our rooms in quiet communion with God.

JUNE 8

*"Assuredly, I say to you, whoever says to this mountain,
'Be removed and be cast into the sea,' and does not
doubt in his heart, but believes that those things he says
will be done, he shall have whatever he says."*
MARK 11:23

*J*esus said these words on the road between Jerusalem and Bethany. The terrain is flat. There is no mountain. When he said "this mountain," He could point toward nothing as being a hindrance on the way.

The mountains of difficulties and obstacles are all in our imagination. We have promises: "Nothing shall by any means hurt you" (Luke 10:19), and "All things work together for good to those who love God" (Romans 8:28). Things and events never touch our souls but remain outside their door. What troubles us are our opinions and our attitudes toward persons and events. Over these we have authority. These we can throw into the sea.

The circumstances in which the Lord said these words show that they don't apply to material mountains. How would the world look if each one of the millions of Jesus' disciples would move mountains to the right or to the left according to his or her pleasure? Every disciple would have a different opinion about where the mountain should be. Jesus speaks about spiritual realities when He teaches us how to remove mountains.

Let events come. Let persons act toward you as they will. Don't regard anything as a mountain in your way. Two and two make four. Fruits contain juice. Men sometimes behave badly. Events can be unpleasant. Yet all things will work together for my good. Difficulties on my way to heaven belong to the world of imagination. I can throw them off.

JUNE 9

"Simon answered..., 'Master, we have toiled all night and caught nothing; nevertheless at Your word I will let down the net.'"
LUKE 5:5

William Chalmers Burns went out as a missionary to China in 1847. After seven years he wrote, "I do not know of a single soul brought to Christ through me." The Lord had made him pass through the school of perseverance.

Fishing as it was done 2,000 years ago was hard work. Would we have thrown our nets into the water again after a whole night of vain labor? Reason and the desire to rest pleaded against it; but there exists the magnificent word, "nevertheless." Simon Peter threw in the nets again and did not pause to rest even after the miraculous but tiring fishing. He and his comrades brought their ships to land and did not go to bed. "They...followed Him" (Luke 5:11).

We should remain at our place of labor in spite of unhappy experiences and unsatisfactory results.

Archbishop Fenelon wrote, "If one were not upheld by the spirit of faith to work on without seeing the fruit of one's labor, one would be disheartened, so little does one accomplish whether in winning others or in amending oneself."

I am president of a worldwide mission. I was brought to Christ by a carpenter, Wölfkes, who had prayed for years—without result —that he might not die before bringing one Jew to Christ. God granted him two, my wife and myself. We brought to the Savior a few other Jews; and these, in turn won more. The result can be seen now in thriving Hebrew-Christian congregations in many towns of Israel. Many of the believers come from Wölfkes' homeland, Romania. Once when I told the story of my conversion in a Romanian village, I noticed that a very old man in the audience was weeping. He told me at the end, "God used me to bring that carpenter to Christ. I thought that I had toiled all my life uselessly. I heard from you now that I am the grandfather in faith of many Jews." You also continue on your post, "nevertheless."

J U N E   1 0

"Christ who is our life..."
COLOSSIANS 3:4

*T*he relationship between Jesus and a believing soul is unique and cannot be well explained in words, there being no real equivalent. In a transfusion, the blood of one man becomes another man's blood. If the latter man is injured and there is a shedding of blood immediately after the transfusion, not the blood of the donor is shed, but that of the recipient. It has become his. In a heart transplant, the heart is no longer that of a corpse, but that of a living man. So it is between Jesus and the believing soul. A transfusion, a transplantation, a change of personalities takes place.

Luther puts it like this: "The Father says to Christ, 'You become Peter who denies, Saul who persecutes, Judas who betrays, Magdalene who sins. Then the law sees Jesus full of all these offenses and tells him that he must die.' Jesus is the greatest murderer, thief, liar, adulterer mankind has ever known. Not in the sense that he committed these crimes, but that he appropriated them to himself." He has become my sinning personality. In exchange, He gives me His personality. In his commentary on the Epistle to the Galatians, Luther daringly says: "The Christian is Christ."

Luther stands here on biblical ground. The greatest teachers of Christianity have taught the same thing. Ignatius wrote, "Christ is our inseparable life." Thomas Aquinas said that Christ and the Christians are "quasi one mystical person." The Scottish Catechism (Craig's) teaches: "Christ is not another person from his people properly."

Jesus was delivered to be crucified. It is Jesus who continues to be delivered to be crucified today in the person of His disciples. All your sufferings are His.

"Lord, teach us to pray."
LUKE 11:1

*S*t. Francis of Assisi prayed like this:

LORD!
Make me an instrument of thy peace;
Where there is hatred, let me sow love;
Where there is doubt, faith;
Where there is despair, hope;
Where there is darkness, light;
And where there is sadness, joy.

O Divine Master, grant that I may not so
much seek to be consoled, as to console;
to be understood, as to understand; to be
loved, as to love; for it is in giving that
we receive, it is in pardoning that we are
pardoned, and it is in dying that we are
born to eternal life.

How is it that most of us don't act like this? It is because we
have the "I." In English, all substantives and pronouns are written
with small letters; only the "I" is written with a capital letter. Having
an "I," much discomfort can happen to me, because of which I
become unhappy and unloving. If you have no "I," what evil can
come upon you?

Therefore the Lord says, "If any man will come after me, let him
deny himself"—that is, let him deny the "I." I will be saved only
when there will be no more "I" to be saved.

J U N E   1 2

"One thing is needed."
LUKE 10:42

*T*he greatest complaint one hears is that people have no time. It is surely so because, like Martha, they are busy with too many things. You would never have heard Mary saying that she had no time. She needed only one thing: to listen to her Beloved and from time to time to do the one thing commanded by Him. He never commands us to do two things in the same moment. There is just one task for each moment of our lives. While fulfilling this one task, I have no other duty. Believers, therefore, always have time.

A new evangelist came into a village and astonished all by his powerful preaching. The news quickly spread, and the next Sunday the entire village gathered in church. He delivered exactly the same sermon. On the third Sunday, when people had come from neighboring villages, again he preached the same sermon. Also the fourth Sunday. The church elders said to each other, "This must be a crook who has learned just one sermon by heart."

"Don't you know how to deliver another sermon?" they asked.

"I have not yet seen you fulfilling what I taught in the first sermon," he replied. "So why should I burden you with another one?"

Why read so many newspapers and listen to so much news, instead of responding to one tragedy near us by offering our help? Why read so many new books when we have not put into practice any of the good things already read? Why do I answer another telephone call, when I did not take time to be attentive, compassionate, and kind toward the man who called me first?

How little our Lord said and did! You could compile the essentials in the sixteen chapters of Mark. But every single act and word was pure, beaten gold. Examine your words and actions. You will find that most of them are not needed. Control them and you will have time and serenity. Examine your conscience every evening. Review the day, asking yourself step by step whether the things you did were necessary. Eliminate all useless thoughts and deeds.

J U N E   1 3

"As many as received Him, to them He gave the right to become children of God."
JOHN 1:12

Once when Napoleon was riding in a parade his horse went beserk. Seeing that the emperor was about to be thrown, a foot soldier, at the risk of his own life, grabbed the loose reins and through sheer strength stopped the wild horse and held it still.

Napoleon said, "Thank you, captain."

The newly made captain understood and went directly to the officers' dining room. Sitting down he began to address the officers as his comrades.

"How dare you?" they asked.

"Why not?" he answered. "I am a captain."

They mocked, "A captain? You? But you don't have a captain's bars, neither the schooling, nor a company to command."

"I have none of this yet," he replied confidently, "but I am a captain, because Napoleon called me one."

No child of God should be dismayed that he does not have the behavior of a saint; that he does not have the necessary knowledge; that he may not be acknowledged as a fellow believer by those around him. He has been called "a child of God" by the King of kings. This is enough.

He who has given you this name will lead you through life, through its ascents and descents, even through death to the fulfilling of your high calling. Only believe that you are a child of God. The rest will come.

"Do this in remembrance of Me."
1 CORINTHIANS 11:24

*J*ohn Chrysostom said, "If we were non-corporeal, God would give us the spiritual things in their simplicity without material form. But because our souls live in bodies, He gives us spiritual gifts in the shape of visible things." He spoke about the ordinances. No Christian life is possible without them.

Augustine wrote, "You cannot gather men in the name of a right or a wrong religion, if you don't unite them through the common use of visible signs or sacraments."

Baptism, communion, the laying on of hands—all are visible signs of an invisible grace that is given to you.

A cheap ring given by a bridegroom gets a new value. The same is true of any metal made into a coin that bears the stamp of the state. So it is with the water of baptism: it becomes a symbol of the cleansing of sin.

By the same token, in communion the bread and the wine are symbols of the body and blood of the Lord.

It is wrong to look around during communion to see whether someone is taking it unworthily. Examine yourself. Everyone takes it on his own responsibility. Don't hesitate to take communion from a pastor whose life you know to be bad. The value of the ordinance does not depend upon the character of the one who gives it, any more than the value of a letter from a loved one depends upon the character of the mailman.

Do not imagine that the ordinances in themselves will help you. They strengthen us on the path toward heaven only if they are taken with faith.

If you have these things in proper perspective, they can become true food for your soul.

J U N E   1 5

"Then Jesus came from Galilee to John at the Jordan
to be baptized by him."
MATTHEW 3:13

S t. Ignace said that Jesus was baptized "to cleanse the waters." Most theologians would say that He did it to show His compassion toward sinners. Did Jesus feel Himself to be a sinner? Did He wish to be cleansed?

From the genes of Mary's ovule, by which Jesus was conceived, He inherited physical characteristics from many ancestors, all sinners. Seventy percent of man's character is inherited. If Jesus is God who has become man in the fullest sense of the word, He was subject to the law of heredity. As man He could be influenced. "He had been brought up" (Luke 4:16). His teachers and all those around Him were sinners. He was tempted like all of us. He had our instincts and impulses. As man His knowledge was limited. To save the humble, He had to hit merchants and Pharisees.

He never committed any sin, but He felt as His own all sins committed against Him since He was a child, beginning with the heredity imposed upon Him and the slaughter of the babes in Bethlehem. He felt as His the sorrow of all who had committed crimes. No one ever had felt guilty like Him. Taking all our sins upon Himself, He became the greatest criminal of history. The sense of guilt is the acutest in the most innocent. Paul calls himself the chief of sinners. We would have said that the greatest sinners were Caiaphas, Pilate, and Judas. The completely innocent One felt the paroxysms of guilt.

Therefore He felt the need to be baptized.

Don't wallow in the innocence granted to you by Jesus. Just because you have become whiter than the snow, appropriate to yourself everyone's sin.

JUNE 16

A bishop committed whoredom. No one knew it. Yet he confessed it before everyone in church. Putting his pallium on the altar, he said, "I cannot be your bishop anymore."

Everybody wept and replied, "May the sin be ours, but keep your bishopric."

He then lay on the floor of the church just inside the door and said, "Whoever will go out without treading on me shall have no part with God." So they did. When the last had trodden on him, a voice came from heaven: "Because of his great humility, I have forgiven his sin."

This happened in the fourth century. At that time the Christians were a gathering of saints. But today I would recommend that no man with a position in the church, or any church worker, do what that bishop did.

I know the case of a Soviet heroine of the faith. She was in prison for having taught children about Christ. She had behaved courageously at interrogations and before the court. In her cell a fellow Christian she had always looked up to as a great leader confessed to her a hidden sin. This made her lose her faith. She did not expect a fellow Christian to have sinned so grievously. She forsook the church and married a Communist. There are times when confessing your sin can hurt someone else. Confess your sins to the Lord. Take your burden to Him.

Only be careful to be considered a sinner by your brethren and sisters. Do not pose as a saint and God will forgive you your sins for your humility.

JUNE 17

*"When . . . you do not speak to warn the wicked from
his way . . . his blood I will require at your hand."*
EZEKIEL 33:8

One stormy, winter day on Lake Michigan, a ship sank not far
from the shore. A good swimmer succeeded in saving ten
persons, one after another. His colleagues had prepared a fire on
the beach. Exhausted, the "savior" warmed himself. Seeing others
still wrestling with the waves, he prepared to enter the water again.

His friends advised him not to do it. "You are too tired," they
said. "You will drown, too."

"I cannot see men perishing!" he answered.

Gathering all his strength, he saved another five. He had done
his utmost. He himself was pulled from the water with difficulty.

Lying exhausted near the fire, he saw two men trying hard to
keep themselves afloat on a plank. "I must save these, too," he
cried.

"It is folly," the others exclaimed. "You will commit suicide!"

He did not listen to them, and saved also these two.

Now the last of his strength was gone, but he could not excuse
himself. He was in agony. In the delirium of fever he asked again
and again, "How will I present myself before the Lord having saved
only seventeen? Could I not have saved at least one more?"

We are responsible for the blood of everyone whose physical or
spiritual life we could have saved, but have neglected to do so. Are
we not all murderers?

Seeing a criminal being led to the gallows, Philip Neri said,
"Were it not for the grace of God, I would have deserved to be in
his place."

JUNE 18

"God... gives to all liberally."
JAMES 1:5

*I*n his important book, *The Power and the Glory*, Graham Greene has one of his characters say the following to the poor priest whose story is the subject of the work: "I can't think how a man like you can believe those things. The Indians, yes; why, the first time they see an electric light they think it's a miracle."

The priest responds: "And I dare say the first time you saw a man raised from the dead you might think so too. Oh, it's funny, isn't it. It isn't a case of miracles not happening—it's just a case of people calling them something else. Can't you see the doctors round the dead man? He isn't breathing any more, his pulse has stopped, his heart's not beating: he's dead. Then somebody gives him back his life, and they all—what's the expression?—reserve their opinion. They won't say it's a miracle, because that's a word they don't like. Then it happens again and again perhaps—because God's about on earth—and they say: there aren't miracles, it is simply that we have enlarged our conception of what life is. Now we know you can be alive without pulse, breath, heart beats. And they invent a new word to describe that state of life, and they say science has again disproved a miracle. You can't get around them."

See the miracles of God in the daily work of doctors, engineers, technicians, psychiatrists, inventors, farmers, factory workers who improve and ease our life on earth. They are the tools. The donor, the performer of miracles is God.

JUNE 19

"You cannot serve God and mammon."
MATTHEW 6:24

A Christian had received great gifts from God. He had been famous for his holy life. His renown came to the attention of the emperor, who called for him to hear his teachings. The emperor was very satisfied and gave him gold, which he accepted.

When he returned home, the Christian bought some land and houses.

As had often happened in the past, someone possessed by a demon was brought to him. The Christian commanded the demon, "Leave the man!"

The demon scorned, "I will not obey you."

Having never heard such refusals before, the surprised believer asked, "Why don't you obey me?"

The demon replied, "Abandoning your sole preoccupation with God, you have become like us. Therefore I don't obey you."

A rich church is powerless in the fight against the devil. So is a rich Christian. A Christian can administrate great riches, but only on the condition that they are not his, but God's, who has given him the gift of multiplying and using them for His glory.

The moment you consider the riches to be yours, you fall under the curse pronounced by the Lord: "It is easier for a camel to go through the eye of a needle than for a rich man to enter the kingdom of God" (Matthew 19:24).

Think thoroughly about these things before you go about managing what you believe to be your money.

"Suffer it to be so now."
MATTHEW 3:15 (KJV)

We know what Jesus said at the age of twelve. About the following eighteen years of his life, the Gospels keep perfect silence. They break it when He reached the age of thirty. His first word is, "Suffer."

John the Baptist could not conceive that the Savior should be baptized by him, as so many sinners had been. Jesus said, "Suffer it."

"Suffer little children" to come to the worship service, though they might disturb it (Matthew 19:14, KJV). "Suffer [in Greek it is the same word, *afiemi*] the tares to grow together with the wheat" (Matthew 13:30, KJV).

"They are blind leaders of the blind." We would have added, "Don't allow them to continue." Jesus says, "Let them alone" (Matthew 15:14).

A certain man wished to cut down a fig tree because it gave no fruit. The dresser of the vineyard, who represents Jesus in the parable, answers, "Let it alone this year also" (Luke 13:8).

Suffer men and things. Let them alone.

Instead of worrying about the evil that others do, learn from the bees. They care about no one, but feed mankind with honey. Do the same.

JUNE 21

*"The Spirit of God was hovering over the
face of the waters."*
GENESIS 1:2

Augustine wrote, "If we had been commanded to build for the Spirit a temple of wood and stones, we would have had a clear proof of the Divinity of the Spirit, because worship is due only to God. But we have an even clearer proof in the fact that we are not to erect, but to be a temple for him."

The Spirit must be God if blasphemy against Him is the only unforgivable sin.

The presence of the Spirit in the life of the believer must be essential. Jews who went to Samaria risked their lives because they were hated by the Samaritans. Notwithstanding, Peter and John risked their lives and went there with the sole purpose of imparting the Spirit to believers.

Without the Spirit, all religious acts are as useless as light to blind men or melodies to the deaf. Christ was baptized because He knew that afterward the Spirit would descend upon Him. This must be our purpose, too, in every religious practice.

"If anyone does not have the Spirit of Christ, he is not His" (Romans 8:9). On the other hand, there is no condemnation to those who are in Christ Jesus, who do not walk according to the flesh, but according to the Spirit (Romans 8:1).

"Amen."
REVELATION 22:21

*A*fter Jesus was baptized, He desired to have the Holy Spirit descend upon Him. And the Spirit did so.

When you ask some gift from God in prayer, don't abandon prayer until you get an inner experience, until you see the demand descending upon you in a quasi-material shape and hear from God's mouth the approval of your request.

This is the sense of the word "Amen." You have spoken to God, but God lives within you and uses your mouth to answer your prayer. "Amen" is His approval to what you have requested.

A girl overheard the doctor telling her father, "There is no more hope for your wife." The girl went into the adjoining room, knelt down and prayed for the recovery of her mother.

Then she changed her voice and said, "Yes, Mary, I will surely heal her."

Changing her voice again, she said, "God, I thank You."

Entering the other room, she told her father, "God has just promised me He will heal Mother."

The mother was healed. This is the sense of our "Amen." It is God's seal of approval uttered through your mouth that your intercession has been accepted.

Every prayer should be followed by an "Amen."

JUNE 23

"Thus it is fitting for us to fulfill all righteousness."
MATTHEW 3:15

No commandment in the Old Testament obliged a Jew to be baptized. Jesus says that it becomes us to fulfill all righteousness by doing things that are not commanded.

There exist no commandments of God forbidding us to smoke, to wear jewelry (what did God make the emeralds and rubies for?), to go to beauty shops, to pass hours watching television. There are no commandments of God that forbid petting or trying drugs. Righteousness is fulfilled not by obeying commandments, but by asking ourselves the simple question, "Would Jesus like it or do it?"

If you threw some dust at a man, you would not hurt him. Neither would he suffer if you poured water upon him. Nor if you threw straw at him. But earth, straw, and water together make a brick. Throw that and you can crush his head.

So there are many little things, which by themselves are harmless. When they gather in our life, however, they become a heavy weight that might destroy our souls. "The little foxes...spoil the vines" (Song of Solomon 2:15).

There is no commandment in the law of God to fight little foxes, but it is good for the possessor of a vineyard to do so. It is good for you to fight certain habits. Even though each one by itself is a mere trifle, together they become a weight that hampers your spiritual life.

179

JUNE 24

"He saw the Spirit of God descending like a dove."
MATTHEW 3:16

The dove is gentle, friendly with men, like the Holy Spirit, and therefore a fit symbol for Christ. They also have something else in common.

In order to observe doves, one must be very attentive and quiet. These little creatures of nature don't show their ways to noisy men. He who wishes to know them must develop the qualities for observing without being observed, for listening without being heard.

It is the same with the Spirit. One must be quiet, remaining silent before Him (Habakkuk 2:20). The Holy Spirit does not behave the same way when He feels observed as when He is at His ease.

In the first case He is suspicious, worried about how His actions will be interpreted. The Lord says of the Jews, "I would have said, 'I will dash them in pieces, I will make the memory of them to cease from among men,' had I not feared the wrath of the enemy...lest they should say, 'Our hand is high; and it is not the LORD who has done all this'" (Deuteronomy 32:26,27).

The Spirit knows Himself to be observed by His enemies, and He depicts Himself as fearing to be misunderstood and acting otherwise than He normally would. The Lord said, "Because of the people who are standing by I said this" (John 11:42). To know the words Jesus intended to say, if uninfluenced by those standing by, we have to keep reservedly aloof.

When observed by enemies, complainers, or the curious, the Spirit, like the dove, does not have normal reactions.

Keep silent, don't interfere, and let the Spirit do as He pleases.

"Others save with fear."
JUDE 23

*I*f you see someone drowning, throw him a rope and try to pull him out of the water. If he is much too heavy for you, abandon your endeavor. Otherwise he might pull you into the water, and two will perish instead of one.

The path of endeavoring to bring men to eternal salvation is also fraught with danger. The effort of many a young man trying to bring some girl to salvation has ended with both falling into sin.

Missionaries have gone to Asian countries to tell people about Christ. Instead, some have been converted to Buddhism or have ended up with a mixture of a foreign religion and Christianity. Mission boards have been formed to proclaim the gospel to other nations; and then Christians have become so busy with financial matters of the institution that Christ disappeared from their lives.

Some Christians have entered the slums, places of poverty, to bring Christ's love—but instead they have become infected with the rebellious spirit prevailing there and are now members of rebellious organizations. When speaking with a profane man about things spiritual, there is a danger that he may pull you down into his profane manner of conversation.

How will you save the souls of others if you are not careful about keeping your own soul pure? Leave the castle of your own loving fellowship with the Lord only rarely, after much preparation in prayer.

Be wary of every maneuver of the enemy. Avoid battles that are too dangerous for you. Foolhardiness is not courage. Save with fear.

*"Behold! The Lamb of God who takes away
the sin of the world!"*
JOHN 1:29

*I*f you sent a child to the grocery store to buy something with a dollar and the grocer demanded two dollars, you could not punish the child for not fulfilling your command. A teacher cannot expect a child in the primary grades to solve complicated problems of algebra.

Neither does God ask us to save our souls. We don't have the capacity for this. We are not guilty of not saving ourselves. Our guilt consists only in not coming to Jesus, who has the immeasurable power to save the whole world. If the whole world, why not me?

Augustine wrote, "If there had been in the world only one sinner, Jesus would have gladly brought for him the same sacrifice which he brought for the entire world."

Jesus never demanded that you should do for yourself what you cannot do. Just leave your soul to Him. He will do the work.

Leonardo da Vinci, painting the scene where John the Baptist exclaimed, "Behold! The Lamb of God who takes away the sins of the world," gave John the eyes of a drunkard. He went so far in this that some believed he had painted Bacchus, the god of wine.

John the Baptist must have been drunk with joy when he discovered that such a Savior had appeared.

Appeal to Jesus for the salvation from all your sins.

"Can anything good come out of Nazareth?"
JOHN 1:46

Nazareth was a town with an immoral reputation. But Nathanael, who spoke the words of our text, was guilty of one of the most destructive sins: contempt toward an entire group of men. Every group of people contains a variety of persons with different personalities and characteristics.

A Lutheran pastor told me, "I have an emotional complex against the Baptists and Pentecostals." He did not realize that he had confessed to a much graver sin than if he had said, "I have lived many years in adultery." His duty was to give up his prejudice immediately for we must forsake every sin.

Every prejudice excludes the man holding it from any possibility of right thinking.

Many will not accept Jesus because He was Jewish.

The Pharisees could not admit that a prophet could come from Galilee (John 7:52).

Others took offense at His belonging to the lower class. They asked in mocking tone, "Is this not the carpenter's son?" (Matthew 13:55).

Some ask themselves if the church about which so many bad things are said can give anything of value.

God is the Father of all men. There is good in all groups.

The Moabites, on the whole, had behaved badly toward the Jewish people. But from them came Ruth, one of the Bible's saintly women.

The Samaritans had gone astray from the true religion, but Jesus tells us about a good Samaritan.

Flee any racial, national, or denominational prejudice. Judge every person on his or her own merits.

JUNE 28

"Let each esteem others better than himself."
PHILIPPIANS 2:3

While praying in his cell, St. Anthony heard a voice: "Anthony," it said, "you have not yet arrived at the stage of that tanner." Anthony immediately went to see the tanner to learn from him the ways of sanctification.

The tanner bowed, bewildered that he could have been found worthy of such a visit.

Anthony asked him, "What is your Christian exercise?"

He answered, "In the morning, when I awake, I say to myself, all in my city are much better than I. They are pleasing to God. I am the biggest sinner and deserve punishment."

The sins of others are not our business. Who am I to judge? Only pride judges and condemns fellow men.

A man came to his pastor and asked, "What should I do? I am much tempted by pride."

The pastor answered, "Just accept it. You have plenty to be proud of, seeing that you created heaven and earth."

The young man did not understand.

The pastor dismissed him with the words, "If the One through whom the world has been made came in humility, why should you, who are only dust and ashes, be proud? What are your works, you unhappy man?"

JUNE 29

"Though we have known Christ according to the flesh,
yet now we know him thus no longer."
2 CORINTHIANS 5:16

*A*ugustine writes, "The face which Jesus had when he was in the flesh is shaped by men in various forms. It is completely unknown how the face of Jesus looked."

We know exactly from sculptures and ancient coins the faces of Julius Caesar or the emperors of Jesus' time, Octavian Augustus and Tiberius; but not that of the King of kings. God's providence has arranged it to be so. This is because the Caesars were only historic personalities. Jesus is God, the Eternal stepping only briefly into time. We should not associate Him with a certain face expressing the specific features of an age, a sex, a race, a climate.

Jesus lives within many men: some of them beggars, others emperors; some white, others black or red or yellow; some children, some old men; some saints, some beginners in sanctity, some who have fallen in gross sins which they regret. We must learn to see Jesus in all of these.

Therefore there has been great opposition in the church to the introduction of icons. Becoming familiar with a certain image of Jesus, you no longer recognize Him in the needy near you.

JUNE 30

"This is the law when a man dies…"
NUMBERS 19:14

*F*ive missionaries to the Auca Indians in Ecuador were killed in one day. Their wives received the news with composure. The norm of Christian living is to die for one's faith. No one really acknowledges a law to be the law of God if he is not ready to die for it.

Not everyone has the privilege of a martyr's death, but every Christian has to die before he dies. He must be dead to the world, its laws and its sins, before he dies.

Macarius was asked, "What does it mean to be dead to the world?"

He answered, "Go to a cemetery, praise some of the dead and curse others. Then come and tell me what happened."

The inquirer did as commanded. He returned telling Macarius, "None answered a word."

Macarius replied, "Do the same."

The five martyrs had guns on them when they died. They could have defended their lives, but they chose to die rather than to shoot the Indians. They had died before dying. How could a corpse shoot anyone? They were alive only for God.

These martyrs gave their lives to bring the gospel to a tribe which at that time numbered only fifty-six people. Men of all tribes have to be among the saved, those of small tribes, too.

The blood of the martyrs brought seed. The Auca Indians already have their first martyr, one of them who went to evangelize a neighboring tribe.

Let us pray regularly for the many men who are still in the stone age not touched by civilization.

J U L Y   1

*L*et us learn from the great saints.

John de la Salle is the father of modern pedagogy. He founded the first free high school and teachers' seminary in France. Because he loved much, he did much. He said, "I cannot think about the many children who perish from ignorance without shedding tears." We are upset by trifles in our personal lives, but how many of us would shed tears for the ignorant?

Unable to bear this burden idly, he distributed his great wealth among the poor and became a poor teacher of the poor. I compare his spirit with that of teachers who are dissatisfied with large salaries and strike to get more. They are examples of selfishness to their students. The catastrophe that they produce in the minds of children by their greed will never be erased by the beauties they teach.

De la Salle had to suffer much from fellow Christians and unemployed teachers.

Pacificus of San Severino was obsessed by the words of the Lord that the harvest is big and the laborers few. He said, "The world needs apostles not doctors of theology." He had decided to become one, going as a missionary to the heathen. But God had appointed him to another apostolate, that of suffering. His feet swelled until he could no longer counsel the souls he loved so much. Then he was afflicted by blindness. His soul was ravaged by inner tempests. Friends insulted him, calling him accursed of God, convinced by his suffering that it was so.

He bore all this suffering valiantly knowing that God's will, not his own, must be done in all things. Pacificus still brings souls to Christ three centuries after his death. Through the story of his sufferings lovingly borne, many more have been won to his Lord than if he had gone to preach among the heathen.

Let us learn to be unselfish and submissive to God's will.

JULY 2

"Seek, and you will find."
MATTHEW 7:7

*I*n daily life you find Jesus through prayer. Teresa of Avila wrote, "The devil knows that he has lost the soul that perseveringly practices mental prayer." She also gives a definition of this exercise: "Mental prayer is nothing else than an intimate friendship, a frequent heart-to-heart conversation with Him by whom we know ourselves to be loved."

This is something entirely different than saying your prayers in the morning and evening and at meals. He prays very little and very poorly who prays only when he is on his knees. We have to remain in contact with Jesus the whole day, through short prayers and meditations about everything which occurs. Be aware that in all circumstances God is present and discuss with Him, your best Friend, what would be the best thing to do. Thank Him also in all things.

We read in *The Imitation of Christ*: "A man does himself more harm, if he seeks not Jesus, than the whole world and all his enemies could do." We are upset about having been offended, or about the catastrophes of war and revolutions provoked by wicked men, without realizing that the greatest enemy we each have is self.

There was a man who never succeeded in anything he did. An invisible enemy thwarted all his purposes. One evening, lying on his couch and brooding about all his failures, he saw a hand stretching out from behind the curtain to strangle him. He said to himself, "Now I can see my enemy face to face. I am powerful. I will overcome him." With a swift movement, he drew aside the curtain and saw the enemy. It was himself—his neglect to seek Jesus.

JULY 3

"With God all things are possible."
MATTHEW 19:26

When I was a little child I did not think about God. I had been taught that He is an all-powerful being. This was all I knew. At the age of perhaps eight, another child mocked God in my presence. "If He is all-powerful," the child scoffed, "can He make a weight He cannot lift? If He can, He is not all-powerful. If He cannot, again He is not what He claims."

I liked the joke and the idea of an all-powerful God never occurred to me again.

At the age of twenty-seven, I read the New Testament and found out that God had made a weight He could not lift. He had made of Himself a babe, weighing just a few pounds. He could not lift Himself. His mother had to lift Him, to take Him from the manger to her breast to feed Him. God had His ears washed. He was too small a child to do it Himself. His jacket which He had torn climbing some tree was patched by His mother. He did not know how to sew.

God had made a weight He could not lift. He had become incarnate as the Son of man. And this Son of man was given into the hands of men. They mocked Him; they crucified Him. The only real subject had become a simple object. People around jeered Him for His lack of power. He could not descend from His cross. Then He became even more of an object—a corpse. If Joseph of Arimathea had not buried Him, His flesh would have been eaten by eagles.

Having made a weight He could not lift, God showed His almightiness by lifting the unliftable. Jesus was resurrected in power and ascended into heaven. Once lifted from the earth, He attracts all men toward Him.

I had been wrong as a child. God is almighty. He can make a weight He Himself cannot lift and is almighty notwithstanding.

JULY 4

"He was hungry."
MATTHEW 21:18

One billion people hunger. We give a figure, but every number represents a person. Ten thousand die daily of malnutrition and starvation, 9,900 of them without having heard of Christ. People of developed countries consume five times as much food as the minimum necessary to save the hungry. In some part of Africa 25 percent of the children die before their first birthday. Their chance of dying is forty times higher than in the U.S. or Australia. Among those who hunger are the children of thousands of Christian martyrs in the Communist camps.

The Christian philosopher Aristides wrote in the year A.D. 125 to the emperor Hadrian: "With Christians, he who has gives to him who has not, ungrudgingly and without boasting...If they find poverty in their midst and they do not have spare food, they fast two or three days in order that the needy might be supplied with necessities."

Fast. Renounce. On the Day of Judgment, the Lord will tell you, "I was hungry and you gave Me food" (Matthew 25:35).

JULY 5

*"From him who takes away your goods
do not ask them back."*
LUKE 6:30

A Christian surprised burglars stealing his belongings. He told them, "Hurry and finish before the police come. Here, I will help you load the goods into your car. It is my fault for possessing them. I am a Christian and we were meant not to gather treasures on earth. Our Lord has warned us that thieves might steal them. It was my fault not to rely on the Father to take care of my needs. Please forgive me for having given you such a bad example!"

The robbers became interested, asking him one question after another. They did not steal from him, but were converted. The Christian had learned a lesson, too.

"The love of money is a root of all kinds of evil" (1 Timothy 6:10). Money must be totally despised by Christians.

An old legend says that Christ once taught His disciples, "Beware of money." They asked, "Why?" He replied, "Because often it is dishonestly acquired."

They asked again, "Suppose it is honestly earned?" Jesus said, "Beware of money even then, because it usually is sinfully spent."

The disciples asked for the third time, "What if it is honestly gained and well spent?"

The Lord replied, "Even then, beware of money. It always pollutes."

JULY 6

*"Nathanael answered and said to Him, 'Rabbi,
You are the Son of God!'"*
JOHN 1:49

*I*slam and Reformed Judaism accept Jesus as a great prophet. They object to His being worshiped as Son of God. We owe them light in this matter.

In Hebrew, the adjective is little used. The Hebrew would not say "a talkative person," but *Ish dvarim*—"a man of words." For "divine," he could only say, "Son of God." In Aramaic, the language the Lord spoke, the adjectives were used even less. Therefore we find in our Bibles the strange expressions, "children of light," instead of "luminous"; and "son of perdition," instead of "lost."

We have to explain to the Jews and Muslims that we don't believe in Jesus being the Son of God in the usual sense of the word. God has no wife and does not conceive children. The Hebrew of the first century simply did not have another expression to show the degree of Christ's affinity as man and substantial unity with the Father as God than calling Him "Son of God."

Modern science supplies us with a new image of what "Son of God" means. We speak about the family of radioactive elements and about a radioactive filiation. Emanation of electrons changes uranium I into uranium II, then into ionium, etc.

We can use different images to exemplify what is meant by the expression "Son of God." What is certain, however, is that Christ is God. The ancients said, *"Aut Deus, aut homo non bonus."* He was either God or not a good man.

Great authors of the twentieth century try to convince us that Jesus was only man. What kind of being must Jesus have been, if after 2,000 years such great effort is still needed to convince men that He was only man. Such a being is God incarnate, in whom we can have full confidence.

"He who receives a righteous man in the name of a righteous man shall receive a righteous man's reward."
MATTHEW 10:41

*M*acarius of Corinth is considered a saint in the East, not because he died a martyr's death himself, but because he trained men for martyrdom. He encouraged those who were entering the martyrs' arena, and thus lit in their hearts the flame of love for Christ and the aspiration of suffering for His sake.

Just as the crown of righteousness is laid up for the martyrs because they finished their course like Paul and kept the faith—so it is laid up for all the coworkers of the martyrs, their fellow contenders and helpers.

In our day also there are many martyrs: in the Communist world, under the reign of Islam, and in heathen countries. Many Christians, including well-known leaders, compromise with the persecuting powers and sympathize with those who prefer sacrificing incense before Caesar's statue to dying, as many Christians did in the first centuries. At that time those who sacrificed were called *lapsi*—"apostates." Now they are called "wise." And today those who, filled with the Holy Spirit, choose prison and death, are called "full of wine" as the apostles were at Pentecost.

Let us be on the side of those who sit in jails and are sentenced to death for their faith. Let us pray for them and help them. So we will get a crown like theirs.

"You are the King of Israel!"
JOHN 1:49

*I*t would seem that this name, "King of Israel," which Nathanael gives to Jesus, would cancel any interest non-Jews might otherwise have in Him. What does a European or an American care for a king of the Zulus of 2,000 years ago?

A King of the Jews was born and wise men came from abroad, while He was still a babe, to worship Him. And today after twenty centuries men of all races still bow before Him.

There must be something special about the Jews that makes their King so important. Paul wrote, "To whom [the Israelites] pertain the adoption, the glory, the covenants, the giving of the law, the service of God, and the promises; of whom are the fathers and from whom, according to the flesh, Christ came, who is over all, the eternally blessed God" (Romans 9:4,5).

The Nazis were consistent when they rejected Christianity as being Jewish. They understood the connection between the church and the Jews better than many Christians do.

Outside the church Israel can do nothing that will last. And without Israel the church cannot triumph. It is only "their receiving" Christ that will be "life from the dead" (Romans 11:15).

A look at the world reveals Israel's chosen role. The great fight is going on between the world that believes in the Jew Jesus, and the other world that believes in the Jew Marx. In science, the universe bears the name of another Jew, Einstein.

It is every Christian's duty to pray and work for the conversion of Jews and for the peace of Israel. We must all contribute our energy toward this.

JULY 9

*S*aints are men and women completely apart, each in his or her own way. They cannot be judged by applying common measurements.

John of the Cross was not capable of any manual work because he was so preoccupied with God that he could not pay attention to a hammer or scissors in his hands. Joseph of Copertino was so lost in God that he had to pinch himself when called to come back to the awareness of the world. For whatever thing was asked him, he brought something else, because his mind was not tuned to the words of men.

Only some saints are like this. Elisabeth of Hungary was a saint who was attentive to every need of the most humble men, though she was a queen. A human saint, she was the human being Elisabeth at her best, sacrificing everything in order that the ideal Elisabeth might live on earth.

Like Jesus Himself, many saints are considered to have been psychopaths. They were theopaths in the etymological sense of the word—suffering for God. They had died to the world before dying.

Some saints have been warriors, like Joan of Arc. Others have gone to extremes of asceticism. But Therese of Lisieux said, "If the food tastes good, I thank God for it. If it is bad, I accept the mortification. The surest way to holiness is to accept as mortification whatever occurs."

Find out your calling from God, the ideal "you," the purpose for which you have been elected from before the foundation of the world. Then follow Jesus in your own calling, though it may seem strange to others.

JULY 10

"Remember the prisoners as if chained with them."
HEBREWS 13:3

A Christian in Russia was sentenced to ten years in prison for his faith. He left behind a wife with nine hungry children. The mission "Jesus to the Communist World" helped them with a small sum of money and received the following amazing response from the wife.

"Glory be to the Lord that He has given us, too, to bear a little chip of His cross." (We complain about many trifles as being unbearable crosses. For her, a husband in prison and nine children to feed, without any source of income, was just a little chip of His cross.) "We must eat our bread with tears, but the Lord be praised for everything. I thank you with tears that the Lord has opened your hearts at such a big distance. Love has a long arm and stretched it out toward us. (When Paul enumerated all the attributes of love in 1 Corinthians 13, he forgot to mention that it has a long arm.)

"When we remained alone, the wicked ones said that we would not have wherewith to live, but praised be the Lord that He takes care, as He took care of Elijah, Daniel, and all who served Him.

"God has given me nine children who wait now for their father to come home, but their father put his life at stake for Christ and left his children to suffer for the faith once for all delivered by God to the saints."

Acts of the Apostles in the original is the only biblical book that ends abruptly in the midst of a sentence. It is an unfinished book. The heroism of the first Christians continues to this day.

Let us always remember in prayer our brethren suffering in prison for their faith. And let us not forget their families.

"We . . . are being transformed into the same
image from glory to glory."
2 CORINTHIANS 3:18

*F*rom philosophy we receive two axioms, which on the face seem contradictory, but in fact complement each other. The first is *Omne quod recipitur, per modus recipientis recipitur*—Whatever we receive, we receive in the manner of the recipient." Hence the variety of religions and opinions about everything.

We all perceive the same reality, but according to our differing backgrounds, heredity, education, character, strength, and the specifics of our intelligence. We never see God as He is, but as He appears to each of us in our own eyes.

This axiom applies even to God. He knows everything about us as we appear from the viewpoint of a divine being. This was not enough, however, for a righteous judgment. Therefore the Son of God became the man Jesus. Now He knew in His flesh poverty, oppression, sorrow, opposition, torture, temptation. When He ascended to heaven, Christ enriched the Godhead with a new dimension: human experience.

Therefore it is written in Song of Solomon 3:11, "And see King Solomon with the crown with which his mother crowned him on the day of his wedding." From eternity past Christ possessed the crown of divine glory. Mary gave Him one more crown: to be God incarnate. She gave him the possibility of uniting with human nature and human experience.

The second axiom is: *Anima quodammodo fit omnia*—"The soul has the capability somehow of becoming everything." It can identify with what it understands and with what it loves and ardently desires.

Christians know their limitations. They know that their spirit lives in the cage of the personality, but they yearn to see God at last as He is. Our soul has the capacity for this. We will reach our aim.

"God has chosen... the base things of the world."
1 CORINTHIANS 1:27,28

From among the many persons to whom the Lord could have appeared, He chose the chief of sinners, Saul of Tarsus—a wicked man who had made havoc of the churches, killing some of the believers and forcing others to deny their faith.

The capacity to do evil is a potential capacity to do good.

At one time Niagara Falls was the source of many disasters for the United States and Canada, flooding great territories of both countries and making agriculture impossible. Then one man decided: "If these falls have such potential for destruction, they must have the same potential for good." So dams were built, turbines were installed. Now Niagara Falls supplies electricity to both countries.

When William Booth wished to evangelize Britain, he looked around for suitable men. He considered most pastors to be either professionals who had not been born again, or real children of God who were much too meek and gentle to be capable of revolutionizing their surroundings. So he appealed to prison inmates. Once converted, they became the soldiers and officers of the Salvation Army. They did the great work.

In Hebrew, *Kedeshah* means both prostitute and saint. The sinful woman who washed Jesus' feet with her tears was always a *kedeshah*, first with a minus, later with a plus. The love that she had squandered in sin was now shed in abundance upon the Savior.

Seek the worst of men, pray for them, and do your best to bring them to conversion. They might become the greatest blessing.

This may apply also to yourself if you are base.

JULY 13

"They were strangers and pilgrims on the earth."
HEBREWS 11:13

An American evangelist, John Morrison, returned home after preaching in many countries where he had brought tens of thousands to Christ. He happened to travel on the same ship as President Theodore Roosevelt, who was returning from a hunting expedition in Africa where he had shot a number of wild hogs.

On the dock at New York thousands cheered. Whom would you say they cheered? Of course they cheered the killer of hogs, who was also the president of the United States. No one was interested in the man who had saved souls. They traveled on the same train. On the station platform again thousands cheered Roosevelt, not Morrison.

An evangelist is human. Morrison felt envy and discontent growing within him. "Is this all the welcome I get when I return home after such an exhaustive journey?" he fretted. A divine voice corrected him: "You are not yet home."

Miserable are the Christians who hope for recognition in this world. Here we have to shun success. What would the value of General Eisenhower or Winston Churchill have been if they had been cheered in Nazi Germany?

Jesus said, "Woe to you when all men speak well of you" (Luke 6:26). It would be a sure sign that you belong to this world which is hostile toward God.

Let us wait for our full reward in heaven.

JULY 14

"Do not be conformed to this world."
ROMANS 12:2

We are told in Luke 7 that John the Baptist, while in prison, had doubts concerning whether Jesus was really the Messiah. The uncertainty came though he had proclaimed Him to be the Lamb of God who takes away the sins of the world. Prison often casts shadows on men's spiritual life.

John communicated his doubts to two of his disciples, who until then had been sure that Jesus was the Savior. But because someone had planted a doubt in their heart, they traveled far to tell Jesus about another's doubts and to question Him. They might have spoken to Him in the presence of others, thus further disseminating the doubts.

Jesus replied, "Go your way" (Luke 7:22, KJV). Don't allow yourself to be infested by someone else's wrong attitudes, even if he is a great prophet.

Christian sisters worked in a concentration camp in a Siberian forest, where they had to fell trees. Far away were other barracks with prisoners who did the same work. One evening, while the Christian ladies were gathered in prayer someone knocked at the door.

"Open! Nothing bad will happen to you," a rough voice shouted. The sisters did not dare obey. "Open, or we will smash the door," several voices yelled.

When they opened the door, twenty men with overcoats covered with snow entered. One of them said, "We heard you were Christians. Speak to us about God. We have seen no pastor for thirty years. Tell us something."

Their barracks became an underground church where the prisoners gathered regularly. The sisters instructed them in the faith, taught them the gospel and prayers long forgotten, and baptized some of them. In exchange, these men sentenced for crimes did the hard work of the sisters, thus giving them more time for prayer.

These were souls who in a Bolshevik surrounding went their way. You go yours, whatever the difficulties of your surroundings.

JULY 15

"Where is the promise of [Jesus'] coming?... all things continue as they were from the beginning of creation."
2 PETER 3:4

*S*coffers challenged the Christians in earlier times with these words. They cannot say so anymore. Today entirely new things happen in this old world. Man has interfered artificially with the nucleus of the atom, piling up fifteen tons of explosives for every living inhabitant. The destruction of mankind could happen in a few minutes. Men walk on the moon. Dictators and money-grabbers can change the minds of men at will through drugs and mass media. Population explosion, famines as never before, the unbreathable air in the towns of the privileged nations are all here. The power is no longer in the hands of those who helped bring about Christian civilization. Representatives of the Third World have the majority in the United Nations, and generally vote as China or other Communists dictate.

The state of Israel is an unshakable fact. God brought His people back to the Holy Land. The whole of Jerusalem is theirs, a further sign of the end time.

Anti-Christian forces have invaded the church. *Capital Voice*, August 1, 1974, published the results of a recent poll: "51% of the Methodist ministers in the USA do not believe in Jesus' resurrection; 60% don't believe in the virgin birth; 62% contest the existence of Satan; 89% of Episcopalian priests don't believe the Bible to be the Word of God. They believe there is no truth." Again a sign of the end time. The abomination of desolation is in the holy place (Daniel 9:27).

These are all signs of the Lord's coming. Things do not continue as they were from the beginning. "He who endures to the end shall be saved" (Matthew 24:13).

*"What kind of man was it who came up to meet you
and told you these words?"*
2 KINGS 1:7

When Elijah sent a message to Ahaziah, king of Israel, the king did not ask his servants the details of the communication, but the question above. The value of a message depends on the quality of the messenger. A sermon on the words, "Woe to you who are rich" (Luke 6:24), delivered by a man who strives to become rich, would make a ridiculous impression.

The Christians of the first centuries were the right manner of men.

Stripped naked and hanged on walls by four rings to which their ankles and wrists were tied with ropes, they were attacked with truncheons, pincers, and torches. They bore the torture and did not deny Christ nor betray where and when the brethren met together for prayer and worship services.

No machine devised by human mind could have withstood what our brethren and sisters withstood during centuries of persecution. Their underfed bodies resisted better than those of overfed wrestlers. It is because they were the right manner of men.

In sufferings, they did not pity themselves but their torturers. They saw even in those who beat or slandered them angels of grace, who, through humiliations, sanctified them for the future kingdom.

We do not need a new theology, but this old breed of Christians.

What about ourselves becoming such men, whose manner of being would give credibility to our Christian message? With Elijah, even his outward appearance, his simple manner of dressing showed the earnestness with which he spoke.

JULY 17

*"Teach us to number our days, that we may
gain a heart of wisdom."*
PSALM 90:12

$\mathcal{A}$ ugustine wrote in his *Confessions*, "If nobody asks me about time, I know what it is; but if I am asked, I don't know what to answer." The Russian astronomer Koziereff calls time "the most important and the strangest quality of nature."

I will not enter into the philosophy of time. It is what makes men belong to different generations, it is the gap between men and their children. They have been born later in time. This makes them look upon parents as symbols of everything old, no longer relevant, unfashionable, hypocritically tied to a now worthless moral code. Therefore Freud said, "One of the most difficult professions in the world is to be a parent."

Some parents are surely not worthy of the honor due them according to the Bible. The American killer Charles Manson was the son of a sixteen-year-old prostitute, who gave birth to the child only because she had no money for an abortion. Soon after his birth she entered prison. He was given to relatives who fed him little but beat him much. From the age of fourteen, Manson grew up only in correction houses and prisons.

Some respectable and religious parents have been rewarded by their children with titles like "capitalist swine" or similar expressions. These are extreme cases. Also extreme are the suicides among teenagers. Their number has increased in the last twenty years by 250 percent. In between is the multitude of youngsters dissatisfied with their parents.

Let us all remember that the problem of children is a problem for the parents who forget that time passes quickly and another generation rises. We must give our children the best of godly examples. Giving them an affluent life is not sufficient. They need the example of a holy life united with a wise education.

JULY 18

"Showing yourself to be a pattern of good works."
TITUS 2:7

A candidate for ordination presented himself before the examining commission and the bishop. He had good credentials, including the best marks on all theological subjects. He answered the usual questions well. The pastor of his church also confirmed that he was involved in all of its activities.

The godly bishop then asked him some questions which were put to ordinands in the first centuries:

"Is despite as welcome to you as profit?

"Do you love foreign people as much as your relatives?

"Do you accept with the same joy sickness or health, liberty or prison, beatings or caresses, opposition or applause?"

The candidate answered, "No."

"Then go and study some more," said the bishop.

Many pastors believe they are called upon to interpret and preach the Bible. This is a secondary function. Jesus said He had come "to fulfill the Law and the Prophets" (Matthew 5:17). He fulfilled what others merely used as subjects for sermons.

Seek for a pastor who is a fulfiller, not a debater, of God's will.

JULY 19

"The day of the Lord so comes as a thief in the night."
1 THESSALONIANS 5:2

Russian dictator Leonid Breshnev shows his mother his luxurious offices, his villa in the Moscow suburbs, his Cadillac, his vacation home at the Black Sea, and asks her, "Are you satisfied?"

She replies, "I am happy that you have it so well; but what if the Communists come to power? They are bad guys. They hate the rich and insist upon equality for all."

It is easy for us to laugh about the inconsistencies between the lifestyle of the Communist leaders and their teachings. The joke could be changed. What if we should show the surroundings in which we live to a godly mother, and she should ask us, "All is fine, but how will it be when Jesus returns?"

A story says that Jesus came to Rome. He saw the army parading, everyone with his gun. He asked them if they were Christians. When they all nodded, Jesus said, "I have taught that My disciples should not even say a bad word to anyone. I never thought that Christians would use weapons!"

He saw signs in shop windows proclaiming, "Here are the best shoes, or the best cars." Jesus entered the shops and said, "I have taught that everyone should put another's honor above his own. Why don't you rather recommend the products of your competitors?"

He saw the prostitutes. They were all baptized and confirmed. He saw Christians split into different political parties. He saw a Catholic church, a Baptist church, and a Lutheran church. He wondered which was His church. The others He had never heard of.

He wished to speak with the pope, but could not receive an appointment. He had to slip past the Swiss Guard. Before being received by the pope, He was told that He must call him "Holy Father." Jesus replied, "I thought this was a name reserved for God!"

What is your standard of life? What is its moral and spiritual level? Everything seems fine now—but what about when Jesus returns?

"I send you out as sheep in the midst of wolves.
Therefore be wise as serpents."
MATTHEW 10:16

*S*ovietskaia Rossia, of May 23, complains that in the Christian assemblies, "Men kneel and arrive to ecstasy" (how good it would be for Western Christians to arrive to the same state when they kneel). They had listened to sermons broadcast over foreign radio, and distributed tapes of these sermons; they had taught the Christian youth to spread propagandistic letters. The article says that the Christians "hunt with the stubbornness of youth." The sentences were of three and five years.

Pravda Ukraini, of July 12, 1966, has an article entitled "They Received What They Deserved," telling about the condemnation of Christians to five years of prison.

Sovietskaia Rossia speaks about the orthodox priest Turkovskii. He and his Christians attempted to prevent the Communist youth from playing volleyball in the church yard during the divine service. For this he was sentenced to four years of prison.

Komsomalskaia Pravda, of March 22, 1964, describes a teacher's horror when she sees that nine of the children are wearing crosses. The article says that we must compel the Christian children to read anti-religious books and learn modern dances. Thus we save a man and bring him out of the dark underground. What Communists hate the most is that sometimes the secret meetings of the underground church take place in the houses of the Communists, who are Communists only on the surface and in their hearts believe in God. They also help the Christians. So it happened in the town of Shushcinsk, as *Kazatstankaia Pravda* reports on May 17, 1962.

Sovietskaia Kirghizia, of November 1966, speaks about the trial against Nina Bikova, who ran secret religious schools for children below seven years of age. The children were told to keep the rules of the conspiracy, and they have kept them. The Communist newspaper itself says that only accidentally they have discovered the schools. In Russia even children know to be "wise as serpents" in the service of the Lord.

J U L Y   2 1

"You will be hated by all nations."
MATTHEW 24:9

*T*here is something wrong with Christians who are not hated.

Henrik Ibsen, the renowned Norwegian playwright, was the most rejected artist of the nineteenth century. This was because he did what we should do. He shook sensibilities by bringing up in public subjects that were utterly taboo, and he championed attitudes unpopular in the society of his time. His main message was that in questions of conscience men have to stand firm and not compromise.

Because of this, he and his family had to suffer much. He puts in the mouth of one of the personalities of his plays, *The Enemy of the People*, words of reproach that he must have heard often from well-meaning friends: "You are a madman; you are insane with egotism. And don't excuse it with humanitarian slogans, because a man who'll drag his family through a lifetime of disgrace is a demon in his heart, a demon who cares more for a public cause than for the lives of his wife and children."

Men who suffer in prisons for Christ's sake in our century have often heard similar reproaches.

Ibsen's reaction was simple. He wrote, "In a storm there's just one thing to remember: it will pass...Before many can know something, one must know it...The majority is always wrong...I am in revolt against the age-old lie that the majority is always right."

When an irritated mob threw stones through his hero's windows, Dr. Stockmann said, "I'm going to keep these like sacred relics."

"The strong man must learn to be lonely."

Let us learn to confront public opinion. Jesus never yielded to the blindness of the masses. He is the light. He influences without being influenced. He was hated, but His acceptance of this gained Him friends who loved Him unto death.

*"Contend earnestly for the faith which was once
for all delivered to the saints."*
JUDE 3

When Nelson, as a teenager, came home from a birdnesting expedition, his aunt chided him for being out so late at night. She said, "I'm surprised that fear did not make you come home."

"Fear?" replied Nelson. "I don't know him."

We don't know the fear of conflicts. When Spurgeon, the renowned Baptist preacher of Britain, alarmed at the increasing spread of heresy within the denomination, forsook the Baptist Union and took up the fight for biblical belief, he did not expect success. He said, "I am quite willing to be eaten by dogs for the next fifty years, but the more distant future will vindicate me."

Abusive and shameful titles were given to him. He replied to his opponents that since there was no language sufficiently strong to express the abhorrence he had for them, he would let them pass in silence.

He craved no tolerance. He demanded submission, being sure that his message was from God.

A black preacher in a village said that he abstained from preaching against stealing chickens because such preaching dampened brotherly love. I was rebuked once by a pastor, to whose church I had been invited, for having preached about Herod's sin of taking his brother's wife. This was the sin of the richest supporter of his church, whose contributions he did not wish to lose.

We have to fight this spirit of compromise and everything that is wrong in the church and in mission work, though it may be at the risk of provoking great conflicts. Traitors to Christ's principles should never be our friends.

A king once told a favorite, "Ask whatever you like and it will be given to you."

The favorite thought it over. "If I ask to be a general, I'll become one, and then I will regret not being the prime minister. If I ask for half of the kingdom, I will get it, and then I will be sad for not having the other half." Therefore he said to the king, "Give me your daughter as wife."

In Hebrew and in Greek the word for "soul" is feminine. Being feminine, the believing soul asks from God Christ to be her Bridegroom. So we become heirs of all things and all angels will serve us.

How glorious and yet how modest our Bridegroom is. Nathanael called him "Son of God" (John 1:49). Jesus answered, "Hereafter you shall see heaven open, and the angels of God ascending and descending upon the *Son of Man*" (John 1:51). In the measure in which men discovered the divine in Him, His modest and good heart made Him emphasize His humanity, in order that His brides, who are human and sometimes much too human, can come to Him with confidence. He belongs to them. Our prayer that He should be ours has been fulfilled.

He is not only a divine, but also a human Bridegroom, interested in human things, concerned even that there should be wine enough at a marriage feast. How unlike some saints, who, because of their sanctity, become apathetic toward the needs of their fellow men.

Christ does not only deliver sermons; and He does not rebuke continually. He quietly takes supper with us, as a Bridegroom would do with a bride.

Bernard of Clairveaux said, "A quiet God quiets everything. To see Him as quiet, means to be quiet." The most quieting thought is, "The Beloved is mine."

> *"Jesus said to him [a criminal], 'Assuredly, I say to you, today you will be with Me in paradise.'"*
> LUKE 23:43

A world that very much needs our love and our prayers is the world of criminals. Society can give them only the punishment they deserve. We can give them the divine message of forgiveness through the blood of Jesus.

Criminals are continually haunted by their victims—some consciously, others unconsciously. Behind all other words, they hear the last words of their victims. You might speak kindly to them but they know what you think about them: they are murderers.

Even if they have not confessed to the police or to a priest, the words break out of them in their dreams, in their involuntary speech. The victims are near their beds at night.

Emile Zola describes in *Therese Raquin* a painter who had killed. No one knew what he had done. He continued to paint, but now all faces resembled each other. They were like his victim. Children's faces, women's faces, all reminded him of them.

Criminals have not killed only the men now dead. They have killed also the pity toward themselves in fellow men. They are despised by everyone, except by Jesus, the friend of sinners. He chose to share the fate of criminals, being crucified like them. He preordained that when Pilate offered the release of a prisoner, the mob should choose freedom for a murderer, Barabas. Jesus was glad to die in his place.

He does not despise thieves. He compares Himself with them. "The day of the Lord will come as a thief in the night" (2 Peter 3:10).

Criminals receive salvation from Jesus. They find also understanding and compassion among His true followers.

JULY 25

*"Wandering stars for whom is reserved the
blackness of darkness forever."*
JUDE 13

The Epistle of Jude accredits one of the many pseudepigraphic books, the book of Enoch.

Enoch wrote, "I saw seven stars like seven great burning mountains. When I asked, the angel told me, 'This is the place where heaven and earth end. This is a prison for the stars and the host of heaven. The stars which turn over the fire are those who at the start of their rising trespassed against the commandment of God, not rising in time. So he became angry with them and bound them . . .'"

Remember that this day there are angels who have been in chains for thousands of years. They are surrounded by darkness and await the judgment of the great day.

All prison life is terrible. Hell, for men, is even worse. But who can imagine the torment of a prison for angels, winged beings, used to flying from star to star to fulfill God's will?

Some angels have arrived there because they did not keep "their proper domain, but left their own abode" (Jude 6). Did you keep your high estate of being a Christian? Do you keep your own habitation, the church, or do you mingle with the sinful world? God did not spare angels; will He spare you?

"Those who turn many to righteousness [shall shine] like the stars forever and ever" (Daniel 12:3). Are you a shining star? Do you turn many to righteousness?

Fear and trembling is a vital contributing part of the Christian life.

JULY 26

"He has put down the mighty from their thrones,
and exalted the lowly."
LUKE 1:52

Strindberg's play *Miss Julie* is the story of a love affair between a very rich girl and her servant. At a certain moment they tell each other their dreams.

The rich girl: "I'm sitting on top of a pillar that I've climbed up, somehow, and I don't know how to get back down...I have to get down, but I don't have the courage to jump...I want to fall, but I don't fall. I know I won't have any peace until I get down, down on the ground. And if I ever get down on the ground, I'd want to go further down, right down into the earth."

The servant: "I used to dream that I'm lying under a tall tree in a dark wood. I want to get up, up to the very top, to look out over the bright landscape with the sun shining on it, to rob the bird's nest up there with the golden eggs in it. I climb and I climb, but the trunk is so thick and so smooth, and it's such a long way to that first branch. But I know that if I could just reach that first branch, I'd go right to the top as if on a ladder."

Many rich people have a guilt complex because of their privileged situation, though they might not be conscious of it. This makes many of them become revolutionists or supporters of revolutionist causes. They feel that their duty is to descend. The poor, however, envy the rich and would like to ascend.

These normal feelings, if brought to light, could become positive factors in social life. The rich could learn from Jesus to go about doing good and sharing with the underprivileged. The poor could emulate the rich, learning from them how better to use their talents for the good of their families.

"He who follows [Jesus] shall not walk in darkness, but have the light of life" (John 8:12). The unbelievers love darkness rather than light (John 3:19). Their feelings are repressed and surface not only in dreams, but also in foolish acts of terrorism, riots, and revolutions. The result is that privileged people lose their positions which they did not enjoy fully, and are replaced by those of low degree, who soon will become disenchanted too.

JULY 27

"[Jesus] went about the villages in a circuit, teaching."
MARK 6:6

*M*any of us feel frustrated. We are not successes. Neither was Jesus. He was a small-time country preacher. Caiaphas had mass rallies with more than a million in attendance at the great festivals, when Jews from all over the world came to worship in Jerusalem. However, he was not a success. Pilate could depose him whenever he liked. Neither was Pilate a success. Caesar dismissed and exiled him. Neither was it a success to be a Caesar. Julius Caesar was killed by his own son. Nero was killed, too, after his successes in uprooting Christians.

Don't envy men who can achieve much. It only seems so. Great men may make history, but only such history as it is possible for them to make. They stand under the dictate of their surroundings.

Even more than that we are conditioned inwardly by our own past. Robespierre, the bloody dictator of the French Revolution, had been abandoned by his father soon after his mother's death. He had to struggle hard for an education. He had been offended in his youth by the young King Louis XVI and the queen. He had been chosen to deliver an address of welcome when they came to his town. They did not say one word of approval, neither did they make a gesture showing appreciation, but drove on. This turned him into a hater of men. He reveled in killing thousands of innocents. He enjoyed seeing the blood of men at the guillotine.

God did not destine us to be killers. To be a killer is always contrary to nature. Therefore, murderers make big mistakes. Robespierre, too, behaved senselessly and died on the guillotine himself. He had achieved nothing. The republic had paved the way for an emperor, Napoleon.

Don't seek successes as the world considers success. They only increase vanity. Bear with resignation your own burden and that of your heredity. Learn from Jesus who was "meek and lowly in heart," content to be a carpenter, an unloved rabbi who went around villages teaching and then was crucified. A resurrection followed.

JULY 28

"I will make a covenant of peace with them."
EZEKIEL 34:25

The Jewess Simone Weil escaped from Nazi Germany to Britain. There she died from malnutrition and tuberculosis because she had decided to eat only the ration that the population received in the Nazi-occupied regions. She left behind many books of deep Christian thought, though she was never baptized. She did not join a church so that she would not put a distance between her and the unhappy multitude of unbelievers. She was a soul with a special calling.

She could not endure what is wrongly called the traditional in the church. She thought that tradition did not consist in faithfully keeping old ashes, but in keeping the old fire burning by continually adding new fuel.

She could not imagine what would happen if Jesus would suddenly appear on the front between the lines dividing armies and tell the Christians on both sides, "Love one another as I loved you." He would fall dead riddled with bullets from both sides. On Sunday, the Christ-killers of both armies would worship the One whom they had killed and each would pray for the victory of their fatherland, which would mean the defeat of the adversary.

Many Christian thinkers suffered because of our inconsistency in love. War, class struggles, revolutions, as well as dissensions among Christians are great blasphemies because they are at the opposite pole from the words, "God is love."

"Blessed are the peacemakers, for they shall be called sons of God" (Matthew 5:9). Let us seek peace with all men, insofar as it depends upon us.

JULY 29

"God blessed the seventh day."
GENESIS 2:3

*I*n the Bible the figure 7 is the symbol of holiness. "Now Enoch, the seventh from Adam, prophesied" (Jude 14). Every seventh year the land had to remain untilled. When seven times seven years passed, the Jews had the year of Jubilee, in which all the land sold in the meantime returned to its first possessor. The days of the creation were seven; seven of each clean animal were saved from the flood. In the Gospel of John, Jesus says in seven ways who He is. On the cross He pronounces seven words. The Book of Revelation contains letters to seven churches, etc.

Why is just the figure 7 the sacred figure? The Chaldeans did not have our decimal system, but a heximal one—six figures and a zero. The decimal system is arbitrary. In computers men use the binary system, having only a 1 and a 0. In the heximal system, our 7 was written 10, because there were no more than six figures. Seven became the holy figure because in looking to its written form "10" it symbolized the fact that if you put before the 0, sign of human nothingness, the 1, sign of the one God, the insignificant man becomes important, more important than all the simple figures.

The Jews were descendants of the Chaldeans. So the 7 became their holy figure. In opposition to 7, 6, being the last simple figure, became the symbol of everything petty. The number of the apocalyptic beast is six, six, and again six (Revelation 13:18), which means a trifle, a trifle, and again a trifle. A lamb can destroy it.

If you are an impersonation of the 7, a man who has denied himself and has become a 0, and if God, "the one," has put Himself as a shield before you, then don't fear huge beasts. They are paper tigers. You will be the victor.

JULY 30

"Blessed are the meek, for they shall inherit the earth."
MATTHEW 5:5

*C*ompare Washington to Napoleon.

Washington was modest. He desired freedom for a country and obtained it. With this he was satisfied. When the crown was offered to him, he refused. He left behind a new, free state.

Napoleon was eager for his own renown. Being general of the republic was not enough. Consul was not enough; it must be prime consul. In the end he became emperor. He had to depose other kings and replace them with his family. He fought in Egypt and in Moscow, where he had no business to be. He died in exile, a prisoner. His empire is no more.

How many are your preoccupations? No one can do everything without bringing everything into a mess. No one can seek his own renown without getting the reputation of being self-seeking and arrogant.

"Be fruitful and multiply."
GENESIS 1:28

*J*esus did not marry, though it was considered shameful for a rabbi in His time to be a bachelor. He might have been loved by many women. He who was "in favor with God and men" (Luke 2:52) must surely have been in favor also with women. He was human. He might also have had some preferential love, but renounced it for the calling He had from the Father.

He did not impose the same attitude upon others. To the contrary, He honored the marriage feast in Cana with His presence. God's Word also teaches, "Marriage is honorable among all" (Hebrews 13:4), not only in conversations between marriage partners and common meals, but also in the sexual sense.

Rank and file Christians may choose to be or not to be married. Bishops are obliged by the Bible to have a wife (1 Timothy 3:2). Chrysostom said, "The first degree of chastity is pure virginity, the second is faithfulness in marriage. The chaste love in marriage is a second kind of virginity."

Enjoy fully sexual life in marriage. Overcome medieval prejudices that cause people to consider sexuality as something dirty. The One who made sexual organs, who commanded, "Be fruitful and multiply" and inspired the Bible which teaches that "they shall be one flesh," surely likes it when you exercise your sexual functions in marriage, as He likes every other good thing you do.

There is nothing wrong or shameful about sex in marriage. Let us thank God for this beautiful gift He gave to mankind.

Let spinsters and bachelors also be thankful for their estate. It is a calling apart with its own blessings, and often contains opportunities that married people don't have. It is a simple fact that under persecution, bachelors and spinsters resisted better than those who had to be concerned about a family.

A U G U S T   1

*E*very marriage is an adventure. Only great love can make possible the happy cohabitation of two very different persons. Where love is missing, marriage can become fornication with legal documents.

Let us free sexuality from any connection with commercialism. No one can sanctify a marriage whose motives were the wealth of the girl, or the high position of the man. Let us free marriage from problems that are foreign to it: denomination, nationality, race, and party. Romeo and Juliet chose to die because they belonged to families that had quarreled. Must love die because Catholics have quarreled with Protestants, Jews with Arabs, and blacks with whites? Cannot two persons love and live in harmony even if they do not agree in all matters?

Women are used unnaturally when they are treated as mere objects for pleasure; when they are used as dolls or dressed and ornamented as advertisements for your high social position; when they become idols for which you give up moral duties; when they are made into slaves.

You cannot impose upon today's woman—who can be a doctor, an engineer, or an officer—injunctions 2,000 years old, that say she may be treated as chattel by her husband. It was the backward situation of women at that time that led to the commandment for husbands to love their wives as their own bodies. A woman must be treated by her husband with awe and love, as Christ loved His church.

AUGUST 2

"The just shall live by his faith."
HABAKKUK 2:4

*I*n the Talmud (Makkoth) it is written: Rabbi Simla said, "613 commandments have been given to Moses...David came and reduced them to 11. They are: 1) to walk uprightly, 2) to work righteousness, 3) to speak the truth in your heart, 4) not to back-bite with the tongue, 5) not to do evil to the neighbor, 6) not to take up a reproach against the neighbor, 7) to have contempt for a vile person, 8) to honor them that fear the Lord, 9) not to swear, 10) not to put out money for usury, 11) not to take reward against the innocent. (Psalm 15)

"Isaiah reduced them to six: 1) to walk righteously, 2) to speak uprightly, 3) to despise the gain of oppression, 4) not to take bribes, 5) to stop your ears from hearing of blood, 6) to shut your eye from seeing evil. (Isaiah 33:15,16)

"Micah came and reduced them to three: 1) to do justly, 2) to love mercy, and 3) to walk humbly with God. (Micah 6:8)"

Rabbi Nachman, son of Isaac, added: "Habakkuk reduced them to one: The just shall live by his faith" (Habakkuk 2:4).

Faith is the great principle of which all the commandments are the elaboration, and which gives them value. Commandments fulfilled without faith do not please God.

Paul mentions this verse of Habakkuk repeatedly. Luther rediscovered its value at the time of the Reformation. If the many commandments are cumbersome for you and you are disoriented, stick to one: have faith in the Lord Jesus and you will live.

AUGUST 3

"Go, sell what you have and give to the poor."
MATTHEW 19:21

*I*t is said about Father Serapion that he found in Alexandria a poor man bitten by the cold. He said to himself, "How can I, who am considered to be an ascetic, wear a garment while this poor man, or rather Christ, suffers from the cold? Surely, if I allow him to die from the cold, I will be condemned for homicide on the Day of Judgment." He undressed himself and gave to the poor his garment.

Then he sat down with his Gospel to read. A police constable passed, and seeing him naked, asked, "Father Serapion, who has deprived you of your garments?"

He answered, "It is the one about whom this book speaks."

Later, he saw a man led to prison because he could not pay his debts. So Serapion sold the Gospel and paid the debt.

When he re-entered naked into his cell, his disciple asked him, "Abba, where is your garment?"

He answered, "I sent it where we will need it."

The disciple asked again, "Where is your Gospel?"

He replied, "He who told me every day, 'Sell all you have and give to the poor' asked me for it. So I sold it in order to have more confidence on the Day of Judgment."

Why should we be satisfied with little faith or wavering faith, when we have before our eyes so many splendid examples of consistent faith? Gamblers put all their possessions on a card. We know in whom we have believed. It is the eternal God, Creator of heaven and earth. Let us rely on Him fully and do to our utmost what He commands.

"You are a chosen generation."
1 PETER 2:9

*H*ow do we recognize one of God's elect? By his humility.
The Lord made Abraham a great man, yet the "friend of God" said, "Indeed now, I . . . am but dust and ashes" (Genesis 18:27).

Though Moses and Aaron dealt with powerful rulers in the name of God, they acted like servants when they spoke even to rebels: "Hear I pray you," and "What is Aaron?" (Numbers 16:8,11, KJV).

God made David the greatest king on earth, yet he said, "I am a worm, and no man" (Psalm 22:6).

The Lord called Paul to become the greatest of apostles, yet he wrote, "I am the least of the apostles, who am not worthy to be called an apostle" (1 Corinthians 15:9).

The elect of God do not feel superior to their fellow men. They fulfill, in its strictest sense, the commandment, "You shall love your neighbor as yourself" (Leviticus 19:18). The sentence in Hebrew could be translated literally, "Love your neighbor: he is as yourself"—of the same caliber, of the same value, with sins and virtues like your own. That should be reason enough to love him.

Election is by grace, without any merit of ours. It does not justify a feeling of superiority. It reduces us rather to the state of servants of our fellow men.

A U G U S T   5

"Present your bodies a living sacrifice."
ROMANS 12:1

When the Earl of Morton, regent of Scotland, told a committee of the General Assembly that they were holding a convocation of the king's subjects and that it was treasonable for them to meet without the king's permission, Andrew Melville answered, "If this be so, then Christ and His apostles must have been guilty of treason, for they called together great multitudes without asking permission of the magistrates."

The regent growled in anger, "There will never be quietness in this country until half a dozen of you will be hanged or banished."

Melville replied, "Threaten your courtiers after this manner. It is the same to me whether I rot in the air or in the ground. The earth is the Lord's. I have been ready to give my life where it would not be half so well expended. Let God be glorified."

The Huguenot Admiral Coligny had been wounded for his evangelical faith. The surgeon had amputated his finger and cut the bullet from his arm. "Nothing happens," Coligny said, "but by the will of God. Why do you weep? I am happy in being thus wounded in God's cause. Pray that He may strengthen me. I forgive with all my heart him who fired upon me and those who incited him."

A thrust of a sword to the hilt into the admiral's heart finished him. Then his corpse was thrown from the balcony.

With this infamous deed the night of Bartholomew started, when thousands of men who also thought like Coligny were killed. Monks encouraged the murderers with the words, "The church revives by the death of heretics."

The Evangelical church has had great men like Knox, who prayed, "O God, give me Scotland or I die." May we learn from them to be men and women of faithful prayer, ready to suffer and die for the holy cause.

> *"Therefore, whether you eat or drink, or whatever*
> *you do, do all to the glory of God."*
> 1 CORINTHIANS 10:31

*I*t is not true that men are converted only through sermons or books or personal witness, which means through words. If you eat and drink and do all things to the glory of God, men should be able to arrive at the truth through watching your behavior at meals, in business, or entertainment.

Someone came to a believer and asked him about the way of truth. The answer was, "Do you hear the murmuring of the brook? There is the entrance." He could have pointed toward every other phenomenon of God-created nature or any manifestation of a saint.

The mystic is—in the words of John of Ruysbroek—a man who has climbed the tree of faith, which grows from above downward, because its roots are in God. Not only words, but also the grotesqueness of every moment of such climbing speaks about the source. There was a time when God had not created me, though in His plan I had been an elect person before the foundation of the world. I was in His thoughts. Then He created me. So I became a creature and He became my God.

When I will arrive at the top in my climbing, that is, to the root from where I came, I will have become a partaker of the divine being. This oneness, this uniqueness manifests itself in everything I do, even if it is far away from religion. It manifests itself though this treasure is contained in earthly vessels.

If someone does not see my participation in the divine nature, it is because a man who has not been born again cannot see the kingdom of heaven (John 3:3). He would not have recognized Jesus to be the Son of God.

Continue to be what you are. Angelus Silesius says that our bodies are shells, in which the Spirit of eternity wishes to brood His little ones. For those illuminated by God, our manner of eating, drinking, and other things of daily life reveal the mystery of our divine nature.

AUGUST 7

"The LORD gave, and the LORD has taken away;
blessed be the name of the LORD."
JOB 1:21

There was once a man who, when his son died, did not exhibit the terrible grief customary at such occasions. His friends said, "You loved your son dearly. How is it that you are so composed now that he is dead?"

The man replied, "There was a time when I had no son. I did not grieve on that account. Now that he died, I am in the same condition as before. Why should I not keep my peace?"

Believers can remain strong in difficult circumstances.

Confucius once met a man clothed in a deerskin, girdled with a rope and playing on a lute. He asked him, "What makes you so happy?"

The man replied, "I have many things to make me happy. Man is the crown of creation. Lo, God made me a man, not an animal. Some die in childhood. I have become an adult. Many are in prison or bound to a sick bed. I am free and healthy. I ate this morning. I have food enough for tonight. How else could I be than content?"

Only when someone is thus free of earthly cares can he make real advances in spiritual life.

Many a man has unreasonable fears. If your speech is sweet, how can the echo be otherwise than sweet? If you walk with the body straight, how can your shadow be otherwise than straight? A Christian is not afraid of anyone or anything.

Jesus was anointed with an oil of gladness above His comrades. He anoints His disciples with the same oil. We never lose anything. He is the Lord who takes from us some things in order to multiply and then restitute them.

*"Some of those of understanding shall fall, to refine
them, purge them, and make them white."*
DANIEL 11:35

*J*esus foretold His disciples that on the evening of His betrayal
they would forsake Him. He foretold Peter that he would deny
Him. The strange thing is that none of His disciples begged Him to
save them from such a fate, though it seems that this would have
been the time to say, "Lead us not into temptation."

The pronouns in the Lord's Prayer are plural. We say, "Lead us
not into temptation" for the whole church of Christ that she may not
fall away. As for me, I let God decide if He wishes to pass me through
the experience of a fall.

If He decides it, we even fall gladly, knowing that God's bottom
waits for us. If He pushes me, the fall will not hurt me. It is part of
God's providence and it fulfills a good purpose.

Jesus told Peter that not only would he fall, but also that after
recovery he would strengthen the brethren. Just after the fall and
because of this experience, he was of an unequaled boldness, chal-
lenging the people on the day of Pentecost with harsh words that
could have cost him his life.

Church history tells us that when sentenced to death, together
with his wife, Peter's last desire was to be crucified head down. He
did not feel worthy to be crucified head up like his Master. On the
cross he said, "In this topsy-turvy world I am now in the right position. I look up toward heaven as men should always do."

The child Jesus "is destined for the fall and rising of many in
Israel" (Luke 2:34). Accept both destinies.

"If we say that we have fellowship with Him, and walk in darkness, we lie and do not practice the truth."
1 JOHN 1:6

*T*he apostle deals here with the heresy widespread today called antinomianism (anti-law). The adherents of this doctrine believe that a man can live in sin or compromise with it and at the same time have fellowship with God. Antinomians never state their doctrine bluntly like this, but as a matter of fact this is their attitude in life.

The apostle deals gently with antinomians in his day. He writes, "If *we* say" this wrong thing, not, "If *you* say." He includes himself in the possibility of thinking falsely.

The verb for "to walk in darkness," which is a synonym of "to sin," is in the present subjunctive in this verse, indicating habitual action. The simple fact is that Christians sin, some of them often and gravely. This is so much the reality that the apostle writes, "If we say that we have no sin, we deceive ourselves" (1 John 1:8). "And if anyone sins, we have an Advocate with the Father" (2:1). But for the Christian, sin is not the usual attitude. It is a deviation from his habitual course. Children of God sin, but they don't allow sin to dominate them so much that righteousness would be excluded from their life. They walk in the light, not in the darkness. Just because they walk in the light, they are aware of their sinfulness and regret it.

As for those for whom sin is the program of life, no religiosity is of any avail. They cannot have communion with God.

We live in the last days. Morality, laws, and standards break down. The heresy of antinomianism, of lawlessness united with religiosity, is very dangerous today. Let us beware of it.

A U G U S T   1 0

*"What is a man profited if he gains the whole world,
and loses his own soul?"*
MATTHEW 16:26

Niccolo Paganini was one of the best violinists the world has ever seen. Even highly intelligent people like the German poet Henrich Heine believed that Paganini had made a pact with the devil, giving him his soul for eternity, in exchange for genius, riches, and fame.

Paganini's rise to fame and fortune was difficult. Pursued by creditors he could not pay, he fled from Venice to Vienna, where he had to earn his living playing at marriages or going from saloon to saloon in the slums. He would not be accepted in better restaurants because of his poor clothing. Once while he played the violin in a third-class restaurant, a student gave him a few coins on the condition that he "stop this unbearable noise."

The insult fired Paganini with a mad ambition. He won a competition in the palace of the crown prince. Henceforth a splendid career opened for him. He had world fame and unspeakable riches. Women offered themselves to him. Paganini had succeeded in life, but only through damning his soul. He was an unhappy man, seeking adulation, a money-grabber of unspeakable stinginess and, above all, full of envy of all other artists of the past, present, and future. Only his own art counted in his eyes.

He wrote his music in such difficult combinations of notes that no one except himself, who had a very large hand, will ever be able to play it. Although a millionaire, Paganini would pick up nails, bits of paper, or rope that he found on the street, to save buying such articles. He ate the cheapest food. He refused women who loved him, because they might have cost him money.

Success at the price of happiness, costing the ability to enjoy it and to put it in the service of the One from whom it comes—this is the sad story of Paganini. Multiply your talents; seek success: but don't allow the tares of sin to grow in your heart. Relax when you seek success, enjoy it and help others to enjoy it.

"Sit down in the lowest place."
LUKE 14:10

*E*very one of us wishes growth, growth in wealth, a bigger house, a bigger business, a bigger church or mission, a bigger position. Why? Growth for growth's sake is the philosophy of the cancer cell.

There are many recipes for success. Jesus studied none of them. Instead He sought to be pleasant to His father and to faithfully fulfill His duty, whether it involved a cross or a crown.

Don't give up biblical principles. Don't marry for money, nor earn money dishonestly. Don't rise in politics through demagoguery. Don't call people to become church members without instructing them in the fact that this implies a Christian life. Don't lead a missionary work so that you might have a big income or a large number of converts, but so that the truth might remain in all its purity.

Never give up any slice of truth for ecumenicity's sake. Love everyone but acknowledge as a brother in faith only the man who stands for the truth as contained in the Bible.

Don't be apologetic about being poor, unnoticed, belonging to some small church. Being ashamed of these, you will become big in the wrong way. Jesus was not ashamed of being a babe in a manger or a man crucified between thieves.

Don't try to be great through producing splits in someone else's family, business, church, or mission. Let the other one enjoy the leadership. Be ready to play the second violin. In this way you will enjoy your modest position much more than the unhappy "successful" people.

AUGUST 12

"Let all the earth keep silence before Him."
HABAKKUK 2:20

The prerequisite for apprehending God is silence. The radio and television have to be switched off, as well as the noise of air-conditioners, dishwashers, and much talk.

Many souls never find the silent God because of the much noise in their homes.

There is much vain talk. I know no vain silence. Silence is a fullness of which words are only crumbs.

When you appreciate the Word or someone's words as being profound, remember that they come from deep silence. So why should you not come to the source of the river? Why do you stop at the words, "He will bring us *to the source* of living water"?

I have traveled around the world many times, but the most interesting journeys have been those I made in silence in the depths of my own heart, the only place where God wishes to meet me.

Forsake the outward noises, also the inward ones, the inner debates, the obsessions, the worries. Enter through the golden gate in the realm of silence where the Bridegroom waits for you.

"Mary said, 'Behold the maidservant of the Lord.'"
LUKE 1:38

*T*he virgin Mary has many virtues for which she is worthy of admiration. One of them is her spirit of independence.

She must have been a young peasant girl when the angel appeared to her. When the angel told her that she was chosen to give birth to the Lord, she knew what she risked. Everyone, including her bridegroom, would consider that she had sinned. The punishment for unfaithfulness in betrothal was stoning. Twenty centuries have passed. She still is the subject of mockery in Communist countries, and not only there. She knew also the prophecies. Her song proves it. So she realized that becoming the mother of the Lord, she would become also a mother of sorrows. She knew that a sword would pierce her heart, too, when nails pierced the hands and feet of her Son.

One would expect that she would have asked from the angel time for reflection and would have consulted with her bridegroom, her parents if they still were alive, her relatives, or a priest.

The plan of salvation would not have been fulfilled through her if she had taken counsel from men. Like Paul later, who when he had seen Jesus, "did not immediately confer with flesh and blood" (Galatians 1:16), the young girl Mary also asked no one, but said spontaneously to the angel, "Let it be to me according to your word."

A chaste woman, she took upon herself the shame of a premarital pregnancy. She knew that what she did was right.

The biblical ideal is that of submissive womanhood, of a silent woman. However, the submissiveness of a Christian woman is not one of weakness. She is obedient to her husband because she can give him an example of humility. She can be silent because she has much to say and can show everyone that deep silence speaks. She can be dependent because she had inwardly acquired a great independence, which is her love-gift to her husband.

> *"[Jesus] spoke of His decease which He was about to accomplish at Jerusalem."*
> LUKE 9:31

*E*nemies of Christ spread the lie about the collusion of the church with Nazism. They hide the fact that Hitler killed four thousand Catholic priests and kept in prison many thousands of others. The number of Protestant pastors who have met the same fate is not known. Not only priests, but tens of thousands of laymen also gave their lives for Christ in this period. As is always the case, the church had at that time its Judases also; but those who represent the church are its saints.

August 14 is the day of the execution of the priest Jacob Gapp. Before being led to death, he wrote: "I consider this day as the most beautiful of my life...I naturally passed through many difficult hours, but I could prepare myself well for death...Everything passes except heaven. I pray for all; I pray also for my fatherland."

The priest John Steinmeyer wrote in his last letter, "My demand for pardon has been refused. Today at 1 P.M. the flight to heaven... I die gladly."

The priest Bernhard Liechtenberg told a fellow prisoner, when both had been beaten with sticks and had their heads put in barrels filled with excrement: "I wish nothing else than what my Savior wills. Quiet. He was spat upon on the way to the cross." He died praying.

Jesus has accomplished many things. The most important was that He accomplished the right death in Jerusalem. His death had a purpose: He died for our sins. It had the right manner. He died praying, caring for His beloved, opening the kingdom for a thief who was a fellow sufferer.

Not everyone is called to martyrdom. But every Christian can give a good testimony by dying in a dignified, hopeful, and loving manner. Your death should be an accomplishment.

*"Do not forget to entertain strangers, for by so doing
some have unwittingly entertained angels."*
HEBREWS 13:2

*T*hose who entertain the greatest number of angels, being unaware of it, are the Communist prison directors. Here is one such incident.

An Orthodox priest in the Soviet Union worked in a garden. He observed a boy sneaking in to steal apples. He caught him with a strong grip. The boy was deadly afraid, expecting a beating, but the priest filled his pockets with apples. He put a few more in his hands and told him, "You are welcome any time. Only enter through the gate and bring other boys with you. I have plenty of apples for all of you." Soon some thirty boys gathered regularly in his garden. He instructed them in the gospel, though it is strictly forbidden by the Soviet authorities to teach religion to youth. He also taught them religious songs. After a time the converted boys brought their parents to these meetings. An underground church had begun.

A teacher discovered the "crime" and denounced the priest. He disappeared forever in a Soviet prison. Like an angel, he appeared from nowhere, then went out of sight, but he left behind him a fragrance of heaven and souls inebriated with the love of God.

This was a priest of the True Orthodox Church, followers of Patriarch Tikhon who had refused to cooperate with the Communists. Metropolitan Venianmin and innumerable other priests have been shot, but this church lives and conquers through love. We pity the Communists who do not know that they, unaware, keep angels in their prisons.

The Baptist pastor Odintsov did not allow the atheist government to dictate to him how he should lead Christ's church. He was arrested and literally thrown before dogs to be torn to pieces. The director again had had an angel in his jail.

A chill passes through a Christian's spine when he receives a brother. What if he is an angel? The Galatians received Paul as an angel of God, even as Christ Jesus (Galatians 4:14).

*T*he German mystic Meister Eckhart wrote, "Woman is the noblest name for soul." Staupitz, Luther's confessor, wrote, "The man who wishes to bring fruits for eternal life must become a woman." With Jesus, "woman" was a name of honor. He addressed His mother in this way, because she was the woman predicted in Genesis 3:15, whose seed would bruise the head of the serpent.

The words surely are not words of rebuke. The only evangelist to report them is John, who must have heard the story from the Lord's mother herself. He had taken her to his house after the crucifixion (John 19:27).

Jesus then explains to her, "My hour has not yet come." His time to do a miracle will have arrived only when the last drop of wine has been exhausted, so He should not be under suspicion that He mixed water with wine. Man's extremity is God's opportunity.

However, his mother has interceded. So He does not wait longer. How will He who yielded to the prayer of a Canaanite woman (Matthew 15:28) not yield to the request of His mother?

She knew what He would do; so she said to the servants, "Whatever He says to you, do it." She was sure that He could only order something good, even when what He ordered was strange, like filling pots with water as though the guests were desirous to take a bath, when they needed wine.

Let this be our principle of life also: to do whatever He says.

"Michael the archangel, in contending with the devil . . .
dared not bring against him a reviling accusation."
JUDE 9

*H*istorians of old, Philo of Alexandria and Flavius Josephus, describe Pilate as guilty of corruption, insults, plunder, plots against the people, arrogance, murder of innocent victims, and constant savagery. The Talmud has strong words about the high priests of Jesus' time.

The Gospels use absolutely no epithets. It is because the evangelists did not hate. They said only what was needed to stimulate faith and action, not what would make the adversary despicable in the eyes of men.

Love is the only possible attitude for a Christian. The tree does not withdraw its protecting shadow from the woodcutter, nor the moon its light from the dwelling of the outcast.

In Lamentations 2:21, Jeremiah tells God, "You have slain [virgins and young men] in the day of Your anger." He prefers to accuse God, who is not reached by our mean words, in order to avoid the great crime of speaking mean words against the actual killers.

Criminals deserve our pity, our love, yes, our respect, for the great suffering they bring upon themselves. To call them names is not a Christian trait. The most terrible waste is the waste of mind. It is such a waste to invent something that would put an adversary to shame.

Christ's death was not the work of some murderers. It was the fulfillment of a plan of God. God the Creator of all beings is also the One who dissolves them in order to resurrect them again. He might sometimes use wicked men to bring to Himself His elected ones. They see all as coming from God, and therefore use no bad words against their murderers.

How much less should we use mean words against those who wrong us.

AUGUST 18

"You shall not make for yourself a carved image."
EXODUS 20:4

When we read in the Bible about the idols to which men bow, we think that these belonged to the past. We don't realize how backward a great part of humanity still is. Animism and fetishism are among the most widespread religions even today.

One example is the Konkombas in Ghana (Africa). Their highest worship is given to a fetish, which they have to forsake when they become Christians. This is not easy. They still believe that the fetish wields great power. It makes the owner rich, gives him many wives, health, etc. They bring chicken, goats, and sheep as sacrifices to the fetish.

The Grumade fetish asks from time to time for blood of men. Missionaries testify that a witchdoctor, in service to this fetish, poisoned a man. His body was completely swollen in agony. Then the chief of the tribe ordered the witchdoctor to bring him back to life or he would be in trouble. Soon the swelling passed.

The natives value this fetish above their families.

Some Konkombas would like to combine the Christian faith with keeping the fetish, which is not accepted by missionaries.

Let us keep in prayer those primitives who bow to fetishes, as well as the many superstitious among modern men who have a belief in luck-bringing amulets and other idols.

"Abraham begat Isaac."
MATTHEW 1:2 (KJV)

*T*he King James Version says, "Abraham begat." We would like to translate in the present tense, "begets." The Greek form of the verb used here is called "aorist," which means etymologically, "without horizon." It is much used in the New Testament and has the connotation of an eternal present, of events outside of time.

In Greek, the aorist is used in the genealogy of the Lord because what we have in this chapter is not only a historical record of what happened once. A comparison with the genealogy of Jesus in Luke 3 shows that they don't match. They do not have to match because they are not only history.

The artificial reduction of the number of ancestors to forty-two and the willful omission of some ancestors from the genealogy shows that this list has another purpose. It was a ladder of initiation. Mature souls in early Christianity, when taught to change from simple believers into men who, like the virgin Mary, would have Jesus living in them, meditated successively on the lives of Abraham, Isaac, Jacob, and all the others until they came to Mary and identified spiritually with her. The genealogy in Luke is another procedure of initiation looking retrospectively from the height of Jesus-likeness to the whole past history.

Even if not in a sophisticated and methodical manner as in times before, every Christian passes through such processes. The Abraham state begets the Isaac state. Therefore the Greek does not use the past tense, but the aorist, the tense without horizon. We are meant not to be slaves of our time, but to live outside of time.

AUGUST 20

"If anyone desires to come after Me, let him deny himself."
LUKE 9:23

A mocker asked a believer, "If you say that Godhead is everywhere, is it also in this dog?" The answer was, "Bow-wow." A wise answer, the answer the dog would give to such a question asked of him.

To every question you ask someone else, you will obtain an answer according to that person's constitution. In this respect, men are not different than dogs. You ask high questions about Godhead. No man has any other answer than the "bow-wow" of a very small creature.

We all see things from our limited point of view. Every point of view is a point of blindness because it incapacitates us totally for every other perspective. Lifting up your eyes, you see the ceiling, but not the floor. Looking to the door, I exclude the window from my sight.

Jesus gives manifold salvation, a salvation from points of view, too. The Christian denies himself, which means that he denies himself. He does not look on things anymore from a certain position, because he has no position. The foxes have their holes and the birds their nests, but the Son of man does not have a place to lay His head.

Not having a certain place for your head frees you. You don't see things anymore from one side or the other. Your answer about the Godhead will not be one of the common "bow-wow." You will have the intuition of the whole, and you will be its witness.

"This Man receives sinners."
LUKE 15:2

*D*evil's Island" is the common name of a cluster of little islands ten miles from the South American coast. They are surrounded by an unruly sea infested with sharks. For years it was populated only by hardcore criminals. They did not work much because the climate makes work almost impossible.

For most of them, drink had been the first cause of their downfall. (Men of the liquor industry should be compelled to spend a year with the victims of their vice in a place like this.) A poll established also that 80 percent are children of alcoholics or syphilitics. The vice of their fathers sentenced them to hard labor.

In 1933, officers of the French Salvation Army offered to live and work for Christ among the most rotten and decayed, exposed to insects and pests. One officer said, "Without the love of God it would be impossible to love such men. I shiver to let my thoughts go into this infected place."

Notwithstanding, they went. Here is the description of a meeting: "Criminals with shaven heads, bare breasts and sleeves rolled up showing the tatooing. One bears the picture of his wife and child, remarkably done, in two medallions. Others have inscriptions such as, 'Child of sorrows,' or 'Oh, my mother, if thou but saw thy son.' They listen silently with impassive faces."

They did not remain impassive forever. The Salvation Army had a recruit among the criminals. He had committed murder. The police knew nothing about him. Converted at a meeting of the Army, he confessed his crime and was sent to Devil's Island. There he helped the Salvationists. He said, "Would that I had known the one Son of man who saved me, before knowing the sons of men who destroyed me!"

Thanks to the missionary Charles Pean and his colleagues many were saved and their situation was improved. Now Devil's Island has ceased to be a penal institution. The Salvation Army has learned from Jesus love toward criminals.

"Whatever He says to you, do it."
JOHN 2:5

*T*herese of Lisieux was the last of several girls in a poor family. One Christmas, a case with toys left over from her older sisters was presented to her and she was asked which one she would like to choose. She answered, "I choose all of them." At the age of fifteen, she entered a Carmelite convent and had to fix her intention upon one specific Christian virtue which she would have to practice above all others. She said again, "I will choose all of them."

Even so the mother of the Lord teaches us to do whatever her Son says, without any discrimination. If you choose among the commandments of the Lord, you really say, "I will not do what He commands, but what I like." We have to obey like soldiers, to go into battle when commanded even if it means sure death and to obey also when He commands what we consider to be shameful retreat.

Moses told the people, "You shall be careful to do as the LORD your God has commanded you; you shall not turn aside to the right hand or to the left" (Deuteronomy 5:32). Do commandments have a right and a left side?

The commandment says, "Do not steal." You can steal in order to enjoy more pleasures. You can steal in order to help the poor. You shall not lie. You can lie in order to deceive for selfish reasons. You can lie in order to save lives. There exist sins of the right side and of the left side, but we are meant not to reason at all when He commands. We are simply to obey and to avoid sin.

We have general rules of conduct which are absolutes, unless we have a special command to do otherwise in exceptional circumstances. Love is the supreme standard. Do everything He commands you, however strange or unsuitable His commandment might seem to you.

> *"I am ... the truth."*
> JOHN 14:6

*T*wo men, Truth and Falsehood, went swimming. Falsehood stole Truth's clothes, and Truth, rather than lower himself to wear Falsehood's clothes, chose to go without. Hence the expression "the naked truth." Falsehood, in the guise of Truth, goes about deceiving mankind to this day.

Truth can never compromise with Falsehood. They can never walk the same way. It is something else with the man taken in falsehood. Toward him, Truth is full of love and tries to convince him to leave behind the stolen clothes and start walking naked, too.

Henry IV of England was a brave man. Therefore he is known as Henry the Great. He was truthful himself and great in kindness toward those with false attitudes.

He once was told about a certain captain who had spread slander against him and had rebelled. Though he had been pardoned and had obtained many benefits, yet for all this he continued not to love the king. Henry IV said, "I will do him so many kindnesses that I will force him to love me whether he will or not." It is thus that naked truth wins false men who disguise themselves as sincere.

Henry IV used to say to those who admired his proceedings, "A man catches more flies with one spoonful of honey than with twenty tons of vinegar."

Love the man in error; love also the man who lives in deliberate falsehood. Just remember: truth is truth and falsehood is falsehood. Never confuse or mix them.

AUGUST 24

"There are diversities of gifts."
1 CORINTHIANS 12:4

*A*round A.D. 165, Bishop Carpus was burned alive because he had refused to offer incense to the heathen gods. While the henchmen arranged the stake, he said, "We all have the same Eve as mother, and what things men do to men." When he was mounted on the stake, his face shone. He was asked about it. He answered, "I have been raptured from this world and have seen the glory of the Lord."

St. Mechthild of Magdeburg knew how to write exquisitely about divine mysteries: "The sweet dew of Trinity sprinkles the flower of the elect maid with water from the well of the eternal Godhead. The fruit of the flower is an immortal God and a mortal man and an eternal warrant of life eternal. Our Savior became our bridegroom."

She knew how to write otherwise, too. She wrote to her bishop, "Your honor has rotted in the mire of vices. You are poor like a beggar, because you want the kingly treasure of love. Jesus will come against you with judgment." For letters like this she was much hated.

Frederic the Wise, duke of Saxonia, when told to conquer the town of Erfurt which had rebelled against him, and when assured that it would cost at the utmost the life of only five men, answered, "One would be too much for me." He preferred peace. He protected Luther, though this was dangerous for his throne. When warned about it, he answered, "I would prefer to take a stick and to leave as a beggar than to act knowingly against God."

Different saints, different callings, but everyone an example of obedience for us.

A Russian revolutionist, Zasulitch, in Czarist times shot General Trepov for flogging a student in the Paviak prison. In 1907, another revolutionist woman, Ragozinikova, fashionably dressed, called the Central prison in Petersburg and asked to speak with the commandant. She had come to protest the government's policy of flogging her imprisoned comrades. Inside her dress were sewed thirteen pounds of dynamite and a detonator. When the commandant appeared, she killed him with her revolver. The dynamite was for another purpose. She knew that she would be arrested and taken to the headquarters of the Secret Police. Not knowing any other way to penetrate it, she intended to blow it up with herself. But she was searched and the dynamite discovered.

She was sentenced to be hanged. Awaiting execution, she wrote to her family, "Death itself is nothing... Frightful only is the thought of dying without having achieved what I could have done." When she was hanged, Ragozinikova was twenty years old.

Christian brethren and sisters are flogged today in many Communist, Muslim, and heathen countries. Worse, they are tortured. Surely, we will not imitate the methods of the revolutionists. Notwithstanding, we need souls as resolute as Zasulitch and Ragozinikova to defend their fellow believers, to protest, to help, to fight for them. Today Jesus says that our courage and zeal should exceed that of the revolutionists and terrorists, as we seek to help our Christian brethren and sisters in bondage.

*D*uring the great terror when Tito first came to power, one of his purge victims, a lay assistant in an Orthodox church, hanged himself before he could be shot. He left this note for his wife: "I have gone to remind God of a world He has forgotten."

"Where is God?" Many believing men have asked this question when passing through great sufferings. Job and David questioned God. Even Jesus did it when hanging on a cross.

You may have some heavy sorrow, and doubt about God may nag you.

When Saul of Tarsus, the persecutor, was converted, the first thing the Lord showed him was "how many things he must suffer" (Acts 9:16). Parents and professors and clergy should teach children and adults sufferology, without the knowledge of which it is impossible to lead the right life. "Man is born to trouble, as the sparks fly upward" (Job 5:7). We are taught many useless things. We are not taught to suffer with understanding. Therefore the despair in sorrows.

Life and reality are hidden behind veils. The Jewish high priest had to pass through two thick veils before entering in the most holy place of the temple in Jerusalem. We don't know whether a veiled Muslim lady smiles at us or frowns, and we don't see the intentions of God because of the veils that cover Him.

The curtain was torn at the death of Jesus. Soon after this, He was seen resurrected. The veil was torn for you, too. You will see that all things work together for your good. God is very near you. He does not forget you.

"He...became obedient."
PHILIPPIANS 2:8

When Bibles were written by hand, a king of France asked a monk to write for him a Scripture without the verses in which whoredom is condemned.

If it were left up to most of us, we would leave out of the Bible everything that enjoins obedience. Once this is missing, everything else is bearable for us.

Obedience to Christ must be total. Once He orders something, we should not ask ourselves what the results will be. A soldier who advances in obedience against a well-armed enemy in the face of cannon fire knows that he has a great chance of dying if he obeys the orders. This is what obedience means.

Can obedience to a commandment of Christ make us lose many possibilities of doing good? We don't have better minds than Jesus. He surely has weighed also the pros and cons. If He says something, we obey without reflecting. We don't delay, saying that wise men think things over before doing them. The psalmist writes, "I made haste, and did not delay to keep Your commandments" (119:60).

In our day Christians do not help the poor because welfare agencies do it. Hospitals take care of the sick, orphanages take care of the fatherless, but institutions don't have the touch of personal love.

In former Portuguese Africa, blacks were observed walking miles with their sick past the government hospital to a much more primitive Christian clinic. When asked why, seeing that the medicines were the same, they replied, "This might be so, but it is not the same hands."

Obey and love and add your personal touch to the good done in the world.

A U G U S T   2 8

"This beginning of signs Jesus did in Cana."
JOHN 2:11

*M*issionaries who have lived among savages all report that they seemed to the natives to be miracle workers. Missionaries knew how to make water burn, even stinking water (gasoline); they made fire in a minute through lighting a match, whereas the natives had to rub two pieces of wood together for a long time. Missionaries could hunt with guns; they could sew; they could talk to each other without opening their mouths, by inscribing some strange signs on paper.

Pearl Buck tells in her novels that the Chinese in remote regions disbelieved her when she said that in England houses were built over houses (she meant apartments) and that carts needed no horses to make them go. The Chinese considered these to be fairy tales.

When Marco Polo, the first European to return from China, said that he had seen yellow men with slanted eyes and pigtails, he got the nickname "Marco Polo the liar."

What then is the miraculous? It is what a being who is superior physically, intellectually, and spiritually knows and can do, which the inferior being cannot know and do.

Jesus was a superior being—God living as man among us. He could do what men normally cannot do.

Now He is in heaven and has all power. Don't limit His possibilities to normal human experience. He can do above all we can imagine. Come to Him with all your problems and those of mankind. Have confidence in His miraculous power. He can change water into wine. He can change tears into cause for joy.

"Eat, drink, and be merry."
ECCLESIASTES 8:15

*T*he Talmud, one of the holy books of the Jews, says that men will be accountable before God for every pure joy they could have had and have missed.

This thought is right. Everything God created is good—the bacilli that produce the fermentation of grape juice, too. Sin has changed many things into occasions of sadness, but there has remained still "a time to laugh . . . and a time to dance" (Ecclesiastes 3:4).

When Jesus changed water into wine in Cana, He showed us that well-understood religion does not exclude human pleasures and joys, providing that they are not inherently evil or that they are not the prominent preoccupation of life. Within these limits, a Christian should share the joys of the world.

Never believe that Jesus, who changed an enormous quantity of water into wine at Cana, reproaches you for a joy. Remember also that His wine, because it was made out of water, might not have had the intoxicating effects of the everyday wine.

The Christian must thoroughly renounce sin, but not the things that make life to be really life. Beauty, art, joy unite man with God. Religion contains an ever-fresh love that is grateful for the happiness in life.

AUGUST 30

*M*en are trying hard to be clever and smart and modern, when what is needed is adherence to the timeless turths.

When Queen Victoria's ministers were urging on her certain matters of state as being wise procedure, she said impatiently, "Don't talk to me of what is expedient. Tell me what is right."

Some Christians joined the Communist Secret Police in order to use their positions to help the church. They had not foreseen all the consequences. They were commanded to murder. If they obeyed, they would retain their rank and a slight possibility of mitigating other horrors. If they refused in the name of truth, they would die without anyone ever learning of their stand. The murder they were ordered to commit would be carried out anyway. They would die without being useful to anyone through their death.

So life is sometimes rooted in horror. Every grain is dunged with filth before becoming an ear of wheat.

What has one to choose when he has before him only tragic alternatives? Don't choose the expedient. Choose God's commandment: "Do not murder."

In a concentration camp in Nikolaev, a Jew was ordered to hang six other Jews who had committed no other crime than being Jewish. If he did it, six innocents would die. If he refused, seven Jews would die and seven old mothers would weep. He thought about his helpless mother and hanged his fellow Jews. He could never forgive himself. Had he refused, there would have been no regrets. Choose always God's commandment.

AUGUST 31

"Your word is truth."
JOHN 17:17

What guarantee do we have that our New Testament is the same as that which was revealed in the first century to the apostles?

Well, the New Testament can claim one advantage over all the writings of old Greece—the age of its manuscripts.

The oldest complete manuscript of *Homer* that we possess is from the tenth century A.D., which means it dates from 2,000 years after the death of its author. There is an interval of 1,600 years between the date when the poetry of Pindar was written (450 B.C.) and the oldest manuscript (A.D. 1150).

In contrast, the New Testament was finished by the year 100. The oldest complete manuscript dates from about the year A.D. 300, only two hundred years separating the two dates. Even for these two hundred years there exists a chain of rich quotations in the early writings of Christians that guarantee the authenticity of the first manuscripts. We possess 4,000 old manuscripts of the New Testament, which can be compared with each other and give us the modern correct text.

We can rely on the teachings of the New Testament. Let us take heed to its principal teaching: "Unless one is born of water and the Spirit, he cannot enter the kingdom of God" (John 3:3).

When we are born physically, we come in a sack of water. We all are born from water, but being born into this world does not make us heirs of heaven. The teaching of universal salvation can be dangerous. Jesus tells those who have been born from a sack of water that they need to be born from the Spirit, too.

Wesley preached endlessly about the same subject: "You must be born again." When asked why, he answered, "Because you must be born again."

Jesus said it. We can be sure that we have in our New Testament His authentic words.

SEPTEMBER 1

"Immediately, coming up from the water..."
MARK 1:10

*S*oldiers begin to march the second they hear the command, "March."

The Gospel of Mark is characterized by the astonishing repetition of the word *eutheos*, which in Greek means "immediately." Some feel that Mark was the rich ruler to whom the Lord had said, "Sell what you have and give to the poor." He had too many possessions. He left the Lord with sadness in his heart; he could not renounce so much. Later he regretted his disobedience and did what the Lord commanded him, although he had remorse for not having done it "immediately." If so, perhaps this made him repeat this one word again and again, when needed and when not needed in his Gospel.

It is said about the cavaliers of earlier times that they slept with the spear and shield near them. So the Christian must be ready to obey a commandment the moment it is pronounced, even if it is at night. The bride says in Solomon's Song, "I sleep, but my heart is awake" (5:2).

Mary at the marriage in Cana said, "Whatever He says to you, do it" (John 2:5). Be attentive. The words are not, "Do whatever He has said before."

It is written, "The word of God spread" (Acts 6:7) and "The word of God grew and multiplied" (Acts 12:24). Christ did not speak only 2,000 years ago. He has not become dumb since. He gives teachings in every generation. He is a wonderful counselor (Isaiah 9:6) in your personal life today. Listen daily to Him and obey immediately what He tells you.

SEPTEMBER 2

Our text makes a comparison between men on the one hand and oxen or donkeys on the other. The comparison is in favor of the animals.

The comparison would not be favorable for us even if we were measured with mice. Mice know how to establish a cause-and-effect relationship between the eating of a food and death. If poisoned food has been given to them, the death of one of them is a warning for others. They would not touch the food.

Experiments were made with mice to whom poisons with delayed effect were given. The mice still found out the cause and transmitted an attitude of refusal toward this poison to others. Moreover, if mice that knew about a poison and had an adversity toward it had other mice put in their cage who knew nothing about the matter, the wise mice hindered those without knowledge from touching the poisoned food, using even violence, as we would try to overpower someone who wanted to commit suicide.

Mice know enough to beware themselves and to warn their comrades of what is deadly for them, even when death is a delayed effect. Yet we men, the crown of creation, do not beware of sin though it brings with it eternal death. We do not have at least as much zeal as mice have to warn others about sin. On the contrary, we sometimes attract others to sin and encourage them in it.

Jesus teaches us to learn from birds (Matthew 6:26). Isaiah teaches us to learn from donkeys and oxen. Let us be ashamed to have to learn even from mice. Sin is poison. Abstain from it and restrain others.

SEPTEMBER 3

"Forgetting those things which are behind..."
PHILIPPIANS 3:13

*S*hema Israel, Adonai Eloheinu Adonai ehad. "Listen Israel, the Lord your God is one God." It was this prayer (the words are their Hebrew original) that was on the lips of many Jews who went to Eichmann's gas chambers while he looked on smiling.

Some twenty years later he was captured by the Israeli Secret Police in Buenos Aires. In his provisional prison, he amazed the guards by reciting this same prayer—which was even more amazing since he claimed not to be a believer at all.

I have known well the world of murderers and big criminals. A mysterious identification with their victims happens in their souls. Mass murderers of Jews became much more obsessed with Jewishness than any Jew would be. Professional abortionists will be haunted by a world of children who point at them, asking the question, "Why did you kill me?" The man who dropped the atomic bomb on Hiroshima, when asked by reporters, "How do you feel about it?" answered, "How did they feel about it?"

We have many victims in life. Jesus became the ideal victim, the innocent lamb betrayed, insulted, wronged, killed for our misdoings. And He died with the words, "Father, forgive them, for they know not what they do."

Then He addresses Himself to us and says, "I, the victim, have forgiven you. All your victims are now in a world where forgiveness reigns. You are the only one who does not forgive yourself. You are haunted by what you have done. Accept forgiveness. Forgive yourself. The unhealthy identification with the men whom you have wronged will cease. You will have a new personality."

"The love of money is a root of all kinds of evil."
1 TIMOTHY 6:10

*I*t surely is. The possession of much money can be a great evil, too. Usually men cannot handle it without being polluted.

Another great evil is the lack of money. A hungry man is an angry man. Revolutions accompanied by mass killings are made by men without money.

Jesus teaches us to give alms, which means that He wishes the poor to get some money from us. Through this we bring them from one endangered sphere into another.

Money is dangerous. Its simple mention produces harm. Having it as well as not having it can produce trouble.

The solution is to live as if money did not exist, not allowing it to play a role in your making of decisions. Do not seek the job that produces much money, but the one in which you can be most useful to society. Marry not the girl or boy who has more money, but the one whom you can make the happiest. Do not buy the most expensive things, which would give you the occasion to boast, neither the cheapest thing which would prove your detachment from the world. Buy what is needed.

May your sanctified mind decide about having or not having of this nonentity, money. Never allow the having or not having of money determine the state of your mind.

SEPTEMBER 5

The British publication *New Society* has conducted a psychological survey of players in symphony orchestras. This shows that brass and string players usually have bad opinions of each other. Woodwind players, especially oboists, are considered as neurotics by their colleagues in the orchestra. Violin and viola players have uneasy, mutually deprecatory attitudes.

The wonder is that people who tend to be mutually hostile to each other can produce an effect of order and harmony.

The moment the conductor lifts his baton, all these emotions are set apart. Only one thing counts now: the success of the concert.

The children of this world sometimes are wiser than the children of light. It is unavoidable that Christians, men and women of such different backgrounds, temperaments, experiences of life, cultural levels, nations, races, and social classes should disagree in many things and feel even, however slightly, some hostility toward each other. We are not only partakers of the divine nature; we are human, too. But the human side should be put aside for the common worship and the common action in the service of the Lord.

Ask yourself which is greater: the cause that we serve in common or the matter in which we differ? Then you will have the right attitude of love.

SEPTEMBER 6

"I sleep, but my heart is awake."
SONG OF SOLOMON 5:2

*T*he time of sleep must not be lost time.

The renowned Russian chemist Mendeleev did not succeed for a long time in finding the definitive form of the periodicity and quality of simple elements. Once after having worked at it a whole night, he fell asleep in his laboratory. And, lo, he dreamed it was the table. When he awoke, he jotted it down immediately. Much of the music of the opera *Snegurotchka* of Rimski-Korsakov came to him in his sleep. The psychiatrist Bechterev always concentrated on the most important problem in the evening in order to have the answers ready when he awakened from sleep. The chessmaster Karpov dreamed a move that made him win a tournament.

Sometimes more neurons are active during a dream than when one is awake. Therefore the morning is always wiser than the evening.

One evening, New Testament Joseph considered leaving the virgin Mary, believing she had sinned. He did not sleep well. His heart remained awake. An angel spoke to him. In the morning he did the right thing. He took Mary as his wife. In a dream he learned how to save the child from Herod and also when to return to Palestine. Pharaoh and Nebuchadnezzar both received important warnings in dreams. So did the Old Testament Joseph as well as many others.

Use the time of your sleep well. Let your last thought be from God's Word. Finish the day with prayer. God will speak to you sometimes as you sleep.

SEPTEMBER 7

"Brethren, if a man is overtaken in any trespass, you who are spiritual restore such a one in the spirit of gentleness."
GALATIANS 6:1

*A*natoli Krasnov-Levitin is a Hebrew-Christian writer from Russia who three times has been imprisoned for his heroic attitude. He told his interrogators simply, "You cannot buy and you cannot frighten me."

When freed, he was sad because Krasin, another Christian writer and godson of his, while in prison, cracked under stress and betrayed some names.

Krasnov-Levitin was called as a witness for Krasin's trial. He had hard feelings in his heart toward the Christian who had betrayed others. In court he met an acquaintance, Mrs. Hodorovitch. He asked her what she was doing there. She answered, "Though I don't call myself a Christian, I sympathize with those who suffer, even if they have broken down under the burden of a cross that was too heavy." Krasnov-Levitin became ashamed of his evil thoughts and he himself published the story of his sin.

Not only under torture, but under all temptations and pressures, some Christians are strong and others weak. Some yield. Men who are strong in some circumstances are very weak in others. It is not for us to judge and condemn those who have fallen, but rather to stretch out toward them a helping hand to restore them with words of meekness.

"My enemies reproach me."
PSALM 42:10

*C*hristians have to be warned against anti-Semitism, as well as against white and black racism. One of the great dangers is the widespread anti-American feeling. It is just like the anti-Jewish hatred in the past generation, unreasonable and unpleasant to God.

The United States provides 80 percent of the finances and 60 percent of the staff for the world mission of the church. The collapse of America would be a collapse of the entire missionary effort. Therefore criticism of America is propagated by the devil.

As the Jews were described as usurers and deceivers, now the lie is spread that rich America is ruining the poor nations. When the West established its first contacts with the Third World it was already far ahead of them. The white settlers of South Africa also were far ahead of the black population from the beginning. They do not owe their privileged economic situation to the exploitation of the backward nations.

It is true that Americans and other whites consume too much. It is to be noted, however, that per capita production in America exceeds production in India by more than the difference in consumption, allowing it not only to pay for the consumption, but also to give foreign aid.

The whites did not cause the Third World to become poor. They are the only help for these people to overcome poverty.

Beware of anti-Americanism as the devil's tool to destroy the greatest support of mission work and of freedom of religion in the whole world.

SEPTEMBER 9

*"Unless one is born of water and the Spirit,
he cannot enter the kingdom of God."*
JOHN 3:5

*J*esus does not say that a man who has not passed through new birth *will not* be in the heavenly kingdom. He says that this man *cannot* enter. A mineral cannot enter into the sphere of living beings except it is absorbed by them. A plant cannot become an animal. If the animal eats it, it becomes a part of the animal's body. An animal cannot become a man. Man belongs to a superior realm. Only if a man eats an animal will it become part of a human body.

So a man cannot become a child of God through any deed of his. The distance between a child of God and a man is much greater than that between a man and a monkey, because man and monkey are both creatures, whereas the child of God is a partaker of the divine nature. Men cannot become heirs of the kingdom through their endeavors. They are absorbed into it by the all-embracing love of God.

The man has to die—die to the world, to its laws and to sin. He has to cease to exist as an "I." Jesus says that we have to deny ourselves (Luke 9:23). A Christian dies before he dies. Then he is absorbed by the divine nature. He becomes a child of God. The new birth has happened.

Die in order to be alive. Someone who has died is not conscious of the human voices around him and is not interested in what is happening.

We remain human even after the new birth and continue in the world, but the child of God has an inner sanctuary in which he is dead to the passions, the temptations, and the labor of this world. If a child of God would remain with his old preoccupations, he would be like a corpse kept in the house, which spreads only stench.

Don't give undue importance to all other religious things. To be born again is the most important of all.

SEPTEMBER 10

"I will have mercy on whomever I will have mercy, and I will have compassion on whomever I will have compassion."
ROMANS 9:15

A man was brought to a psychiatrist. His madness consisted in believing that he was a corpse. The psychiatrist was sure that it would be easy to cure him by showing him that corpses do not bleed, whereas from his body blood would flow even when stuck only with a needle.

The psychiatrist took the patient to morgues and made him attend autopsies. He thus convinced him that dead men do not bleed. Then, to convince him that he was alive, he pricked his finger with a penknife. Blood flowed. The man cried, "So I have been mistaken. Corpses do bleed."

We sometimes are dismayed about the many to whom we have witnessed about Christ, some of them beloved members of our families, who do not accept the message of the gospel. We cannot attribute it always to our fault.

There exists a vincible and an invincible ignorance. Reactions of men usually are irrational. The most powerful arguments rarely succeed in changing a viewpoint which a man has because of circumstances of birth and education or because of belonging to a certain religion or nation. Prejudices are often more powerful than facts.

It is our responsibility to witness for Christ and to pray. Some will receive the testimony, fulfilling what has been ordained for them before the creation of the world. Cases of vincible ignorance can be helped by dialogues and good examples. Where the ignorance is invincible, we have to leave the case in the hands of a loving and righteous God. Don't destroy your own peace of heart with unjustified continual reproaches about your inability to convince others.

SEPTEMBER 11

"You shall not murder."
EXODUS 20:13

*A*braham Lincoln was the first man to buy a machine gun to protect himself. It did not help him. He was shot.

The machine gun was invented by the American R. J. Gatling. He hoped that by enabling one soldier to do the duty of one hundred, there would be no more need for large armies. But the armies became bigger than even before.

Hiram Maxim patented a much better machine gun, after he was advised in Europe, "Hang your chemistry and electricity. If you want to make a pile of money, invent something that will enable these Europeans to cut each others' throats with greater facility." He really made big money. Not only Europeans killed each other, but Africans, Asians, and Australians, too. Americans gave their part of sacrifice of blood.

The Middle Ages was a time of chivalry in war. It was said already during the American Civil War that shovelry had replaced chivalry. After the atomic bomb on Japanese cities, there remained not even corpses for whom to shovel a grave.

Einstein said that he did not know with what weapons World War III would be fought, but that World War IV would surely be fought with sticks and stones by primitives.

The solution is so simple. It is God's word: "You shall not murder." God does not forbid you to get murdered, but to murder. The knowledge of eternal life chases fear. Children of God can afford to be good. While in the world an arms race is going on, we have to run in another race set before us, the race toward Jesus (Hebrews 12:1,2).

As the world has multiplied its weapons of destruction, let us multiply our actions of love and kindness.

"My covenant was with him, one of life and peace."
MALACHI 2:5

*C*hristians keep their peace. Why should they squander energy fighting their enemies? Peacefulness is one of the secrets of longevity. To outlive your enemies is better than to try to beat them. Look to the Jews. During almost two thousand years they had no army and outlived their foes. Since they have an army, they are in trouble.

Christians keep their peace. They count the many reasons to be happy and, while doing so, forget to have a look at the many mischiefs that beset them.

When rains and floods come, they get into the ark. If you are not small enough to get out of the rain, an umbrella will not help you much. You might still get wet and catch pneumonia, too.

Christians live their lives quietly without anxieties. If Jesus is the head of the church, He should also have the monopoly on headaches.

A reporter asked an old lady on her birthday, "What is the secret of living to 105?" She said, "The secret is to keep breathing." Jesus breathed on the apostles and said to them, "Receive the Holy Spirit" (John 20:22).

There is a kind of breathing that communicates the Holy Spirit. There are other breathings. "Saul, still breathing threats and murder..." (Acts 9:1). There is the quiet breathing of faith, which prolongs a life of peace.

SEPTEMBER 13

When Napoleon Bonaparte proclaimed himself Emperor of France, and the English government, ignoring the fact, continued to address him simply as general, he said to a friend, "They may call me what they please. They cannot prevent me from being what I am."

With many people politics befuddle policy. They anxiously seek public applause and fear the disapproval of the mob; they always are trying to overhear what people say about them, and they miss the only chance they have to be themselves once in this single lifetime.

You cannot avoid being misunderstood. Moses, the great man of God, was slandered even by Miriam, a prophetess who was also his sister. It is also true that every child of God is exposed to the gossip of men who often speak without thinking.

Don't be concerned about others' opinions. Be yourself, whatever this may mean. Jesus was a first-class child to His mother and a first-class carpenter before becoming a first-class Savior. Lincoln and Garfield had few friends, but were the right men and became presidents of the United States.

Even stains on your character and sins, if confessed to God, cannot hinder you from being what you basically are, a person called by God to do good.

Francis Bacon twice was arrested for debts. As attorney general he was guilty of torturing at the rack an old clergyman, Peacham, to make him confess to treason in a sermon he had never preached. Later Bacon himself pleaded guilty to taking bribes. But then he came to his senses and became one of the greatest intellects mankind has ever known. He retired and wrote *Novum Organum* and other books which keep him famous century after century, and which have taught many men right statesmanship.

Be what you are—a creature of God sent into this world for a great purpose. Don't allow sayings of others and memories of your past sins to sidetrack you.

SEPTEMBER 14

"His own sheep... will by no means follow a stranger, but will flee from him."
JOHN 10:4,5

*I*n the middle of the seventeenth century, the Jews all over the world went wild with joy. From Spain to Russia news came that the Messiah had appeared. His name was Sabbatai Zvi.

Rich men gave away their possessions to the poor. Some Jews rolled in the snow or lay with heavy stones on their chests or flagellated themselves to become clean of sin and to be worthy to meet with this Messiah who would lead them back to their Holy Land.

Sabbatai Zvi had given the command that all mourning for the loss of Zion was to cease. He would reconquer it. A Jewish Christian girl brought up in a convent in Poland who had always dreamed of being the Messiah's bride became Sabbatai's wife. She, too, believed him to be the Anointed.

The Turkish Sultan had Sabbatai brought before him. "If you are God's messenger, you can prove it and then we will all honor you. Let my archers shoot at you with their arrows and if you don't die, then you will be acknowledged as the Messiah. Or, you have the alternative to accept our religion. Otherwise you will die."

Sabbatai did not waver. He put on a white Turkish turban and accepted Mohammed's religion. He said to the Sultan, "I am not the Messiah. I am your majesty's humble subject."

The Jews had not believed in Jesus. They had believed in Sabbatai Zvi. All men are prone to believe impostors rather than the embodied Truth. In every century, certain men capture the imagination of millions who consider them as saviors. In the end they all prove to have been deceivers.

Jesus, when defied by those in power, allowed the arrows of death to pierce Him. Lo, He is alive and is the giver of life.

Beware of every new name that appears on the firmament of religion. There is only one name by which men can be saved.

"These things I write to you, so that you may not sin."
1 JOHN 2:1

A Christian is not to sin. "Whoever abides in Him does not sin" (1 John 3:6). There might be exceptional circumstances in which a Christian falls into sin but then he should not despair. "If anyone sins, we have an Advocate with the Father" (1 John 2:1). Taught by what has happened, you try to do better next time.

Persecution has not crushed the church, time has not abated its forces, but continual abuses by its members have shaken its stability and credibility. Sin cannot be a program of life for Christians.

We are not perfect, but we should strive to be able to say about the deeds of our life what Sir Walter Scott said about his writings: "I have been perhaps the most voluminous author of the day and it is a comfort to me to think that I have tried to unsettle no man's faith, to corrupt no man's principle, and that I have written nothing which on my deathbed I should wish blotted."

There is forgiveness of sins, but blessings lie not only in forgiven sins. They lie in virtuous deeds that surely will be succeeded by reward, even if sometimes late. One immediate reward of a thing well done is to know that you have done it.

Prefer this small reward to the regrets of forgiven sins. The admonition of the Bible is: "Sin not."

> *"If any of you lacks wisdom, let him ask of God,*
> *who gives to all liberally."*
> JAMES 1:5

*I*f Martians existed and you would ask their scientists about life on earth, they probably would say there was none. So we don't know what is happening on the billions of stars throughout the universe.

We don't even know our neighbors, the animals. In December 1975, *Sovietskaia Rossia* published a few amazing facts. A cat passed a driveway out of which a car came at great speed. The cat did not see the car and would surely have been killed, if a shepherd dog had not stopped the cat with its teeth and brought it at the last second to a halt on the sidewalk.

Near the town of Livingstone in South Africa a man had a dog. A crow had also become friendly and came regularly to be fed from the man's hand. One day, the dog disappeared and could not be found. The crow became gluttonous as never before. When she received a piece of meat she would fly away with it and come back crowing loudly asking for more. After a week the man decided to find out where the crow flew. Thus he found his dog, which had fallen into a trap. It had been provided for by the crow.

A Cairo engineer, Mahmud Vally, was on the sea in an inflated mattress when the currents took him far away from the shore. He would have been lost if dolphins had not pushed the mattress for a whole day the many miles to shore.

The chimpanzee, when he wishes to drink, wraps up a few leaves to make something similar to a cup.

Will not God (who has given much more than instinct to animals) have taken care that there should be plenty of wisdom in store for the crown of His earthly creation?

God says, "My son, pay attention to my wisdom; lend your ear to my understanding" (Proverbs 5:1). Then you will have the light of life.

"Whatever things you ask in prayer, believing, you will receive."
MATTHEW 21:22

*T*his verse seems to blatantly contradict our experience. No man received from God everything he asked for in prayer.

I believe that most of us misunderstand these words of the Lord. We usually express in prayer not what we desire, but what we have desired before kneeling in prayer. We have no promise that these requests will be fulfilled. Jesus speaks about the desires that arise while you pray.

If prayer is really standing before the awesome majesty of God, bowing to Him and speaking with Him; if it is forgetting yourself in His inebriating embrace, all desires which you had before that moment will play no role in it. Only love remains—love to God and love for the eternal salvation of others. This prayer is one of adoration. God never refuses a deeper spirit of adoration to anyone who asks for it.

St. Catherine said toward the end of her life, "God, you know that for thirty-five years I have asked You for nothing." Whatever you desire in this attitude of heart is granted. Whatever, without restriction.

The bride in the Song of Solomon says, "I am lovesick!" (5:8). She asks for no medicine or miraculous healing. Martha and Mary sent word to Jesus that Lazarus was sick. They didn't ask Him to come and put His hand upon him. At the highest levels of faith, all desires cease except the desire of nearer union with Him. Such a desire will be fulfilled.

It would be terrible for us if God would give us everything we desired before prayer and expressed in prayer.

Shakespeare has written:

We, ignorant of ourselves, beg often our own harms,
Which the wise powers deny for our good,
So we find profit by losing our prayers.

SEPTEMBER 18

*"Naked I came from my mother's womb,
and naked shall I return there."*
JOB 1:21

*T*he following anecdote comes from the Soviet Union:

In the Ukraine, where meat is scarce, people stood in line the whole night in front of a butcher shop. In the morning, the director of the State store came out and said, "There will be only pork and even of this not much. So Jews should go home. Nothing for them." The Jews left.

After an hour, he came out again and said, "We were told that the quantity allotted to us will be reduced. So only those who work will get meat. Retired persons have to leave." These also left.

Two hours later came another announcement: "There will be very little meat. Only for the Party members. All the others go home."

A hundred Communists remained, wet because of a rain that had started to fall. An hour later the director told them, "We just received another telephone call. There will be no meat today."

One Communist exclaimed, "It is again the dirty Jews who are the profiteers." "What do you mean by this?" someone asked. "Well, they were the first to go home."

The story has a deep spiritual application. In the end we will all remain empty-handed. We stand in line in this world. When we leave it, we will not be able to take with us even a needle. All our possessions will remain behind. The profiteers, the privileged, are those who renounce them first.

Christians know that everything under the sun is vanity, that we have come into the world naked and that we will leave it the same way. They die to themselves before they die. They renounce what deceived everyone in the end. They go home first and spend their time in their home, in the realm of the Spirit.

*"Release those who through fear of death were
all their lifetime subject to bondage."*
HEBREWS 2:15

*I*n many Japanese homes you can find the hieroglyphs "Shinzo arau" (wash your heart or cleanse your soul) exhibited in the nicest place, though not many are still able to read these Chinese signs.

One of the many stains from which we have to cleanse ourselves is the illusion that we have here an abiding place.

A legend says that a woman with the name of Kishagotami told the Savior, "My only babe has died. I can't give him back to the earth. I asked everybody in vain for help. Now I have been sent to You and hope was given me that You can resurrect the dead. I cannot live without my child."

Jesus answered, "All right, I will bring your child back to life, but I need for this some salt. Bring it." She immediately ran toward the first house to ask for salt, but Jesus shouted after her, "Kishagotami, the salt must be from a house where no one has died." This condition, she thought, was not hard to accept.

She asked for salt in the first home. They were happy to serve her, but when asked, they said that their father had died recently. She ran to another home. There the wife had died. In the third home a child had died. Then her eyes opened and she understood what the Lord wanted to teach her.

She returned to Him and said, "I thank You for having taught me that there is no house in which no one has died. Give to my child and me life eternal."

The clinging to this earthly life, the fear of death, keeps us prisoners of the evil one. Accept the idea of your death and of the death of your beloved one as being as natural as that of life, and seek the resurrection that the Lord Jesus gives.

> *"They had handed Him over because of envy."*
> MATTHEW 27:18

*C*hampollion was a poor pupil in school, except at languages. At the age of eleven he had already learned Hebrew, Arabic, Syrian, Chaldean, Persian, and Coptic. All the other subjects in school were uninteresting to him. At the age of seventeen, he was already a member of the Academy, having become famous through his book, *Egypt Under the Pharaohs*. At the age of twenty, he was a university professor.

His great ambition was to decipher the Egyptian hieroglyphs. When he succeeded, he rushed into the house of a friend with the words, "I discovered," but fell in a swoon when this friend told him, "You are the second. Alexander Lenoir has already published a brochure with the translation of the old Egyptian signs." He discovered afterward that there was nothing to worry about. Lenoir's book was a hoax. However, Champollion's character had been disclosed. He himself might have believed that he worked purely in the interest of science. Not so. He was concerned with his own fame. He was not happy that someone else should bring his contribution to the same science. He was jealous. All of the discoveries must go under his name.

Champollion himself became the victim of envies later. He was even put in prison and denounced by colleagues who could not suffer someone else to have a big name.

The motives for the condemnation of Jesus were complex. One of the main motives was envy. Christ knew how to preach as no one else could. He did miracles. He was beloved, where others were only respected. He dared to be the Messiah, without having doctorates in divinity.

There is in every one of us a tendency to be envious. The envious will not inherit the kingdom of heaven.

"I press toward the goal."
PHILIPPIANS 3:14

I once listened to the testimony of a Norwegian lady, now over seventy, as she told how she had received Christ at the age of fourteen.

She had heard a sermon in which the pastor described the Last Judgment. God would sit on His white throne. Behind Him would be a curtain. Before Him in a line would be all those to be judged. God would make a sign with His hand and from behind the curtain would appear beings of unspeakable beauty, radiating with splendor, and one of these beings would stand before every accused. The men and women who had never seen such splendor before would ask God, "Who are these wonderful beings?"

God would answer, "These are each of you as you would have been if you had obeyed My voice."

Then men will realize what they have lost; and, ashamed, they will flee to hell, to escape the sight of the opportunity they rejected.

This illustration brought her to Christ. I heard it forty years ago. I used it often in my sermons and it brought others to the Savior. The sermon of the pastor still works a century after he died.

There is the real "I" and the ideal "I," the person I am and the person God conceived and planned and intended me to be. I can live my everyday life on the level of what is immediate, or I can run toward the goal, the ideal "I," the being that I have been predestined to become.

Let us be careful not to be ashamed on that day.

"As through one man's offense judgment came to all men, resulting in condemnation, even so through one Man's righteous act the free gift came to all men."
ROMANS 5:18

*S*howing a patient in a sanatorium a huge sycamore tree dead to its roots, a doctor told its story. It had been killed by one small worm.

"Two years ago the tree was as healthy as every other tree in the garden. One day I observed a worm three inches long that tried to penetrate its bark. A naturalist asked me not to kill or bother the worm. He wished to know how much time it would take the worm to destroy the tree. I complied and allowed the black-headed worm to do its work. It made a hole in the bark very quickly. Soon after this, the tree lost its leaves—much earlier than usual. One year later it was dead. The worm had penetrated to the heart of the tree."

Adam and Eve, having committed only one sin, lost Paradise because of this—paradise for themselves and their successors. Moses was excluded from the Promised Land for one sin. Many sit in prisons all their lives because of one wicked deed.

It is the same with righteousness as it is with sin. As one sin of a man can destroy him forever and have a deadly influence upon his children for many generations, so the one deed of Christ, suffering for us on the cross of Golgotha, glorified Him and also gave salvation to all those who believe in Him.

Don't discount as unimportant the one sin that still besets you. Put your faith in the one deed of Jesus Christ.

SEPTEMBER 23

*"The Word became flesh and dwelt among us,
full of grace and truth."*
JOHN 1:14

*A*n American Indian who had just arrived from a reservation attended a party in a nice Christian home in San Francisco. A heated debate went on about grace and law. The Indian listened, trying to understand. In the end he was enlightened and asked to be allowed to state his opinion.

"When I was at the train station," he said, "an ugly, old station, I saw a sign on which was written, 'Do not spit.' So I spit. Then I came to this beautiful house. Carpets, curtains, furniture, as I have never seen before. I looked around to see the sign forbidding me to spit. There was none. So I did not spit. The first case showed me the law, the second was grace."

No law, not even the law of God, can give life (Galatians 3:21). But what the law cannot do was done by God sending His Son in the flesh (Romans 8:3).

How can an inscription "Don't do this or that," even if it is written by the finger of God, keep a man from sinning when he is a sinner through and through? It only antagonizes his innate self-will.

The railway station is ugly and there is nothing attractive about it. So I amuse myself by spitting just because it is forbidden. But Christ brings me to another realm. He makes me to sit with Him in heavenly places. I am in the communion of saints and see around me only examples of love and beauty. No one forbids me anymore to spit. But why should I?

Pass from the sphere of law to that of grace.

*"You must continue in the things which you have
learned and been assured of."*
2 TIMOTHY 3:14

*M*any base their unbelief on the writings of Darwin. The only one who did not draw atheistic conclusions from his writings was Darwin himself.

It is said that Lady Hope, a British aristocrat, had been at his bedside often before he died. He was bedridden for a long time and assiduously studied the Bible. She asked him one day what he was reading.

"Hebrews!" he answered. "Still Hebrews. The Royal Book, I call it." Placing his finger on certain passages, he commented on them.

She made some allusions to the strong opinions expressed by many persons on this history of the Creation, its grandeur, and then their treatment of the earliest chapters of the Book of Genesis.

He seemed greatly distressed. His fingers twitched nervously, and a look of agony came over his face as he said, "I was a young man with unformed ideas. I threw out queries, suggestions, wondering all the time over everything; and to my astonishment the ideas took like wildfire. People made a religion of them."

Then he paused and said, "I have a summerhouse in the garden which holds about thirty people. It is over there," pointing through the open window. "I know you read the Bible in villages. Tomorrow afternoon I should like the servants and a few of the neighbors to gather there. Will you speak to them?"

"What shall I speak about?" she asked.

"Jesus Christ," he replied, "and His salvation. Is not that the best theme? And then I want you to sing some hymns with them. If you take the meeting at three o'clock this window will be open, and you will know that I am joining in with the singing."

Does the whole guilt really lie on one who was a young man with unformed ideas, or on the many scientists who have destroyed the faith of millions by holding up unsubstantiated theories?

Only what we will think on our deathbed counts. Don't be rash in your youth to elaborate theories and to act according to them. Seek the old path of righteousness.

"At the name of Jesus every knee should bow."
PHILIPPIANS 2:10

A young Brahmin came one day to the renowned missionary E. Stanley Jones and told him, "Your speeches have found much response. It would be good if you would preach Christ as one of the many ways. There are others, too. We love Krishna. Others love Kali. If you would accept this, all India would listen to you."

This temptation existed already at the beginning of Christianity. The Roman Empire was very tolerant toward religions. They gladly would have accepted Christ as one of the many gods in their pantheon—on the same footing as Diana, Mars, Apollo, Mithra, and the emperors. What led to the persecution of the first Christians was the insistence that Christ is the only way and that all the others are false.

Personally, I would like it very much if there could be many ways. However, in no regard is the universe constructed according to my wishes. Someone wiser than I, who knows better, has created it. I have to accept it. I have no other choice. I would like to have been born and raised in other circumstances. Again, my life has been predestined without my being consulted. I cannot decide how men should be saved. The Master of the universe has appointed only one way of salvation.

There is no arguing with Him. Receive Jesus Christ and you will be saved. Refuse Him, neglect Him, and you will be damned. It is as simple as this. God did not ask us about our tastes. We would like it if there would only be a heaven. There exists a hell, too. It is so easy for you to avoid it.

SEPTEMBER 26

"He who endures to the end shall be saved."
MATTHEW 24:13

One day a three-year-old child had given her mother a particularly hard day. After one more exasperating episode, the mother said, "Rebecca, I'm getting sick and tired of this!"

The child answered innocently, "Well, you'd better go to bed then."

Her answer was right. A Chinese proverb says, "The day you cannot smile, don't open your shop." I would add, "When you cannot smile anymore, close your shop." We are meant to be always nice and gentle. We cannot be so twenty-four hours a day. We sometimes come to the end of our rope. That is the right time to go to bed or to cease, at least, the opening of our mouths and the writing of letters.

We all have mutually exclusive desires. The same man might like to be handsome, well dressed, an ascetic, a millionaire, a warrior, a peaceful man, have all the pleasures of life, and be a saint. "The flesh lusts against the Spirit, and the Spirit against the flesh" (Galatians 5:17). Within the flesh and within the spirit, different tendencies tempt us. We cannot commit two contradictory sins, to be at the same time stingy and a squanderer. We cannot be two kinds of saints in one: a Joan of Arc and a hermit. "These are contrary to one another, so that you do not do the things that you wish."

William James said that you must review the options carefully and pick out the best.

If you have chosen to be a mother, be motherly to the end, never giving up, never getting sick and tired of what your child or your brother in faith does.

"A merry heart makes a cheerful countenance."
PROVERBS 15:13

*T*wo little boys who had never been to church peeked through the window while a prayer meeting was going on. It apparently was a dry service.

One boy asked the other, "What are they doing in there?"

The other boy replied, "I don't know, but whatever it is, they surely don't enjoy it."

On the contrary, a Hindu once asked a Christian, "What cream do you put on your face to make it shine?"

The man said, "Nothing."

The Hindu retorted, "Yes, you Christians do. Your faces shine."

The Christian religion has many shades. Choose the joyous one. Christians are saved by a deed, by what Christ did for us on Golgotha. May our religion be one of deeds, as that of Dorcas: a "woman . . . full of good works and charitable deeds which she did" (Acts 9:36). There is no better cream for making your face shine than a pure conscience, the knowledge that your response to Christ's deed has filled your own life to the brim with good deeds.

The religion a man has is less important than the man who has the religion. A ritual is less important for a soul than the soul he puts into the ritual. No religion or ritual will ever make you happy, if your whole personality is not in it. "Put on tender mercies, kindness, humility, meekness, longsuffering; bearing with one another, and forgiving one another" (Colossians 3:12,13). Your heart will become free and your countenance cheerful.

SEPTEMBER 28

"When he was yet a great way off, his father saw him and had compassion, and ran . . . and kissed him."
LUKE 15:20

*I*n a village a poor woman had an only daughter. She decided to make her a servant maid in town, hoping to buy a field from her earnings. The girl served in a rich home. She was beautiful and intelligent. She soon discovered that she could earn more by not working than by working. Soon the girl had a car, furs, jewels. However, she had lost her soul and had forgotten about her mother. Ten years passed like this, in parties and fun.

One night the remorse came. "How could I neglect Mother?" she asked herself. Driving immediately to her village, she arrived there after midnight. The gate to her house was wide open. She was sure her mother must be ill and the doctor had come. Crossing the yard, she saw the light burning in her mother's bedroom.

When she put her foot on the threshold, the voice of her mother asked, "June, is it you?"

"Yes," she replied. "How is it, mother, that the gate is wide open so late at night?"

"Since you left, ten years ago, I have never closed it."

The daughter asked again, "How is it, mother, that the lamp burns in your room so late at night?"

The mother replied, "It is because since you left, I have never turned it off. The heart of a loving mother waited for you."

The same will be your experience if, after having walked astray in sin for years, you return to the heavenly home. You will find the gate wide open and the light burning. God waits for your return with Fatherly compassion.

"There is no fear in love."
1 JOHN 4:18

A missionary to Indonesia tells the story of how the natives, being saved from sins, are saved also from fears that literally controlled their lives—such as the fear of continuing down the trail after hearing a certain bird call out from the jungle because it had special power from *iblis* (the devil). They would turn around and go home because they were afraid of the consequences.

There was also the fear of continuing to prepare a rice field prior to planting because they saw a snake. Thus, they would have to sacrifice a pig, rice, money, some chickens, or whatever the *dukun* (witch doctor) requested. If they could not afford to sacrifice to *iblis* they had to abandon the field, even if it was very fertile, or else pay the consequences.

Fear of crop failure haunted them if when they burned their field off, an animal got caught in the fire and died. They had to sacrifice to *iblis* or pay the consequences.

If they had fear of losing their sick child, they would make a *jimat*. This might be a little wooden block, a dove carved on top, a hole dug in from the front in which is placed a stone, and a wooden plug snugly closing the opening. The purpose is to hide the child's soul in the box (represented by the stone) from evil spirits with the dove guarding it.

We modern men don't have these fears, but we have many others of our own: the fear of losses in business, of remaining unemployed, the fear of sorrows, of wars, etc.

The words "don't fear" occur in the Bible 366 times, once for every day of the year. Even the extra day of leap year is covered. If we love God, we are as safe amid the tempests of life as in heaven, because all things work together for good (Romans 8:28). Every day of the calendar is covered. Don't fear.

"He who believes in Me, though he may die, he shall live."
JOHN 11:25

The great German industrialist, Krupp, produced weapons of war. He supplied many countries with the means of killing millions of men. He himself was haunted by the fear of death. His biographer says that he had forbidden the mention of dying in his home. When a relative died in his home, he fled from the house. He divorced his wife when she chided him for it.

When he became ill the last time, he offered to give the doctor a million marks if he could prolong his life for ten years. It was in vain.

How different from this is the attitude of the believer.

I know about the child of the caretaker of a cemetery. Asked if she was afraid to walk through it at night, she answered, "No, because my home is at its end." So we know that our home is at the end of the road on which we pass through death.

We sympathize with all those who strive for a better society, in which men will be richer, freer, happier. Suppose this ideal were fulfilled, who would be willing to die and forsake such a beautiful life? Happy men die with much more difficulty than the poor. The happy inhabitants of any future Utopia also will have to die.

Every party that doesn't give perpetual youth without old age and endless life without death, deceives. A rich life ending in death is like the banquet given to men sentenced to death before being executed.

Jesus has overcome death. He was resurrected from the grave. He gives life eternal. He is our only hope.

OCTOBER 1

"Seek those things which are above."
COLOSSIANS 3:1

A Christian put the inscription *Linquenda* on the front of his house, which means in Latin, "I will have to leave it."

It is good to remember that one day we will have to leave our business, our library, our loved ones, our body.

A beggar knocked at the gate of a rich man and asked for one night's lodging.

The rich man shouted, "I cannot let you in. This is not a hotel."

The beggar answered, "Please, forgive me. I will seek shelter somewhere else. Your house really impresses me by its beauty. I will not bother you, but please satisfy my curiosity. Who built this house?"

The rich man, friendlier now that he knew he would not have to put up with the stranger, replied, "My father built it."

"Very nice. Is he still alive?

"No, he died and I inherited it."

"Do you have children? Who will inherit it when you will die?"

"My eldest son. He just married. He will live in it after my decease."

The beggar then said, "Well, the house is just what I thought it to be—a hotel. It is the first time I saw a hotel owner getting angry when someone asked for a room."

All of our houses are hotels. I don't have the slightest idea who stayed in the house where I write these lines, before I entered it. I don't know who will succeed me. *Linquenda*—we will have to leave all.

Jesus came to invite us to an eternal abode, to His paradise. Detach your mind and your desires from the transitory. You will have to leave it all anyway.

279

OCTOBER 2

"Jesus said, 'Let the little children come to Me,
and do not forbid them.'"
MATTHEW 19:14

*B*efore finishing the complete sentence "Let the little children come to Me," the Lord had to say, "Let the little children come..." They had to be born before being able to come to Jesus.

The question is discussed with great debate today whether the embryo has the right to live. Does a human being once conceived have the right to be born, or should this right be voided through birth control pills? Abortionists and birth planners base their arguments on overpopulation, poverty, and much suffering.

I believe that the problem is not whether the embryo has the right to exist. I would ask rather whether nuclear weapons, hunger, and poverty have a right to exist. A revolution must come in this regard. I am only against revolutionists who are resolute to kill others and to die themselves if necessary, but who have no idea how to change society.

The United States is one of the richest countries in the world. It is first in the world in the percentage of churchgoers, yet the proportion of the total American gross national product which goes for economic aid ranks below that of other free-world nations, according to the World Bank.

We know the secret of successful revolution: perfect love. The determination with which terrorists pursue their wicked deeds is the one thing lacking among those whose weapon is love. Only then will the danger of nuclear war be gone, and the worst aspects of poverty and hunger, too. Why should children then not come into the world in order to come to Him?

OCTOBER 3

*P*aul said to a sorcerer named Elymas, "O full of all deceit and all fraud, you son of the devil," and he cursed him to blindness (Acts 13:10,11). Paul would have sinned if he had been meek toward an enemy of righteousness.

Luther wrote to a duke who opposed the Word: "Ass of all asses, bloody dog, lying mouth, thick sausage, son of the devil." In a later letter he expresses his wonder that he could have written so gently and explains: "A Christian is a man who has hatred and enmity against nobody, but nurtures only love and goodness; but a preacher must have guts, must bite salt, and say the whole truth, because this is what the Word of God does. It hurts the whole world; it puts its hand into the throats of rulers and princes; it thunders and lightens and assaults big mountains... As far as I am concerned, I would do no harm and say nothing against any man, but as regards the enemies of the Word of God, you should know no friendships and no love."

Christians must be fighters against evil in the church and in the world. They must fight for justice in society, for peace and progress. "The kingdom of heaven suffers violence" (Matthew 11:12).

The Christian does not indulge in small conflicts. He would not quarrel with his wife or neighbor, but when he has to fight the evil that has penetrated the church, he must always have before him the image of Jesus with the whip in His hand. He must hit and not have remorse. Jesus never apologized to the merchants He had driven out. Hatred toward sin cannot be expressed in dignified words, as love cannot be cold and formal. There can be no politeness toward sin. Love the sinner and awaken him through striking ruthlessly at his sinfulness.

OCTOBER 4

"[The Israelites] from whom, according to the flesh, Christ came, who is over all, the eternally blessed God."
ROMANS 9:5

*I*n a Soviet jail, a Christian prisoner, A. Petrov, wrote a poem called "If I Were a Jew." Here are some excerpts from it in prose.

If I were a Jew, I would never call myself something else.
We're all brethren. We have our Parises and Romes and Washingtons,
But Israel, it is unique.
Israel is Cain and at the same time Abel, it is servant and master.
From Israel comes freedom and truth and the greatest of sins and the deepest repentance.
Israel is the beginning and end—a miracle—from there comes the salvation for all.
If I were a Jew! By the way, this is what everyone should be, judging and slandering nobody,
Bringing honor to our homeland and nation.
The Jews are the salt, the sense, the essence of things.
Remember, you are the descendants of men like David. The Lord came from you.
Don't spare your forces. In fights, temptations and tempests, In days of triumph and of great sorrows,
Be worthy of your great predecessors, remember that you are a Jew.
Oh, if I were a Jew.

Is it really something special to be a Jew, a member of the chosen people, to have a capital city whose name our heavenly abode also bears, the Jerusalem above? We should be thankful to God that "he is not a Jew who is one outwardly, . . . he is a Jew who is one inwardly . . . whose praise is not from men but from God" (Romans 2:28,29).

Let us bear with joy the beautiful name of Israelites, let us love Israel, the Jewish nation, the Hebrew Christians. Let us remember also that we, having been grafted into the olive tree of Israel, now have a duty to add fame to the beautiful name "Jew" which has been given to us all.

OCTOBER 5

"We also ought to lay down our lives for the brethren."
1 JOHN 3:16

*I*n Boston, a statue honors Mary Dyer, a Quaker who was twice imprisoned, twice exiled, and finally hanged for her faith.

It happened in the seventeenth century. Massachusetts was ruled by Puritans. They were so pure that they could not tolerate Christians who believed in inward light, in direct communication with God, without the intermediary of a clergy or rituals. So a law was passed that every Quaker coming into the colony would be "soundly whipped, jailed, and kept at hard labor during imprisonment." A man who, although not himself a Quaker, had defended a Quaker assaulted by a zealous Puritan, was whipped and exiled. Any Quaker who converted someone had to be exiled, and if he returned, hanged.

Mary Dyer came from Rhode Island to Boston to visit some imprisoned Quakers. She was flogged and exiled with the threat of death should she return. Three months later she was back, to care for her imprisoned brethren. She and two fellow believers were sentenced to be hanged. Mary watched their execution. Then her hands were bound, her face hooded. She ascended the ladder and put her head in the hangman's noose. At the last moment she was pardoned, but banished.

She returned. She knew she had brethren in jail. She risked public flogging and having her tongue pierced through with a hot iron.

Brought before the court, she said, "If you do not repeal your unrighteous laws, after my death the Lord will send others to witness for the truth. My life means nothing in comparison to the liberty of the truth."

There are thousands of brothers and sisters in prisons today in various countries for their faith. We should also be ready to give our lives for them.

OCTOBER 6

"He needed to go through Samaria."
JOHN 4:4

When the bulk of the Jewish people were led into the Babylonian captivity, the remainder left in Samaria intermarried with the new settlers placed in their land by the oppressors and practiced a mixture of Jewish and heathen religion. When the Jews returned from captivity, they despised these people called Samaritans.

The animosity was so great that Jews and Samaritans would not give each other a glass of water. The Talmud taught that to eat bread from a Samaritan was as sinful as to eat pork; that Samaritans had no part in eternal life. Samaritans were considered as devils.

The capital of Samaria was called Shechem. The Jews gave it the nickname "Sichar," which meant "drunkard," as if they themselves had no drunkards.

Jews avoided passing through Samaria. Jesus, though Jewish, purposely went to Samaria. He stood on the side of those hated and despised by His religion. In Jericho, He chose as host Zacchaeus, a tax gatherer despised by the population.

We hurt ourselves when we hate or despise someone. By doing so, we place Jesus on that person's side.

Don't listen to the arguments brought by your mind to justify contempt toward a fellow man. Jesus is the friend of sinners. Be their friend, too.

OCTOBER 7

"Lord, do not trouble Yourself."
LUKE 7:6

*T*he state of the world would be less of a riddle to us if we would understand that it was created by a sad God. It was created just after the fall of a beloved archangel, Lucifer, who had drawn with him in rebellion one-third of the host of angels.

We could understand the relationship between divinity and the world better if we would meditate on the fact that we have a troubled and weary God. God says through Isaiah, "Your New Moons and your appointed feasts My soul hates; they are a trouble to Me" (1:14). Isaiah also wrote, "Is it a small thing for you to weary men, but will you weary my God also?" (7:13).

We always ask God for comfort and deliverance from our troubles, which is all right, but what about reciprocating sometimes and being a comfort to Him?

St. Therese of Lisieux surprised a young nun complaining to another about some sorrow she had. Therese advised her not to do so anymore, not to burden someone else's heart. This nun answered, "You are right. Henceforth I will tell my troubles to Jesus alone."

"Oh, no, not to Him," Therese replied. "Has He not had trouble enough? Keep your sadness for yourself. Give Him rest."

She herself had the habit of laying her crucifix on the pillow in the mornings and saying to Jesus, "You rest now. I will work for You."

God has saved us. Let us save Him, too, from more sadness and weariness than what He already has.

"Let all . . . evil speaking be put away from you."
EPHESIANS 4:31

*D*e *mortuis nihil nise bene*—"Speak nothing about dead men except good." This is a wrong precept. Historic accuracy and justice and the need to learn from other men's mischiefs oblige us sometimes to tell their sins. This proverb dates from the times when people feared the revenge of the spirits.

I would say we should rather determine not to speak evil of the living. The Bible prescribes fixed rules for cases when something blamable is found in a man. The first thing is that you should love a man in spite of his sins. Only lovers are allowed to blame and to criticize. Second, you must tell him first what you find wrong in him. If he refuses your advice, bring others to help you persuade him. Then speak with his church. In cases of public sins, you might be obliged sometimes to press the issue publicly, but never become a slanderer or a detractor.

Slander is an old vice. It preceded the appearance of man. The devil is the "accuser of our brethren" (Revelation 12:10). He accused us before we committed sins, asking that we should not be created.

Jesus was killed by slander. Lies were spread about Him that He was Samaritan, that He had a devil, that He broke the laws and was a blasphemer. Knowing that slander crucified Christ, Christians should abstain from it and never listen to it.

OCTOBER 9

"God has chosen the foolish things of the world."
1 CORINTHIANS 1:27

*M*any people have passed through depressions, neuroses, and psychoses. Some have passed a time in asylums. When they return to normal, they feel branded for life. They know that they have been "mental cases" and feel that those around them might not pay attention to their ideas because of this.

I can speak as one who has lived among many who have passed through states of madness as a result of tortures and doping in Communist prisons. There is no motive to feel badly about a past and not even about an actual "mental case." Bear your state with easy heart if this is your predicament or comfort others who are in it.

Adolf Wölfli's drawings have been exhibited in all of Europe. Innumerable books and studies have been written about his art, because Wölfli was not only a painter who achieved fame, but he was also a writer and a musical composer.

Adolf's father died because of alcoholism when the child was seven. His mother died soon afterward. At age ten, Adolf had to earn his own living. At age thirty he was put in a hospital for lunatics after having tried to rape a girl of three. Wölfli stayed in this asylum thirty-five years and died there in 1930. He never had schooling. No one taught him to draw or paint. He had no occasion for self-education except the few books of the asylum's library and a few musical notes in its possession.

If men, using well the natural gifts of God, can overcome schizophrenia and become useful, even remarkable members of society, even more those who have the Holy Spirit should be able to do so.

If you have been or still are "out of your mind," perhaps it is God who has afflicted you (Ruth 1:20,21). Job has shown that God who takes away can restore sevenfold what you have lost. Madness is not only a liability, it is an asset, too.

You might not be artistically inclined, but you can become a useful member of your family and of the church.

*B*e careful about the music you hear. Rock music can be deadly. The revelation of God consists not only of letters. The Hebrew Bible contains also musical signs. It is not meant to be read, but chanted according to a specific melody. The same word might have different meanings according to the pitch on which this word is sung. Only with its melody does the Bible contain the complete revelation of God.

There is also evil, obscene, and morally corrupting music. Giants like Cervantes, Goethe, and Tolstoy were shocked at the immorality of some music. There is music that wrecks homes today. Understanding between two generations becomes impossible if they listen to types of music that are so contrary to each other. Neither is all of the classical music good. Tolstoy believed that no one listening to Beethoven's *Kreutzer Sonata* could possibly withstand the erotic suggestiveness of the music. Their morals would be in jeopardy and the inevitable would happen, if occasion arose.

It is terrible to hear the beautiful music in Verdi's *Othello* when the Moor chokes Desdemona. You hear Strauss's electrifying music when Salome stripteases and demands the severed head of John the Baptist. Most opera plots could have been written by members of the Mafia. Crime is propagated on the stage, crime accompanied by heavenly music.

People hear Beethoven's *Passion According to St. Matthew*, and whisper to each other, while the artist sings about the whipping of Jesus, "How beautiful a melody."

Many sins are strengthened in our souls this way. Therefore, Christians are careful about the deceit of music.

Jesus went to Gethsemane singing. Sing His tunes. Listen only to music pleasant to God.

"Take, eat; this is My body."
MATTHEW 26:26

*D*uring World War I, almost two million Armenians were martyred for their faith and nationality by the Turks.

At Der es Zor a group of Armenians stood before the firing squad. One of them, Mavy, told the soldiers, "It is written in your Koran that you should not kill anybody without allowing him first to worship his God." Mavy was granted his request.

He gave a short message from Revelation 2:10: "Do not fear any of those things which you are about to suffer...Be faithful until death, and I will give you the crown of life." They sang together and took communion. They had no bread, but distributed some of the glowing sand from the ground saying, "Take and eat. This is My body." Everyone swallowed some sand. Then they were shot. Those who did not die instantly dipped their fingers in their blood. While dying Mavy told them, "Take and drink this. This is My blood given for you."

Christ is a being with two natures: a human and a divine one. He also has two bodies. He has the body of a Jewish carpenter which, after death, was glorified and ascended to heaven, as well as the church, which is also His body. When during communion the words are said, "Eat; this is My body," both bodies are meant. Jesus suffered and bled 2,000 years ago in Palestine in His limited body. It is He Himself who suffers and bleeds also in all those who bleed for Him. They took communion with their own blood, which was also His blood.

You are a member of His body. Behave as such.

OCTOBER 12

*H*ow many years of life do we still have?

A king gave to his clown a marshal's baton and told him, "I nominate you as marshal of the fools. If you ever find one who is more foolish than you, hand it to him."

Years passed. The king was on his deathbed. The clown asked him, "Do you know where you will go?"

"No," answered the king. "I know only that I must die."

"So there is a 'must' for kings, too. Did you store for yourself some riches in the world beyond to which you go?"

"I never thought about it."

"You knew that you would have to die and, notwithstanding, you made no definite choice? You did not prepare for heaven? You did not avoid hell?"

"I never took time even to ponder deeply about these things."

The clown took the baton from the sleeve in which he had hidden it, and returned it to the king. "Now I nominate you as marshal of the fools."

Remember that you will die, and that you do not know when this will happen.

OCTOBER 13

"Nor did we seek glory from men, either from you or from others, when we might have made demands as apostles of Christ."
1 THESSALONIANS 2:6

A Christian is supposed to be humble and submissive. When hit on one cheek he turns the other. The canvas never quarrels with the painter. He is free to paint on it what he likes, be it a beggar or a king. The Christian accepts any condition in life as coming from God. If he is successful, he does not boast of it. Can a brush boast that a beautiful picture has been drawn with it? Only the master painter deserves glory. Such is our relationship with Christ. A Christian seeks glory from no one.

Christ was humble, as was Paul, though their humility had a special feature: it was difficult to make others understand it. Jesus had to say: "I do not seek My own glory" (John 8:50), and, "I am gentle and lowly in heart" (Matthew 11:29). Paul also had to assure men that he sought no glory. Normally, a humble man does not go around boasting about his humility. It is only when he makes an impression of great pride, or even arrogance, that he has to explain what is in him.

A Christian is humble in his own affairs, yet he is sure that he has a message from God. This he asserts with full authority, ready to contend with anyone, even to the point of being considered burdensome or annoying, or giving the impression of being an "I-know-better" man. Apostles of Christ might be burdensome (1 Thessalonians 2:6). Paul was such when he wrote that he sought no glory from men.

Know how to exercise authority in God's service.

OCTOBER 14

"Love your enemies."
LUKE 6:35

*H*ere are some true stories from Romania that show how persecuted Christians are following this teaching of Jesus today.

B. had been a Communist state prosecutor. He fell out of the good graces of the Party and was imprisoned by his own comrades. Once he was transferred from a prison where hunger reigned to a mine where the prisoners were given more food since they had to do hard slave labor. At the prison gate he was met by a stranger who immediately gave him something to eat. The stranger sat near him while he ate. He asked the stranger for how long he was sentenced. The answer was twenty years.

"What for?"

"For having given some food to a fugitive pastor sought by the police."

"Who gave you such punishment for a good deed?"

"You were the state prosecutor at my trial. You did not recognize me, but I recognized you. I am a Christian. Christ taught us to reward evil with good. I wished to teach you that it is right to give food to a hungry man."

Dr. Munteanu's father, an Orthodox dean in Romania, had been killed for being a priest. The doctor eventually ended up in prison with the murderers of his father. When the murderers fell sick, he gave them not only medical care, but also his own food.

The Christian Tsotsea had been sentenced unjustly to twenty years in prison. After awhile, the judge who sentenced him was also imprisoned and fell deathly sick. His disease was repulsive. His waste and urine had to be washed away continually under prison conditions, without running water, cotton, or sheets. Tsotsea, the victim, loved his enemy and cared for him as for a brother until the judge died, reconciled to God and forgiven.

*"Whether it is right in the sight of God to listen to you
more than to God, you judge."*
ACTS 4:19

*P*sychological experiments at Yale University demonstrated the dismaying extent to which ordinary men will obey authority, even to the point of inflicting excruciating pain upon another person for whom they have no personal feelings.

A shock machine and three persons were the setting for this experiment. The experimenter was the authority figure. An actor, posing as a pupil, was in collusion with the experimenter. The third party—the subject of the experiment—was made to believe that he was teaching the pupil.

The electric shock machine looked authentic. It had switches labeled from fifteen to four hundred fifteen volts with the designations "Slight shock," "Strong shock," "Danger: severe shock." The last switch bore the label "XXX." The machine was fake; it gave no shocks to the actor who played the part of the pupil.

The one doing the teaching had to instruct "the learner" in several simple things and then examine him. If "the learner" gave the wrong answer, the subject of experiment, "the teacher," had to shock him, first slightly and then stronger and stronger. The actor screamed, shouted, complained of his heart, and feigned to fall in swoon. "The teacher" could think only that it was all real.

The experimenter would order strong shocks and suggest to the teacher that he must continue in spite of the pain he inflicted upon "the learner."

Two-thirds of the subjects at Yale obeyed the experimenter. They were not impressed by the pain shown by "the learner." They had an order and fulfilled it. In Germany, 85 percent of the subjects obeyed authority.

Christians obey authority only if it does not order something contrary to the law of love given by God. For this independence of mind, Christians are hated by beastly rulers. We should never give up our independence. Otherwise, we could become accomplices of criminals.

"Sarai said to Abram, '... Please, go in to my maid; perhaps I shall obtain children by her.' And Abram heeded the voice of Sarai."
GENESIS 16:2

C ommenting on this verse, the Talmud says that Abram yielded to the authoritative voice with which Sarai requested him to take a servant maid as concubine.

The words "heeded the voice" can be expressed in Hebrew in three ways: *shamoa bekol, shamoa el kol,* and *shamoa lekol. Lekol* is used generally only when one has to consent to what is dictated to him. The Midrash, another Jewish commentary, referring to Genesis 3:17, where God says to Adam, "You have heeded the voice of your wife," explains that Eve, too, has taken a domineering attitude toward him and had imposed her will. So Adam ate the forbidden fruit. This commentary is based on the fact that the term used for heeding the voice is, in both cases, *shamoa lekol.*

You can easily discover that someone wishes to tempt you to sin by the fact that he exercises authority in his manner of speech.

The Lord Jesus said, "The rulers of the Gentiles lord it over them, and those who are great exercise authority over them . . . ; but whoever desires to become great among you, let him be your servant" (Matthew 20:25,26). A servant entreats you humbly to do something; he never commands. You heed the voice out of love or you consider the wisdom of the advice, not because you fear that the person might give you a hard time. The lover leaves you the freedom of choice.

Christians should not yield to the big tyrants, neither to the little tyrannies exercised over them in daily life.

*A*n infidel mocked Christianity. One of his arguments was the bad behavior of some believers. One of these answered, "Did you ever meet anyone who wondered about the bad behavior of atheists?"

The infidel answered, "No."

"Well, this is the whole difference," said the believer.

Christianity teaches the highest moral and spiritual standard of living. Christ was Himself the example of how a life should be lived. It is normal that men born in sin, no matter how hard they try, should fail in their endeavors and that there should often be a discrepancy between the high principles proclaimed and our few achievements.

Atheism has no principles of conduct. Marx wrote in the *Communist Manifesto* that he wished the abrogation not only of all religion, but also of all morals. Where there are no morals, there can be no inconsistency.

For us it is an honor to be mocked on this account. We are sorry for our sinfulness. The fact that, though climbing, we are still far from our goal, shows that we are among that part of mankind which has set for itself the highest aim.

Join us. If we become a larger party climbing together, we may succeed better.

"Avoid ... opposition of science falsely so called."
1 TIMOTHY 6:20 (KJV)

Never allow science to disturb your faith. Science that does not admit the miraculous is not scientific.

In physics, there exists the law of Charles. According to this law, the volume of an ideal gas under constant pressure is directly proportional to the absolute temperature. Since for each degree centigrade of temperature that the ideal gas drops at constant pressure, it loses $1/273$ of its volume, at -273° C, the ideal gas would have zero volume. But this does not happen. First of all because absolute zero has not been achieved, but also because a phase change occurs before it is reached. Balloons made the observation that the pressure-temperature curve drops smoothly as the altitude rises to 40,000 feet, where the thermometer stands at -67° F.

The scientist has to accept either that beyond 40,000 feet a miracle happens, the natural law is transgressed, the law of Charles is broken; or he has to plead that another law, yet unknown, intervenes when the law of Charles leaves off.

In the first case, he concedes that miracles happen. The miracle of the resurrection of Jesus is possible then, too. If the scientist chooses the other alternative, that laws still unknown account for some experiences, then some laws still unknown may account for the miracles of the Bible, too.

Believe the Bible. No science can contradict it.

*"[Life] is even a vapor that appears for a little time
and then vanishes away."*
JAMES 4:14

W hen you feel important, when you are on an ego trip, when you are inclined to believe that you are the navel of the earth and cannot be replaced, dip your hand into a bucket of water. When you have pulled it out and looked for the hole it left, you will know exactly the measure of your indispensability. The water does not keep even a trace of the fact that your hand was in it.

I have known important Christians who played a big role in church work. They were put in prison under totalitarian regimes. When they were freed, they found out that the church had fared without them as well as with them. In some cases their absence gave younger and more capable men the possibility to develop better.

Jesus, the Son of God, lay in a grave. The planets continued their courses. Flowers bloomed and children played. Jesus left the world for a little while without Himself, to encourage us to do the same, to feel a little bit less important. Then He resurrected and He had entirely new powers.

The saints were saints because they did not consider their staying in this world as absolutely necessary. Knowing that he could go, without the church suffering because of this, Basil the Great could answer the persecutor, Modest, "I don't fear deportation because the whole earth is the Lord's. You have no treasure to take away from me. I possess nothing. To die is gain for me, because this will unite me with Christ for whom I live and work."

By not considering themselves important, the saints became important.

> *"I urge you, imitate me."*
> 1 CORINTHIANS 4:16

One evening a father went to a saloon. Soon his little boy joined him. "How did you find out where I was?" asked the father.

The boy answered, "I just followed your steps in the snow."

The apple does not fall far from the branch. Our dependents follow in our steps. Where do our steps lead?

I stood once at the gate of a prison in which a criminal sentenced to life was detained with chains on his hands and feet because he was considered very dangerous. A police van bringing new convicts stopped before the gate. Among them was the son of the criminal, himself also a murderer sentenced to life, kept also with chains on hands and feet. Father and son met there.

The son lifted his chained hands toward the father and asked him, "Was it for this that you brought me into the world?"

The hardened criminal blushed and let his head drop. He did not answer a word.

Where do our steps lead?

We think about the traces that Abraham's walk left. After thousands of years Judaism, Christianity, and Islam still walk in these steps. Winds and floods could not wipe them away. Paul walked in the bloodstained steps of Christ in self-sacrifice. For two thousand years Christians could follow his example.

Be careful of your steps. You will not be the only one to walk in them.

"O Timothy! Guard what was committed to your trust."
1 TIMOTHY 6:20

One of the great losses of the church after the Reformation was the forgetting of the beautiful teachings and examples of the saints of old.

They were humble. When at the Second Ecumenical Council quarrels arose about his being bishop of Constantinople, John Chrysostom said, "I am not better than Jonah, the prophet. Throw me into the sea, only let the strife finish." He withdrew forever from the bishopric, quoting to his parishioners as his last words 1 Timothy 6:20.

He was ready to renounce everything, but he would not yield an inch from the truth. He left us the teaching: "There are splendid divergences as well as harmonious concord...When we are required to act with obvious dishonesty, or with violence and the sword, we must disregard the requirements of the times and rulers (I dare say, not only of secular, but also of church rulers); we must not have communion with evil. We should not touch the contagious. The most horrible thing for a servant of truth is to fear anything more than God, and because of this fear to become a traitor to the faith and the truth."

John Chrysostom was a preacher, though not in the modern sense of the word—one who delivers a speech for twenty minutes once a week—but he daily called men to repentance. He did not spare his audience. He spoke out against shameful dress, against luxury, among other things, but most of all against the clergy's love of power and against divisions in the church. He said, "Nothing provokes God to wrath more than strife. Even if we do the most perfect works, but destroy the unity, we will be punished as if we had torn apart the body of the Lord."

In exile, he finished his life with the words, "God be praised for everything."

OCTOBER 22

"Walk in love, as Christ also has loved us."
EPHESIANS 5:2

*I*n 1969 the Christians in Kenya had a difficult time. They had refused to take the heathen oath of the Kikuyu tribe. Many were stabbed because of this. Others were beaten to death. This had happened to a brother whose wife, also beaten, was lying in the hospital. She was brought from the hospital to his burial attended by a thousand people, among them some who had hated the deceased.

The wounded wife stood near the grave of her husband. The believers sang Christian hymns. Then the widow spoke. Her speech was published the next day in the newspaper.

> Before we finish this burial service, I wish to tell you what my husband told me before dying. He asked me to tell all his murderers that he goes to heaven loving wholeheartedly everybody, his assassins, too. He has forgiven all for what they have done, because Jesus loves them. I, as his widow, also tell all of you, in the presence of my dead husband, that I hate none of those who killed him. I love the killers. I forgive them, knowing that Christ has died for them, too.

This is Christian forgiveness. Make a precise, written list of all men who have ever wronged you. Write over it in large letters, "Jesus loves them." Then burn the list and forgive once and forever all those who have harmed you. Remember how many you have hurt. To bear a grudge is not the Christian way.

"Each one's work will become manifest."
1 CORINTHIANS 3:13

*E*instein, who discovered the last laws in physics, and whose name our universe respects, declared at the end of his life, "If I had known, I should have been a plumber." It was because he had not known how to conceal some of his science from wicked men. His formula served as the basis for the construction of the first atomic bomb.

How unlike this is the conclusion that Paul draws at the end of his life: "There is laid up for me the crown of righteousness" (2 Timothy 4:8).

Like Einstein, Paul had discovered a mystery: that the Gentiles are called into the kingdom and given the same standing as the chosen people, the Jews. He also had other divine mysteries entrusted to him from God. They were all beneficial. He did not have to regret that he had made them known to the world.

As a result of the activity of scientists who did not seek guidance from God concerning how much to reveal to sinful mankind, today the radioactivity in the world is thirty-five times higher than it was in the beginning of the century. Scientists may have contradicted religion. The problem arises now whether mankind will be able to survive the victory of a godless science. The air, our rivers, and the seas are all polluted.

As a result of the activity of every Christian who witnesses for his Lord, multitudes of men pass from transitory life to life eternal.

Will you regret at the end of your life what you have done, or do you serve Christ and are you sure that your end will be a change to glory?

"Woe to you, scribes and Pharisees, hypocrites!"
MATTHEW 23:13

*T*he Lord Jesus scolded the hypocrites, and He told us to beware of hypocrisy. He never told us, however, not to be in their company.

Many Christians have forsaken the church, complaining that there is too much hypocrisy in it. Business is full of hypocrites, too, but no one stops making money because of that. The relationship between sexes, generations, and nations is full of hypocrisy. Notwithstanding, people fall in love, cohabit with children and parents. Nations coexist. How many remain bachelors and spinsters because married life is full of hypocrites?

One place is surely full of hypocrites. It is hell. Instead of not going to church because you cannot suffer those who only pretend to be religious, you had better beware that you don't go to hell which is full of men with false hearts. In church you are with the hypocrites for only an hour; in hell for eternity.

If you loathe hypocrisy, then take decided steps to get to heaven, the only place where full sincerity reigns.

There is no salvation outside the church, in spite of its many human failures. He who has God as his Father has the church as his "mother." A loving child does not forsake his mother when she falls sick. Neither does a Christian forsake the church because he finds in her some faults. She is the keeper of the Word of God and of the ordinances. In her, the communion of the saints is fulfilled.

Regarding hypocrisy, it is best not to look at the speck in your brother's eyes, but rather to take out the plank from your own.

"The mercy of the LORD is from everlasting to everlasting."
PSALM 103:17

*T*he first letter of the Hebrew alphabet is *aleph*. It is in the form of a man who is pointing to heaven and earth in order to show that the world below is the mirror of the world above.

George Cantor, a mathematical genius who died mad, introduced the *aleph* in mathematics as the symbol of the transfinite.

What is this transfinite? Draw on a piece of paper a line of ten inches. Everyone knows that the number of points on this line is infinite. Cantor says, "Obviously no." Cut the line into ten pieces. Every line of one inch has an infinite number of points, so the number of points on the first line must have been bigger than infinity, a multitude of infinites which he calls the transfinite. Only so can we understand the expression of the Bible, "from everlasting to everlasting." There exists a multiple of eternities.

The number *aleph* is the only one that is equal to each of its parts. The number of points on the first line is as big as the number of points on every segment of it, because these can be divided, too. Any part is equal to the whole. A Jewish carpenter said to an apostle, "He who has seen me has seen the Father" (John 14:9). The one Christ can be "the all in all." He is in His entirety in every believing soul.

The first Christians had the proverb, "When you see a brother, you see God." Luther wrote, "The Christian is Christ." The Lord has taught that as often as you are good to a hungry and suffering man, you do your good deeds to Him. He Himself was the hungry or imprisoned person.

This seems absurd to reason. It is a truth of faith and, since recently, a mathematical commonplace.

OCTOBER 26

"O Death, where is your sting?"
1 CORINTHIANS 15:55

There is an old Christian story, kept in secrecy for the elect only. They hear it from a man or from an angel only in moments of supreme suffering.

A believer had devoted his whole life to seeking revelation in nature, in the faces of men, and within his own heart. He sought the sense of the ineffable name Jehovah. Approaching old age, he was condemned for his faith and was to be devoured by a leopard.

While waiting in the arena of the circus, he observed through iron bars the wild beast to which he had been assigned for food. He gazed at the spots of its skin, and behold, a wonder. The rhythm of their design and their pattern explained to him the sense of the name of God for which he had been seeking for decades. At once he understood why he had to be sentenced to this cruel death. It was because this was the only means to fulfill his great wish. God had granted him this meeting with the leopard bearing the secret.

The martyr knew then that such a death was no death.

We all will be swallowed up by death in some manner. The question is, "What have you been looking for in life?" If you have looked for the right thing, death will reveal to you the mystery, and it will be just a veil through which you will enter into the presence of the Lord. This applies not only to death, but also to every great suffering. Seek in its forms the name of God.

*E*very army has had an elite force: the Persian Immortals, the American Green Berets, the German SS, the Soviet Gvardia. The Kamikaze pilots of Japan are probably the best known. They would have a funeral service while alive. After they had entered the cockpit of the aircraft, it would be sealed from the outside. Then they would fly toward some enemy ship and crash with their load of bombs into the ship. It was certain they would die, but they also would destroy many of the foe.

It is as though Jesus had put Himself inside the cockpit of a Kamikaze aircraft. He went knowingly and decidedly to die on the cross for sinners.

We also bring our lives as a living sacrifice to God (Romans 12:1); our baptism is our burial service. We are buried with Christ. Only those who pass through this experience belong to the elite of the church, because having shared Christ's passion they also will know the power of His resurrection.

In 1955, a Professor Singleton showed during an atomic conference in Geneva some carnations which he had grown in the radioactive field of the great nuclear reactor at Brookhaven. They had been white. Now they were a purple-red, a hitherto unknown species. All their cells had been modified and they would continue in their new state.

So is the new man resurrected with Jesus, an avante guard fighter for the cause of the kingdom of God.

OCTOBER 28

"It is no longer I who live, but Christ lives in me."
GALATIANS 2:20

God has given us a great gift: to be personalities on our own. Personality is not a part of the universe. The universe is a part of everything that the personality comprehends. This is because the universe, the energy, and whatever material entities may exist are objects of thoughts. Personality is not an object. It always remains the subject.

Jesus has said, "I am the way, the truth, and the life" (John 14:6). An "I," a divine subject, has pronounced these words. On the basis of these words, we have asserted for 2,000 years that *He* is the way, the truth, and the life, which simply is not true. When we reduce Him to a "He," Christ has become an object of our reflections. An object cannot be the truth. Jesus never wanted to become a "He." Jesus is always an "I." Jesus lives in His fullness as an "I" in every believer. The believer is an "I" also—the same "I" as Jesus. The eyes with which Jesus sees me and my eyes are the same eyes.

A lover knocked at the door of his sweetheart late at night and asked for entrance. "Who is there?" she called.

He answered, "It is I."

The girl from inside responded, "My room is strait and my bed is narrow. I have no room for you. Leave."

He left, not understanding why she had refused him. He knew she loved him dearly. After wandering the world for several years, he had an illumination. One night he knocked again at the door.

She asked, "Who is there?"

He answered, "It is you."

Then the door opened. He heard the words, "For years I have been waiting for you."

When we arrive at the gate of heaven, we must be free people —free from being one of the many objects of this world. We must have become a personality on our own, an "I," but this "I" must have become His "I," a reappearance of Jesus in miniature. We must be able to say at the gate to Jesus, "It is You." Then the door will be wide open for us.

"You do not do the things that you wish."
GALATIANS 5:17

A soldier made great plans how he would fight the foe and conquer him, but when he tried to stretch out his rifle, he found that he could not. When making his plans, he had forgotten to find out first who he was. He was a soldier—but a paper soldier with whom children played.

Many of us make beautiful plans for a life of service to the Lord and mankind. They are futile. We have forgotten that we are born in sin and shaped in iniquity, that even our good deeds are like dirty rags; that we have within us powers incapacitating us so we cannot fulfill beautiful designs. We are no more than toys in the hands of evil forces and of base lusts. We are paper soldiers. Before doing real things, we must become soldiers of flesh and blood.

This miracle is accomplished by Jesus. He gives us new birth. He tells us to eat His flesh and to drink His blood.

He makes us partakers of His spiritual divine nature. He gives us new life, the strength of His grace.

He makes a paper soldier into a real one and only then can the fight begin.

A smith had a son who broke his heart. Every time the son did something wrong, the father would hammer a nail in the door. In time, the whole door was full of nails. The son heard of this in the distant land where he had gone. He was plagued with regrets and it caused him to ask forgiveness from his father. The first nail was taken out of the door. Then the son returned to God and news began to flow about the good deeds done by the same son. At every such news, the father pulled from the door another nail.

One day the son returned as an honest man, yes, as a saint. He became the joy of his father. The last nail disappeared. The father showed the son the door and explained to him what had happened.

The son said, "Yes, the nails are gone, but the holes have remained."

The father was happy to tell the son that there is One who also can close the holes. The Hebrew word *asham* means not only "sacrifice for sin," but also "restitution." In Isaiah 53:10 it is written that Jesus gave His life as an *asham*, thus not only atoning for our sins, but also washing them away. To be justified is to be "just as if I'd" never sinned. We become whiter than snow.

"I will tell you what is noted in the Scripture of Truth."
DANIEL 10:21

*T*he angel tells Daniel about a book of the truth and quotes from it things that were not in the prophet's Bible. Our Scripture is a translation into human language of the inexpressible realities of God, contained in this book of truth. Every true preacher of the Word lifts his Bible, which is a translation from Hebrew and Greek, and says, "This is the book of God." What if the Hebrew and Greek were themselves translations, putting into the primitive languages of men the unspeakable riches of God?

Value the Bible, but don't stop at the words. Jesus said, "I still have many things to say to you, but you cannot bear them now" (John 16:12). Why should we not become men who can bear everything and learn from His mouth these hidden things? Forced to explain again to the Hebrews elementary things, Paul complains that he has no time left to speak about the spiritual explanation of the stories of Gideon, Jephthah, etc. (see Hebrews 11:32). If we would not always return like children to the elementary things of the beginning, we could perhaps learn these explanations that were withheld from the Hebrews 2,000 years ago. Jude said that when he wished to write about an important subject, our common salvation, he had to change his mind and warn against some false teachers in the church (Jude 3). If we would drive these out, we could learn what Jude intended to teach.

Go on from the Bible to the realities toward which the Bible points. There is a book of truth in heaven.

> *"Were there not any found who returned to give glory to God except this foreigner?"*
> LUKE 17:18

*G*od once invited all virtues to a banquet. They greeted and embraced each other. They were good friends, except two who stood aloof from each other. God asked them, "Are you not acquainted?"

They answered, "We never met before." Their names were "generosity" and "gratitude."

There is a legend about a Roman slave, Androcles, who had fled from his harsh master. He hid in one of the caves of the Lybian desert. Once he observed a lion in pain, because a thorn had entered its flesh. Androcles took the thorn out and healed the wound. Afterward, the two were inseparable friends.

In the end, the master found his slave and brought him bound to Rome, where—according to the custom—he had to be thrown before a wild beast in the circus. It so happened that the lion launched against him was the same lion whose pain he had eased. The lion recognized his friend and instead of devouring him, sat down quietly at his feet. Androcles explained this attitude and was pardoned.

It is easier to find gratitude among beasts than among men. A Turkish proverb says, "If you have done good to somebody, avoid him like a raving dog. He will bite you." The experience of centuries is in this proverb. We all complain about the lack of gratitude of others toward us. Let us make a list of all those who have been good toward us and to whom we have not shown thankfulness.

Let us first be thankful to God for His creation. Let us be thankful to Christ for salvation, let us be thankful to the Holy Spirit for His guidance, and let us be thankful to parents, teachers, doctors, bakers, tailors, and farmers. In other words, let us be thankful to all who work for us and also to all those who have stooped down to help us in difficult moments of our lives.

*"Some of those of understanding shall fall, to refine
them, purge them, and make them white."*
DANIEL 11:35

*M*ost people spell the word "disappointment" wrong. The correct way to write it is "His appointment." Paul of the Cross wrote, "Indeed, when an undertaking seems to have failed completely, it is then that we see it succeed wonderfully." On Good Friday, Jesus, the hope of the world, died, crying, "My God, My God, why have You forsaken Me?" Everything seemed to be lost. This was the preparation of the triumphal Resurrection.

Lincoln was a bankrupt businessman—so he could start his career as the biggest American statesman. Many engagements and marriages have been happily healed when they seemed hopeless. Many people who almost died, afterward spent many years in good health. I have been near death many times. Some Christians who have fallen into deep sin have later become great saints of God. Seemingly Peter's career as an apostle had ended in disgrace with the ugly denial of his Lord on the night Jesus was betrayed. There was no hope that he could ever again be a leader with authority in the church, after having failed so shamefully when he was tested. Forgiven by Jesus, he returned, continued to lead a fruitful life, and died as a martyr.

In 1759, Paul of the Cross wrote, "In the most profound recollection of mental prayer, I shall prepare myself for death." He had to change his mind because there were still some towns to evangelize. So the dying saint continued his activity another sixteen years.

He wrote, "The misfortunes which happen in this world, when accepted from the living hand of God with submission to His most holy will, enable us to run in the path of the divine commandments. Besides, resignation to these events serves as a very efficacious means of obtaining favors, even temporal favors."

Cherish your disappointments. They will prove to have been His appointments.

> *"Wine . . . makes glad the heart of man."*
> PSALM 104:15

*G*od saw everything that He had made, and indeed it was very good" (Genesis 1:31). Wine is good, too, as are all the other human joys. Sin has brought sadness and grief, but a time to laugh and a time to dance has remained (Ecclesiastes 3:4).

It is true that Christ teaches us this life is only a vestibule through which we pass to life eternal. But in a well-ordered house the vestibule must be beautiful, too.

Jesus, in changing water into wine in Cana, showed us that well-understood religion excludes no earthly joy so long as it contains no inherent evil and does not receive a prominence causing it to absorb more time and energy than permitted.

Within these limits, it is not wrong for a Christian to lead a life full of joy. The Christian must abandon sin, not things that make life enjoyable.

Many men know only the alternatives of life without God or God without life. Jesus breaks this vicious circle. He gives joyful life with God. The joyful instinct of the healthy child is the ideal example we see in Jesus—not the self-inflicted tortures of the ascetic. The latter may be a special individual calling, but not the rule for the average Christian life.

If you had been at Cana, would you have agreed with what Jesus did, or would you have preferred for Him to deliver a speech scolding those who wished to enjoy themselves at a wedding feast?

N O V E M B E R   4

"It came to pass."
MATTHEW 11:1

*I*t is said that King David once called a jeweler and said, "Make me a ring whose appearance will gladden my heart when I am sad, and make me sad when I am joyful. You have two days for this. If you bring the ring, you will be richly rewarded. If not, your head will be where your legs are now."

The jeweler left in despair. He knew his life would be forfeited. Who could make such a ring?

When he crossed the palace yard, little Solomon, who was playing, observed his grief and asked him what it was about. The jeweler told him of the foolish demand the king had made.

The child laughed and said, "Make him a simple ring of tin and write on it the words, '*Gam ze iavoh*'—'This will pass, too.' Nothing more is needed. In moments of darkness, the king will read that this will pass and find comfort. In revelings, the ring will remind him that joys in this world are transitory."

The jeweler made the ring and received a rich reward.

One of the beauties of the Bible is that the expression "It came to pass" occurs so often. What burdens you have today will pass. Don't be so preoccupied with your present griefs. What were you sad about five years ago, on November 4? You don't even remember anymore. So today's sorrows soon will be forgotten. And when you are joyful, don't forget that you have not attained heaven yet. All joys in this world are temporary.

Christians seek the eternal abode in which all tears will be wiped away.

NOVEMBER 5

*M*uslim tradition recites the following legend from the life of our Lord Jesus:

One day Jesus saw a group of people standing around with a sad expression on their faces. He asked them what their trouble was. They answered that they had heard about a horrible hell and were afraid to end up there.

Then He met another group of people, also showing grief. When asked about it they said that they had another burden: they had heard about heaven and trembled to miss it.

Afterward He met a third group overflowing with happiness. They told Him that they had found the truth and rejoiced in it.

Jesus, blessed be His name, said, "These men have escaped hell and are sure of heaven."

God promises rewards to the righteous and everlasting punishment to the wicked, but the motivation for the actions of Christians is love toward the Lord and enthusiasm for the truth. If the followers of the luminous path of Jesus would be sure that their road leads toward eternal destruction and if the devil would have a splendid paradise to offer, we would still follow Christ's way of the cross. We do not serve Him for His heaven, but out of love for Him.

Madame de Guyon prayed, "Lord, everything which You wish to give me in the next world, give to my friends. Everything You wish to give me in this world, give to my enemies. To me, give Yourself."

NOVEMBER 6

"He got into a boat."
MATTHEW 8:23

*A*n Oriental emperor sat on the balcony of his palace and watched with pleasure the many boats that passed near the shore. Each was a sign of the prosperity that flourished under his rule.

He asked a priest who stood near him, "How many boats do you think leave and enter our harbor during one year?" The priest answered, "Only four." The wrath of the king was kindled. This priest dared to mock him to his face?

"How do you dare to give me such a reply!" exclaimed the king. "I see at least a hundred boats before my eyes right now, and you tell me there are only four the whole year?"

The priest repeated, "It is as I said, only four: the ship 'Desire of adventure,' another, 'Desire of fun,' the third, 'Search for fame,' and the fourth, 'Running after money.' These are the real names of all boats, whatever the inscription on their bow. These are the only forces which drive men."

On the small lake Gennesaret one very small boat sailed. Jesus had entered into it. This ship had another name: "Self-sacrifice for the glory of God."

It is a unique ship. In Mark 4:37–39, we are told that Jesus once rebuked a storm and the wind ceased at His command. But that evening a bigger miracle than the stilling of the storm happened. The waves had beaten into the ship, "so that it was already filling" (v. 37). A ship full of water sinks—but not if it is Jesus' ship. It goes forward when no wind blows in its sails; it glides on when the oarsmen have become lazy and do not row anymore. The church advances even when it is filled to the brim with heresies, schisms, and sins that make her the mockery of men. It advances contrary to the laws of hydrodynamics. It is the only ship that stays afloat and sails on though full of water, because its motivation is the right one.

Choose the right ship in which to make your journey.

315

"If anyone is in Christ, he is a new creation."
2 CORINTHIANS 5:17

*T*his is the day of the Communist revolution in Russia, the most important fact in the political history of the twentieth century. What did it give to souls?

In an atheistic meeting in Moscow, the lecturer showed a glass of water to the audience compelled to attend. He put a powder into it. The water became a purplish wine. He explained: "Jesus, at Cana, had such a powder hidden in His sleeve. People at that time were backward and believed that He had performed a miracle, when as a matter of fact it was only a magician's trick, like mine. I can do even better than Jesus. I can change the wine into water again." Another powder and this change happened. "And now I turn it into wine again." Another powder and his word was fulfilled.

A Christian stood up and said, "Comrade lecturer, you have amazed us by your miraculous power. We would ask you only for one thing more. Could you please drink a little bit of the wine you just made?"

"I am sorry," was the reply, "the powder I put into the water is poisonous."

The Christian then said, "This is the whole difference between you, the Communists, and Jesus. He gives a wine that has gladdened hearts and enlightened minds for 2,000 years. You also change water into wine, but it is a wine that poisons our hearts with fear and hatred."

No revolution that leaves the hearts of men unchanged can bring lasting good to mankind. The revolution needed is the new birth. It makes men into new creatures in Christ Jesus.

NOVEMBER 8

"When you pray, say..."
LUKE 11:2

*L*et us adopt the following prayer of the early church, composed by Eusebius:

O, God, grant that I may be no man's enemy,
But friend of all that is eternal and abides.
That I may never invent evil against somebody,
And if evil happens to me, may I be spared
Without hurting the one who wished to do me evil.
May I love, seek, and obtain only the good,
May I desire the good of all men and envy nobody.
May I never wait for someone else to scold me,
When I have done or said something amiss;
But may I reproach myself, until I become better.
May I never obtain a victory
Which would hurt me or my adversary.
May I reconcile friends who are angry with each other.
May I help with all my might those who need my help.
May I never abandon a friend in danger.
May I respect myself.
And for this may I tame all my impulses that might otherwise
    make me rave.
May I never speak about who is evil and who had done evil,
But seek good men and follow in their footsteps.

NOVEMBER 9

"Blessed are the peacemakers."
MATTHEW 5:9

*I*t is said that in the first generation of monks in the Thebaid desert, Avva Pahone built for himself a hut in the valley, because he had gotten old. His former cell on the hill he gave to Avva George. He soon regretted this, because he saw that hundreds came to Avva George to hear the Word from this saint.

Overwhelmed by envy, Pahone sent a disciple to Avva George, ordering him to leave the cell immediately. The disciple told Avva George, "Father Pahone sends me to you with words of peace and begs for your prayers, because he values your piety very much."

When the disciple returned, Pahone asked him, "Did you tell him what I ordered?"

He replied, "I surely told him what he deserved."

Avva George remained and people continued to flock to him. Pahone sent the disciple a second time. "Tell that hypocrite to leave my cell without delay, otherwise I will drive him out with a stick."

The disciple went to Avva George and told him, "Father Pahone loves you so much. He asked me to assure you of his affection and convey his blessings. He never ceases day or night to pray for you."

Returning, the disciple reported to his master, "I told him everything needed." So also the third time.

Since Avva George remained in his place, Pahone went with a stick to drive him out. The disciple, who was swifter, ran before him on another path and told Avva George, "I could not detain my master. Though old, he ascends the hill to get a blessing from you."

George went to meet Pahone, knelt before him and said, "I thank you for the many messages of love which you sent through your disciple. I am not worthy of them and of your coming up this steep hill especially to bless me."

Pahone understood how the disciple had fulfilled his task. He embraced George and, returning to his hut, said to the novice, "Until now I was your master. You were my disciple. Henceforth you will teach me, because you know better the ways of love."

"The tree of life was also in the midst of the garden."
GENESIS 2:9

*E*very tree is a tree of life. First of all because it is a nature preserve for birds. What the Lord said is true of every tree: "The birds of the air come and nest in its branches" (Matthew 13:32).

Trees are not only for birds. Badgers burrow at their roots. Hundreds of plants, insects, and animals find food and shelter beneath its branches and lovers find a place to enjoy each other.

More than 200 different kinds of insects live in an oak. Innumerable wasps and bugs feed on oak flowers, beetles eat the bark, caterpillars of many kinds eat the leaves. There are the squirrels and the wood mice. Owls in their turn feed on the mice and nest in the hollow trunks of old oaks.

Then there are the ivy, mistletoe, mosses, algae, lichens, and ferns. Near to death, the oak tree is invaded by fungi.

The oak is hospitable to each and every one. Lovers are gladly received to exchange kisses in its shadow. Trees are even places where men can meet with angels. Abraham met angels while resting in the shadow of an oak. Believers are like trees planted by the rivers of water (Psalm 1:2). Not only that they have life in themselves, but they give opportunity of life to hundreds of others. They are trees of life for a multitude of creatures.

When dying, a tree gave its wood for a cross on which the salvation of mankind was fulfilled. The tree served even when dead. Let us be trees in God's garden.

"Many... will betray one another."
MATTHEW 24:10

O ne of the darkest features of the Chinese church under communism has been the denunciation movement, when friends and members of the same family were turned against each other in betrayal and hate, everyone seeking only to save his or her own skin. A "Christian" conference in 1951, attended by 152 Protestant leaders, asked the death penalty for the Methodist Bishop Chen and the Evangelist Ku-Jen-en. The Communist Party was more gracious than the brethren. They gave the bishop only five years of prison. No one heard anymore from Ku. He probably died in some jail.

The Christian pastor Lu Chih-Wei was attacked in a public meeting by his own daughter: "I now accuse my father, for the way in which he has blinded me, causing me to lose my standing with the people." The father wept. She continued, "Do you think that your false tears are able to bribe my conscience?"

Good Christians, thousands of them, could be induced vehemently to denounce their beloved ones. Brother Sun, editor of the *Christian Farmer*, was subjected to such mental pressure that he committed suicide. Only a few resisted, among them Watchman Nee and Wang-Min-Tao.

Your not becoming a traitor and your resistance in times of intensive trial depends upon your earlier Christian life. When, after the conversion of Saul of Tarsus, the Lord appeared to Ananias, He told him how to teach a new convert: "I will show him how many things he must suffer for my Name's sake" (Acts 9:16).

Every Christian church that does not teach its members the main religious science, sufferology, does not fulfill its duties. Impose upon yourself mortification. Learn to suffer and not to yield. The time may come when you will need this knowledge.

*"The LORD ... said to [Abram], '... Walk before
Me and be blameless.'"*
GENESIS 17:1

A story says that the devil and a friend of his were walking along a street, when they saw on the other side a man bowing down, picking up something and putting it in his bag. The devil told his friend, "This man just found a piece of truth."

"This is a catastrophe for you," said the friend.

"Oh, no," the devil replied. "I will give him the idea of creating an institution for its propagation. It will see to it that the truth is neutralized."

We cannot renounce institutions. If Jesus had only given His teachings and died and resurrected without leaving a church behind, there would be no disciples of Christ today. We have the Scriptures from the church. The church guarantees their authenticity, interprets the difficult parts, preserves the rich experience of generations of Christians, and imparts baptism and communion.

We would like every man to be a giant of faith like Abraham, who set out on his own and walked before God, when, except for his family, no one believed in him. We could as well desire every baboon to be a man, every aborigine to be a cultured genius. Men are as they are and they need the institutional church for a life of faith.

We must be aware at the same time that institutions not only convey truth, but sometimes also distort it. They are led by men with shortcomings. Nothing can replace firsthand experience and the discovery of the kingdom within ourselves.

So be faithful to the institution and have your personal walk with God.

"Obey those who rule over you . . . for they
watch out for your souls."
HEBREWS 13:17

*D*on't be a troubler in Zion, one who always finds faults with ministers, who is ready to break away from a church or to produce a split.

Every minister, even one who leads a church like the church in Laodicea, where Christ instead of being in the center was kept like a beggar at the door knocking, is a star in Jesus' right hand (Revelation 2:1). It is for Him and for the rare ones who have a special assignment from Him to reprove and to remove ministers who have gone astray. We can easily be mistaken and uproot wheat together with the tares. We can deceive ourselves into believing that we are doing God's service when we drive a holy man from the pulpit or make his life bitter by continual criticism.

One pastor could achieve nothing good in his congregation because of much gossip directed against him. He left. After this, men were converted through remembering his previous sermons. His value was not appreciated by the congregation while the minister had been with them. The deacon who had hated him most repented and went to see him. The pastor's wife received him with the words, "He is dying. Don't go in to see him. The sight of your face might add to his anguish." How terrible for a Christian to be a source of anguish for a dying saint!

The deacon entered anyway. The dying pastor could only open his languid eyes once and said, "'Touch not mine anointed, and do my prophets no harm.' I have been a sinner. Whatever you have done to me has been right. Don't worry, but you will meet others. Remember these words. The one in whom you find faults might be God's anointed. 'Touch not mine anointed, and do my prophets no harm.'" With this, he passed away.

No minister is perfect, either in his teaching or in his life. Still they must be held in esteem. An unloved pastor cannot do good to his congregation.

"You will be saved, you and your household."
ACTS 16:31

*T*here are privileged saints whose faith is tested to its utter-most and who have the chance to show their loyalty to the uttermost.

In sixteenth-century Spain, Antonio Herrezuelo was sentenced by the Inquisition to die at the stake for his evangelical belief. Julian Hernandez had smuggled Spanish Scriptures and reformed litera-ture into the country, hidden in wine casks. Smuggling is an old habit in the church of Christ. When caught, Hernandez was brutal-ly tortured for three years, but did not betray those to whom he had given the Bibles. Herrezuelo had received such a Bible and had been converted.

When brought to the stake, Herrezuelo was tormented by the knowledge that his wife, also a believer, had recanted for fear of death and that because of this, the generous inquisitors had changed her death sentence to life imprisonment. One word from the mouth of Antonio and he could escape the stake, too. He could go to jail and hope that one day a pardon would be given and he would be reunited with his wife.

He knew of a better hope: the promise of God given to all believers that they and their houses would be saved. Until the gag was put into his mouth, he admonished his wife to repent. He be-lieved that the Word of God, effective in saving sinners, would also be effective in making a backslidden saint return to the fold of Christ.

He died. His wife went to jail, but had no peace there. The inner fight lasted eight years. After this time, she withdrew her recanta-tion and threw the affirmation of her faith in the teeth of the inquisi-tors. She was burned, too, and went to join her husband in heaven.

Believe in the promise of God for all who constitute your house.

*"I have not shunned to declare to you the
whole counsel of God."*
ACTS 20:27

A Bible salesman was refused harshly when he tried to sell a Bible. He then offered a New Testament at no charge to the lady.

Her husband mocked. "We are married," he said, "so half of everything she has belongs to me." He took an axe and cut the New Testament in half.

A few weeks later he asked his wife, "Where do you have the other half of the book? I need it. My half finished with the story of a prodigal son returning to his father and saying something. I am curious to know what he said. His words are in your half."

This was not the only man to divide the Bible in half. Jesus came full of truth and grace. Some preachers speak only about truth, leaving for others only grace. Others do the opposite.

The Bible always unites forgiveness of sins with repentance.

Don't halve the Bible.

Don't stop at the fact that Jesus died for our sins. It is also written that we have to present our bodies as a living sacrifice (Romans 12:1).

> *"...those who have known the truth."*
> 2 JOHN 1

*H*ow can a man find the truth? Do we have the necessary spiritual and intellectual qualifications for finding it? Would we recognize it if we met it?

We are small. Can one catch the sun in a butterfly net or the ocean in a thimble? Send a child of three to a big library and ask him to find and bring to you Dante's *Divine Comedy*. How will the child identify it?

In order to find the truth, I must have an exact definition of what truth is. In order to know which of the many definitions of truth is true, and which of the assertions declaring themselves to be the ultimate truth in religion, politics, morals, etc., are really true, I must know the true signs by which truth is recognized. Whoever does not know the truth beforehand can never find the truth.

We are in a vicious circle. The truth cannot be found. The history of human thought is a graveyard of scientific and other assertions of which mankind once had been cocksure were true, only to later discover they were false.

Possession of truth distinguishable from my person, of truth which I can take or leave, is ruled out. Truth can be only an "I." Therefore Jesus said, "I am the . . . truth" (John 14:6).

The rule of truth in a man can never be the rule of someone or something else.

Truth is the manner of being of a Christlike person. The more Christlikeness, the more truth is indwelling me, a truth that I don't have to seek. It is my character. There is no other answer to the search for truth.

God does not lead us as being someone else, but as identifying Himself with me.

*P*erpetua was in a dungeon for her faith. She could have escaped if she had denied the Savior. Her old father entreated her to do so.

She told him, "Father, do you see this little pitcher here?"

He replied, "Yes."

She asked him, "Could it be called by any other name than pitcher?"

He replied, "No."

Then Perpetua said, "Neither can I call myself anything else than what I am, a Christian."

She remained steadfast when her father asked her to have pity on his gray hairs, not to deliver him up to the scorn of men for having an imprisoned criminal as a daughter, and also to remember her infant child. She could not be shaken, because she could not be something other than a Christian, as a pitcher cannot be something other than it is.

Her unbelieving father was beaten with rods in her presence and her child was taken from her. She remained the only thing she could be.

When she was tossed to the wild beasts, her tunic was torn from her side. She immediately covered her legs, being more mindful of her nakedness than of the suffering which waited her. This was her last gesture before dying a martyr's death.

Christians, simply be what you are. You could not be anything else.

"Let him deny himself, and take up his cross daily,
and follow Me."
LUKE 9:23

A Christian cannot be careful enough in choosing which public events he will attend, what he will watch on television,
or what books he will read. Tertullian, a great Christian teacher of
the third century, told of a Christian lady who went to an indecent
show and came back possessed. In the exorcism, when the unclean
spirit was upbraided for having dared to attack a believer, he firmly
replied, "I did it most righteously, for I found her in my domain."

I concede that in many shows there are things that are both
pleasant and innocent in themselves, even some things that are
excellent. The explanation is simple. No one dilutes poison with
gall. The accursed thing is put into delicacies well seasoned and of
sweet taste. Therefore, be careful before going to a show even if it
seems innocent.

The Christian's joys, his nuptial banquet, are yet to come. We
are not in a hurry to get all the possible pleasures out of life. We
can fellowship with the world in her entertainment as little as she
can fellowship with us in our worship.

The Lord has said, "The world will rejoice; and you will be sor-
rowful" (John 16:20). Let us mourn over the prevailing unright-
eousness, while the world is merry, that in the day of the world's
doom we may rejoice.

No one can have the pleasures of both lives. Don't scan the
newspapers daily to find what fun you can have, but take daily
your cross and follow Him.

*"The bridegroom came, and those who were
ready went in with him to the wedding."*
MATTHEW 25:10

We who live four hundred years after the Reformation can understand only with difficulty the thinking of Christians in the Middle Ages.

In the thirteenth century, no one would have contested the words written by a monk of that time: "All are entitled to enter the family of Christ, when they make a proper use of the blood of their Redeemer and of the milk of the sacred Virgin, their mother; yes, of that adorable blood which encourages the martyrs and soothes their torments and of that virginal milk which sweetens the bitterness of our cup by appeasing the wrath of God."

The Scriptures were almost totally unknown. They tell us about the cleansing power of the blood of Christ. The saving power of Mary's milk is just a human fancy.

Men at that time loved also to venerate lesser female saints. They might have gone too far in this respect, although many of them were beautiful personalities.

Wartburg, remembered now only as the place where Luther preached, had been where St. Elizabeth of Hungary was reared and where she had prayed. She had erected a hospital, which still can be seen at the palace gates, so that she might never forget human misery in the splendor of her queenly rank.

Her last words were, "The moment has arrived when God summons His friend to the wedding feast. The Bridegroom seeks His spouse. Silence, silence."

It was on November 19.

On a Sabbath day, Rabbi Meir had gone to the synagogue. While he was there his two little boys had climbed up a tree, had fallen, and were found dead beneath the tree. His wife, Beruria, took the corpses to an upper room, covered them with a sheet, and went downstairs to prepare the table for her husband.

When he returned home, he said the prescribed prayers, sat down at the table and asked about the children. She answered, "Well, they are children. What can you expect from them?"

When he had finished eating, she said, "I have to ask you a question. A neighbor gave me a pair of costly earrings to keep for her, because her husband was a drunkard and might have sold them. Now her husband is dead and she asked me to give them back. I loved them. When you were not at home, I used to ornament myself with them before the mirror. They were one of my joys. Should I give them back?"

The rabbi answered, "I think you should return them, and thank her for the privilege of having had them for so long a time."

Then she said, "Come with me. I wish to show you how beautiful they are."

She took him to the upper room, drew away the sheet, and said, "These are the gems. We have enjoyed the time with them. Let us now hand them back to their owner with thankfulness."

He answered, "Blessed is a husband with a wise wife. God has given; God has taken. Let the name of God be praised."

Let us take our losses like this.

"God loves a cheerful giver."
2 CORINTHIANS 9:7

A Christian told his brother in the faith, "I put aside every Sunday what I have to give to the church. If I am hindered from going, I give the money to my wife to take along or save it for the next time, and add the tithe to the next week's offering. How do you act in this regard?"

The brother answered, "Before going to church, I kneel with my family at home and thank God for the privilege of living in a free land where I can go to God's house. I thank Him for the pastor, for the missionary effort of our congregation, and for all the other things. Then I decide how much to give and bring it to the altar."

After a time the two Christians met again. The second said, "I tried your method. It is marvelous. After praying and thanking God before deciding about how much to give in church, I found always that the sum put aside was much too small, when I had in view the favors received. I increased my giving. My blessings increased accordingly. I find exquisite joy in giving. I am happier than ever before."

Do you give at random or under God's guidance?

NOVEMBER 22

"I came ... to fulfill [the Law]."
MATTHEW 5:17

Shun Shauk, former president of the Japanese Bible Society, tells the following story.

At the end of World War II American soldiers received a hearty welcome in Shinmanbuke, a village on the island of Okinawa. The houses and the streets in this village were clean, unlike anything seen elsewhere, and the inhabitants looked happier than the other Japanese.

The difference came from the fact that thirty years earlier an American missionary had passed through that village. He could not stay long. He just told them a few words and left them a Bible.

Two brothers, Shosei and Mogon, began to live according to this book, though they had no communication with Christians from anywhere else. They had found the Savior through the book and fulfilled His precepts. They witnessed to others. So the one brother became mayor of the village, the other its teacher. The Bible was read daily in school. The village was administrated according to the Bible.

The American chaplain could see that the thirty-year-old Bible had been well used and had changed the life of a village.

Does your Bible lie often on the shelf? Has it changed your life? Have you decided to learn daily from it and to put to practice immediately what you learn? Do you bring its teachings into your school, factory, and community?

If you have not used the Bible wisely until now, learn from these Japanese brethren.

> *"Today, if you will hear His voice:*
> *'Do not harden your hearts.'"*
> PSALM 95:7,8

A young man told his mother, "I cannot accept the Bible. It contains so many things that I cannot swallow. They simply make no sense."

The mother answered, "When you were at war, you wrote me once: 'Your letters describe a situation which is unintelligible for me. It is true that I have been away from home for three years. I would understand perhaps if I were with you.'"

The measure of how much the Bible is unintelligible for us shows for how long and how far away we are from our heavenly home, whose thoughts are expressed in the Bible. Return to the parental house and you will understand.

Do it at once.

The Greek tyrant Archacus was on his way to a banquet, when someone handed him a letter, saying, "It is very important."

He answered, "Important things we will leave for tomorrow." Shortly after that, while he was drunk, a dagger of an assassin pierced his heart. His blood fell upon the letter containing a warning about the plot.

Evil forces strive to keep us far away and for a long time from the house of the heavenly Father, in order to keep our minds muddled here with eternal death waiting for us at the end.

Heed the warning. Return.

"Lord, teach us to pray."
LUKE 11:1

When I was a young Christian, I was taught that if you go to a prayer meeting for rain in a time of drought, you have to take an umbrella with you. This would be a token of faith.

Later I read in the Talmud that the Jewish high priest, when he entered once a year into the most holy place, always finished his supplication with the words, "Lord, don't listen to the prayers of wayfarers."

Every wayfarer wishes nice weather for the day on which he travels. How would the world look if God would have to give or stop rain according to our having taken an umbrella or not?

I prefer the vicar who, when asked to pray for rain, answered, "Not while the wind is in this direction."

Our Lord said, "The wind blows where it wishes." There are objective laws that reign in nature. To pray against the weather forecast because it does not fit your purpose is as wrong as praying that two times two should not be four.

The great prayer of Christians is, "Thy will be done." Elijah could bring rain. Jesus could rebuke the winds. Do you wish to imitate them? You can't do it on your level. You have to become a powerful, spiritual personality, knowing God's will about the weather. You must know things meteorologists don't know.

*"I have manifested Your name to the men
whom You have given Me."*
JOHN 17:6

When the monk Paulinus was at the court of Edwin, king of Northumbria, in A.D. 627, endeavoring to persuade him to accept Christianity, the king was in two minds about it, until one of his warriors spoke.

"The present life of man upon earth, O king, seems to me, in comparison to the time which is unknown to us, like the swift flight of a sparrow through that house wherein you sit at supper in winter with your nobility, while the fire blazes in the midst, and the hall is armed, but the wintry storms of rain or snow are raging without. The sparrow, flying in at one door and immediately out at another, whilst he is within is safe from the wintry tempests, but after a short space of fair weather he immediately vanishes out of your sight, passing from winter into winter again. So this life of man appears for a little while, but of what is to follow or what went before we know nothing at all. If therefore this new doctrine tells us something more certain, it seems justly to deserve to be followed."

The new doctrine, the doctrine of Christ, answers this quest. Jesus manifested to us the name of the Father (John 17:6). The knowledge of this name opens all doors for a soul here and in eternity. Through all ancient literature of different peoples persists the belief that if the real name of a thing is known to a man, the powers inherent in that thing are under his control. The thought was right. When we know the chemical formula, the last name of a thing, we can act on it.

Through Jesus we know that God is love. God's love is the key for solving the riddle.

NOVEMBER 26

"There was silence."
JOB 4:16

A student went to a great sage and said, "Master, teach me about God."

The sage remained silent.

The student again said to him, "Master, teach me about God."

He still remained silent.

When asked by the student a third time, the sage said, "I taught thee about God. I am silent."

To put God in words is like trying to catch waves with a fishing net. Words have arisen from the necessity of men to understand each other in hunting, production, personal relations. We cannot do without them, but we must be aware that when we apply human words to God, calling Him "Master, Father, Love," they can bring wrong connotations. A master can be an exploiter. Luther had great difficulty in saying the Lord's Prayer, because he did not like to call God "Father." His father had been very harsh. Love? I love apple pie and my dog. Is it the same sentiment that stands for God?

When Livingstone wished to explain to savages that God is love, he could not do it, because they did not have the word "love" in their language. He found out that the thing they most appreciated was the meat from the arm of a man when smoked. They called it "unboy." He delivered his famous sermon, that "God is the best unboy." He was criticized for it. But he did what the apostle John had done before him, calling God "love."

Love is a human sentiment. Does anyone believe that God is a sentiment? Because it was the highest that man knew, John applied it to God, as Livingstone applied to Him "unboy."

As for what God ultimately is, you will know it when you keep silent.

"It pleased God... to reveal His Son in me."
GALATIANS 1:15,16

What can a man do to discover the Son of God in himself? How can he recover God's image in which he was created and which has been marred by sin? There is no way.

An actor plays Othello. Perhaps he never had an occasion to be jealous and has not known this sentiment. He tries to play the role of a personality foreign to his nature: the prototype of the jealous male. The impersonated person, the role Othello, could never change the character of the actor. The actor can always decide not to play Othello anymore.

Every one of us is first of all what he is. Secondly, he takes different attitudes in life—that of a person who plays with sin, that of a hardened sinner, that of a repentant sinner. None of these roles can decide what I should be. It is the fundamental "I" which decides what role to play.

The whole change starts when the Othello played by me does not take himself seriously anymore. He knows that he does not really care for the fake Desdemona and never killed her—that the whole scene has been a play. Then your real personality, the Son of God in you, will appear in its entire beauty. The old man, the acting, will have passed away.

It is written in the parable of the prodigal son that when the prodigal son decided to return to his father, he "came to himself" (Luke 15:17). Every return to God is a return to your real self.

"Weep with those who weep."
ROMANS 12:15

A Christian was severely stabbed. The criminal was caught and taken by the police to confront his victim in the hospital. The police assured the Christian, "This man will get his due punishment. He will sit in prison."

The Christian replied, "What an honor for me to meet him now. Jesus said that visiting one in prison is like visiting Him." The Christian bowed before the criminal and died.

Bow before everyone who suffers, even if he suffers for having wronged you. Jesus, the Man of sorrows, sympathizes with the sufferers.

It is written in the Talmud, "When an unrighteous man persecutes a righteous one, God is on the side of the persecuted righteous man. If an unrighteous man persecutes another unrighteous man, God is on the side of the persecuted unrighteous man. If a righteous man persecutes an unrighteous one, even then God is on the side of the persecuted."

Be always on the side of the hungry, even if they are hungry because they are lazy. Be on the side of the thirsty, even if it was their neglect not to have dug a well. Be on the side of the naked even if they have gambled away their clothes. Be on the side of the sick, even if they have destroyed their health through vice. Be on the side of prisoners even if they are criminals, only being careful not to favor them above their victims who were also men innocently persecuted.

"Sell what you have and give alms."
LUKE 12:33

The rich man in the parable was clothed in fine linen, which according to Revelation 19 symbolizes the righteousness of the saints. This man had the outward appearance of righteousness, but he could not be acknowledged as such because he was callous toward the poor.

All Christians of industrial countries are in danger of committing the same sin. Developing countries receive only fifteen percent of the final selling price of their product. Producer nations get only eleven cents for every dollar worth of bananas sold to rich countries. The colonial pattern by which poor countries provided cheap raw materials and tropical foods for the rich industrialized nations still exists. Between 1963 and 1971 Sri Lanka lost 45 million dollars on exports of tea to Britain alone as a result of falling prices, twice as much as Britain gave in aid.

Within the underdeveloped countries, there is also much social injustice. The richest ten percent of the population in these countries account for about forty percent of the total income, while the poorest forty percent account just for twelve percent of the income.

The individual Christian must use restraint in consumption. The normal thing for a Christian, with whatever income, is not to spend on himself and his family more than the average income of a citizen of his country. Everything above this is luxury.

Ambrose wrote, "If your brother starves while you have the possibility of helping him, you are a thief; and if he dies of hunger, you are a murderer."

"Of such [the little children] is the kingdom of heaven."
MATTHEW 19:14

One of the saddest moments in the life of a parent is when he observes that his child is retarded. For them I recount the following true story, quoted from the book by Fritz Rienecker, *The Best Is Still to Come* (Sonne und Schild, Wuppertal).

> In a home for retarded children, Catherine was nurtured twenty years. The child had been a complete idiot from the beginning and had never spoken a word, but only vegetated. She either gazed quietly at the walls or made disordered movements. To eat, to drink, to sleep, were her whole life. She seemed not to participate at all in what happened around her. A leg had to be amputated. The staff wished Cathy well and hoped that the Lord would soon take her to Himself.
>
> One day the doctor called the director to come quickly. Catherine was dying. When both entered the room, they could not believe their senses. Catherine was singing Christian hymns she had heard and had picked up, just those suitable for deathbeds. She repeated again and again the German song, "Where does the soul find its fatherland, its rest?" She sang for half an hour with transfigured face, then she passed away quietly.

So it had only seemed that she was not receptive to what happened around her. From the medical point of view this case is a riddle. God has lifted the veil once to encourage parents of handicapped children. God makes no mistakes. He who cares for sparrows has arranged that the mentally retarded should have a place in heaven, too.

"The LORD God formed man of the dust of the ground."
GENESIS 2:7

*M*an is not formed simply from earth (*eretz* in Hebrew, from which the English word "earth" comes). He is formed from the ground. The Hebrew word is *adamah*, which meant originally exceptionally good soil. The soil of paradise is called *adamah* in Genesis 2:9. There is also desert or stony ground. God used the best of grounds on which the trees of paradise, even the tree of life grew, to form man of it. The potential of man is huge.

Then God breathed into his nostrils "the breath of life." The Hebrew does not have the singular, "life." The Jews used for it *haiim*, which is a plural, "lives." If you would like to write an infidel book in Hebrew saying that man has only one life, you could not do it because the language has no singular for "life." God endowed man with lives: with bodily and spiritual life, with life in this world and life in the next.

Man must be exceptional in that it should be said about him that he is only a little lower than an angel (Psalm 8:5). In Hebrew the verse says, "Thou hast made him a little lower than God [*Elohim*]."

In bodily size, man is only a speck of dust in the universe, but who can express his greatness? Blaise Pascal wrote, "A breath, a drop of water, can kill man. But even if the universe would destroy him, man is greater than the universe; because man knows that he dies, while the universe does not know that it kills him."

Remember your greatness and thank the Creator who has given it to you.

"My joy may remain in you."
JOHN 15:11

*I*t is said that a man suffering from melancholic depression visited a psychiatrist, who recommended frequent travels.

The patient answered, "I am traveling continuously and it does not help."

"A glass of wine drunk at a happy party is useful," said the doctor.

The reply was, "I drink whole barrels of alcohol and remain sad."

The doctor had an idea. "There is a clown in town who is un-equaled. People cannot control their laughter listening to his jokes and seeing his tricks. Spend your evenings there."

The patient said, "I am that clown. I gladden everyone except myself. And the joy of those who watch me does not last."

The joys that this world gives are illusory, because in the depths of our hearts we realize they are mere escapes from the fact that we are men sentenced to death, men burdened with guilt. When we laugh, there is in us the remembrance that we made others weep.

Only God gives the real joy. He has shown in the resurrection of Christ that He has forgiven all our sins. Jesus our Lord "was delivered up because of our offenses, and was raised because of our justification" (Romans 4:25). The resurrection of Jesus is a pledge that we will resurrect, too, because we belong to Him. We have an inner joy that continues even without external stimulants.

DECEMBER 3

*"The works of the flesh are ... adultery,
fornication, uncleanness ..."*
GALATIANS 5:19

A preacher was asked at a student meeting, "What is wrong with premarital sex? Everyone tries four or five suits before buying one. Why should I not try sex with four or five girls before marrying one?"

The preacher answered, "There is a flaw in your judgment. By the same token, each girl has to try four or five young men before taking a husband. So in the end you buy a used suit instead of a new one."

Premarital sex is not a preparation for marriage. Should theft be the preparation for an honest life? How can the sexual possession of a person, unaccompanied by love, prepare for a life based on the highest sentiment of affection between two beings of the opposite sex?

Sexual sins are frequent today. They can easily be forgiven, like all other sins. Isaiah said, "He [the Messiah] was wounded for our transgressions, He was bruised for our iniquities" (53:5)—iniquities of whatever kind, including sexual ones. But after being forgiven, let us not continue in them. The price for extramarital affairs is much too high.

Think only about the fate of children born without a stable home, abandoned. Think about the grief of your parents and of the other person's parents.

To avoid sexual sin, practice spiritual hygiene. Be choosy in reading books and magazines, in watching TV or movies. Fill your days to the brim with serving the Lord and your fellow men.

DECEMBER 4

"We are members of His body."
EPHESIANS 5:30

*B*ecause we are members of His body, we must be active in continuing His mission today.

Some years ago, a young boy actively involved in sports suffered a diving accident that rendered him permanently paralyzed from his neck down. His mind sent out signals to his members to respond to the desire within his youthful heart to involve himself in further activity, but his arms and legs remained limp and lifeless in the wheelchair.

Even more tragic and heartbreaking is the thought of seeing Christ at the wayside of humanity, His noble mind sending forth signals to His members to show love and mercy, only to find those members paralyzed and silent in fear and neglect.

In earlier times He healed the paralytic. Today He is rendered helpless by the same malady of His body which is the church.

Let us fulfill without delay all the orders issued from His mind, remembering that we are His members.

DECEMBER 5

*"For [Christ] I have suffered the loss of all things,
and count them as rubbish."*
PHILIPPIANS 3:8

You discover easily how much of a Christian a man is if he loses money, fame, health, etc. He was meant to consider all things as rubbish. Who gets angry when he gets rid of rubbish, which makes everything around him smell offensively?

Sadly, these biblical words that were reality for Paul are only a phrase for most of us. Even churches try to accumulate rubbish. There have been attempts at reformation in this regard, but they all failed. Francis of Assisi and Joachim of Fiore, founders of religious orders having poverty as their supreme rule, resigned from the leadership when they saw that they had not succeeded.

Money, love of fame, attachment to creatures are great competitors of God. With most men, God loses in this competition.

A prince boasted once to a company about the great wealth he possessed. A pastor who was present asked him, "Your highness, would you kindly accept this pin and return it to me when we meet in eternity?"

The prince replied, "How can you ask for this? I can take nothing with me."

"That is right," said the pastor. "We boast of what does not belong to us and might be lost today, instead of accumulating what is of eternal value."

An inscription was found in India: "Jesus, blessing be upon His name, has said, 'This world is a bridge. Pass over it, but don't construct a house on it.'"

Die to the things of this world before you die. Count all things really as rubbish, that you may gain Christ.

DECEMBER 6

"The love of God has been poured out in our hearts."
ROMANS 5:5

While Jesus walked once on the streets of Nazareth—so a Muslim story goes—the mob heaped abuse upon Him. He continued on His way quietly, praying with loud voice for everyone who insulted Him.

He was asked how He could do this, to which He replied, "I give them the only thing I have in My purse."

Smash a bottle filled with milk. No vinegar will spill from it, because the bottle did not contain vinegar. How can words of hatred and vindictiveness flow from a Christian heart? The Christian does not have to choose between several options. He does not fulfill a commandment of love because Christ so ordered. If he would like to hate, he would not know how to do it, because God has renewed his heart.

The first disciples asked the Lord, "'Rabbi, where are You staying?' He said to them, 'Come and see.' They... remained with Him that day" (John 1:38,39).

He could not have taken them to an abode on earth. He had none. He dwells wherever love reigns, be it in a humble cottage, or in a palace. Jesus took the inquirers to a couple of such homes. They understood and became His apostles.

DECEMBER 7

"The disciples were first called Christians in Antioch."
ACTS 11:26

*I*t is said that whales once swam near the shore of America and philosophically asked themselves what they really were. Then they heard some children exclaiming, "Look! whales!" Then the whales were happy. They knew their names and they fancied they knew by this also what they were.

Some believers, in the same way, have been given by men on shore the title "Christians," and mistakenly think that this name discloses their inner reality. It is not so. The Lord said, "By this all will know that you are My disciples, if you have love for one another" (John 13:35), not that you "bear a certain name."

In the Italian Alps, peasants have the habit of leaving the door open on Christmas Eve, heating the oven, and having a dinner prepared on the table, in case the holy family pursued by Herod should want to take refuge there.

The Ostjaks, a Mongol tribe in the outer parts of Siberia, the place of deportation under the Czars and under Bolshevism, always put some food outside their door when they go to sleep, in case a fugitive prisoner needs it.

We are what we are, not what we are called. Jesus and the holy ones are always fugitives in this world. Do we show concern for the needy? What we do shows what we are.

DECEMBER 8

One of the oldest problems in religion involves the question of why there is so much suffering among mankind if the world is led by a good God.

The answer is simpler than we would imagine. God is good not only toward the good, but also toward the unthankful and evil (Luke 6:35). Only an all-embracing goodness is good. Goodness shown to the wicked usually does not have the effect of changing them, but often encourages them to continue in their evil. God's goodness is patient and long-suffering, which is used by those who are evil to commit new crimes. God was patient even with Hitler and Stalin and bore with them for decades. During this time they practiced mass slaughter.

In order for the world to be good, God would have to cease to be good Himself toward the wicked. Who of us would dare to tell God, "Stop being good to sinners," when we know the evil in our own hearts?

On the earthly level, with our human mind, there is no solution for the problem of evil. God has made provision. He is not only good, but He knows how to take revenge as well. He has a day of wrath in reserve. Leave philosophizing to God—He has a better head than we do—and flee urgently from the wrath of God.

> *"Enoch walked with God."*
> GENESIS 5:22

*D*on't be afraid to follow a man because he is rejected by the church. Many a saint has been martyred by the church and canonized afterward. Men who would have opposed the church in the saint's lifetime and have taken his defense against the prelates would have served the cause of Christ better than those who obeyed and trusted the church.

Joan of Arc was burned by the church. Celestine V died in prison. There is strong suspicion that he was murdered there by the order of his successor, Pope Boniface VIII. St. John of the Cross was treated like a madman. Huss died at the stake, condemned as a heretic. Thousands of others suffered the same fate.

Our attitude toward the church has to be ambivalent. Whoever has God as his Father has the church as his "mother" and owes her obedience and love. A mother can go mad, too. The church is not only a divine institution; she is also constituted of men who can commit grave sins in her name. Top church leaders are not exempt from this possibility. So obedience toward the church has a limit, which natural reason and the guidance of the Holy Spirit will show you.

The supreme ideal for every Christian is to be, like Enoch, a man who walks with God. Personal contact with God is the guarantee against a life of error.

DECEMBER 10

"Moses said to the LORD, 'O my Lord,
I am not eloquent.'"
EXODUS 4:10

Why did God choose as His messenger a man slow of speech and of a slow tongue? Rabbi Mohliver of Byalystok explained that if He had chosen instead an eloquent orator, such a man would have entered into a long argument with Pharaoh and his advisers about the sociological and psychological evils produced by slavery, about the value of emancipation, about the beauty of a monotheistic religion, and the value of the traditions which the Jews had from their ancestors, etc.

He would have become enamored of his own speeches. More and more dialogues would have been initiated, like the endless and useless dialogues which different religions have with each other. The result for the Jews would have been nil.

Because Moses stuttered and could pronounce few words without difficulty, he went directly to the point and said to Pharaoh. "Let my people go." It is such men that God needs even today.

It is as though the whole Bible had been written by men who had difficulty in speaking. They chose monosyllables.

In John 3:16, the central verse of the Bible, there are twenty monosyllables in one sentence and only six words with more than a syllable. In John 3:17, there are twenty-one monosyllables and only one word with more syllables. I know no other book like this.

It is not a book of eloquence that is important, but one that brings us into the heart of truth.

*T*he Buddhists in Japan have a legend that four eternities ago a king by the name of Amida arrived at the perfection of a Buddha, but refused to enter into the well-deserved Nirvana until all living beings had also entered it. They believe that men who cannot arrive at Buddhahood because of their many sins and cares will arrive at it through the merits of this sacrifice, if they repeat the sacred formula, *"Namu Amida Buddha Butsu"* (I trust fully in Amida Buddha).

God who inspired in many nations aspirations expressed in such legends, has made the hope of sinners a reality in Jesus. The very name Jesus (in Hebrew, *Jeshua*) means "salvation." The Bible assures us repeatedly that whoever calls on His name will be saved. God knows that we are born in sin and conceived in iniquity, that we cannot save ourselves by our endeavors. The sacrifice that Christ accomplished on Golgotha saves sinners, if only they call upon Him, because the calling of their heart is inspired by His love. Don't expect an answer when you call Him. Your call is already His answer.

A concert doesn't really involve two different objects—a pianist and a piano—but rather one unique event, the pianist at the piano. So in the act of faith there are not two parties—the sinner who appeals and the Lord who pities. His pity made you appeal. It is the sign of your acceptance. Believe this and you will live.

Pray also for the Buddhists that they may know the only name in which there is salvation.

> *"Be merciful, just as your Father also is merciful."*
> LUKE 6:36

A Japanese Christian, Endo Shisaku, tells about a missionary, Rodrigo, during the great persecution in the eighteenth century. When arrested, he endured tortures stoically and did not deny his faith. Inwardly, though, he was disturbed by the fact that God kept silent, that He did not answer his prayers. He begged Jesus at least to diminish his pain, but received no answer.

One day he faced the great test. He had the alternative either of seeing dozens of Christians killed before his eyes, or of winning their freedom. They would not even have to recant but he had to give up his faith publicly by treading on an image of Jesus. Out of love toward his brethren, he chose the latter. The moment he did it, he heard for the first time Jesus speaking to him, encouraging him to save the lives of his brethren. It is the character of Jesus willingly to be wounded in all ages so that others may escape. When Pilate offered to release either Jesus or Barabbas, Jesus wished rather Barabbas' release. Would He not wish to have His image trodden under the feet of a pastor so that innocent believers should not die?

Secretly, Rodrigo remained a Christian and brought to salvation even the one who had betrayed him.

The biblical solution is simple. It is to endure everything and never to deny the Lord. On the other hand, life has its complications, in which it is not easy to make the right choice.

Let us remember lovingly in prayer the leaders of the official churches in the Communist countries, commonly referred to as traitors because of their cooperation with the atheist governments. Many of them did it with the thought of saving the churches and their flocks. God understands and is rich in mercy. Let us be the same.

DECEMBER 13

*"Being like-minded, having the same love,
being of one accord, of one mind."*
PHILIPPIANS 2:2

*T*he Greek word for peace, *eirene*, means etymologically, "to speak again with each other." Men don't come to an understanding because they never talk. They only make noises when they are together, believing that this is discussion. They change the expressions on their faces and think they understand each other. We are strangers even within our families and among friends. We live together for decades without the normal receiving and giving of aims and ideas. We make use of one another, each for his own purpose. We don't love and are not beloved. We are alone. Men don't know the way of peace.

It consists in passing from making noises with words to "realizing." I have translated thus the real sense of the Hebrew word *ledaber* as to speak. It has as its root *davar*, which means not only "word," but also "thing, reality, cause." A Hebrew is meant not only to speak in words, but also to communicate reality in words. For "knowing," the Hebrews used the same word as for sexual intercourse. In Greek, too, *gnosis* has both senses. You know only through intimate union, through a loving embrace in which the two become one. You communicate then not only in words, but also in the warmth of the fellowship of burning hearts. There is no possibility of quarreling in that moment.

The bride in the Song of Solomon prays, "Let him kiss me with the kisses of his mouth" (1:2). No one can quarrel while his mouth is covered with kisses.

Seek real encounters with your brother, sister, and fellow man. Let it not be only an exchange of words, but a real melting together. Then we will have fulfilled the commandment, "Love one another as I have loved you" (John 15:12). Jesus not only told us words. He, the Son of God, became man.

"He might fill all things."
EPHESIANS 4:10

*A*rmelle Nicolas was an illiterate peasant woman who lived in the seventeenth century in France. She said, "God has sent me into the world with the sole purpose of loving Him. By His grace, I loved Him so much, that I cannot love Him anymore in the manner of mortals. It is time that I go to Him, that I may love Him in the manner of the saints in heaven."

She came to this high level of love through practicing the continuous presence of our Lord.

She took every piece of food that others despised, rejoicing that she could leave the good things to others. When she prepared food for her mistress, she thought about Jesus as food for her soul. If she saw a dog following its master faithfully, she decided to do the same. When she saw the quiet lambs in the pasture, who meekly allowed themselves to be shorn and slaughtered, she remembered that Jesus was the Lamb of God who had had the same attitude. When she saw the hen gathering her chickens under her wings, she remembered that she was compared with one of them and that Jesus wished her to be under His shelter. When she was enchanted by beautiful flowers, she remembered the words by which the Lord described Himself: "I am the rose of Sharon, and the lily of the valleys" (Song of Solomon 2:1). The fish swimming in the sea taught her to swim in the ocean of His love.

All things were for her allegories of the heavenly realities. So she became an advanced saint.

"Do not be overly righteous."
ECCLESIASTES 7:16

*P*eter wept a few tears about his denial of Jesus. When he met the resurrected Lord he did not even apologize. Judas's remorse was of an entirely different kind. He confessed to the priests that he had sold innocent blood. Peter had not gone back to the servant girl, before whom he had denied Jesus, to put things straight. Judas gave back the money he had received for betrayal. How few are those who make such restitution.

Contrary to all human logic, Peter received grace and became a prince among the apostles. Judas, after having done things much greater than to weep a little bit, remained without grace and committed suicide.

This is always the fate of those who are righteous over much, who overdo in repentance, who accumulate works of penitence instead of simply relying on the sacrifice of Christ, not only for forgiveness of sins, but also for repairing its effects.

In the Book of Leviticus the Hebrew word used for sins among fellow men is *asham*, but the restitution that a thief had to make to the owner is also called *asham*. Jesus is called *asham* in the great prophecy of Isaiah 53. He is not only the sacrifice for our sins, but also the One who makes restitution. He can give pearls for every tear we have caused someone to weep; He can give new life to those whom we have murdered; He can give heavenly riches to those from whom we stole earthly treasures. Do not dig into your past too much—not even in order to repair it—if you cannot do it with an easy and confident heart. Do not make the way of holiness too difficult for yourself.

Judas proceeded like this and failed. Peter did not muse too long over his own sins and won. He shed tears of repentance, met the resurrected Lord, and saw that he had remained Jesus' friend, so the sin of the past was done with. It did not burden him anymore.

*"It would have been good for that man if
he had not been born."*
MATTHEW 26:24

Would it have been better for me not to have been born? Suppose that the soul is preexistent, to have been in some other sphere before being born on earth. Suppose that I could have known beforehand all the sins that I would commit in life, and all the chain of sufferings and sorrows they would provoke. Suppose that I had known all of the sorrows that have been my lot in life and the possibility of an eternity in hell. If I had had the choice, I would have chosen not to be born. Jesus said about Judas, "it would have been better for that man if he had not been born." Did Judas have a choice?

We belong to a Master whose power is absolute. He does not take advice from anyone. We were born without having been consulted. We will live a span of life whose length is not decided by us. It is not decided by us even when we will have a mood that will lead one of us to suicide. We will be judged whether we like it or not. Instead of a useless quarrel with this Master, let us prepare ourselves to meet our God.

There is no other preparation for eternity than to obtain eternal life now through belief in the blood of Christ. In the presence of Judas Jesus said, "This is My blood shed for you." Judas could have had part, too, in the unbreakable covenant in this blood. Jesus is not ashamed to call sinners His brethren. He would not have been ashamed to call Judas a brother either. He had called him friend.

Only when you think about this life as a prelude to life eternal in paradise, does being born become the right choice. I have a choice after all. I can be born again. I say, "Yes," to this. I enter this time into life concurring willingly with God's decision that I should be His elect.

DECEMBER 17

"It pleased the LORD to bruise Him."
ISAIAH 53:10

*T*herese of Lisieux had her place at evening prayers just in the front of a sister who had a nervous affliction. She always made a little curious noise, rather like one would make by rubbing two shells together. This tiny noise got Therese down, but she never chided the offender, not even with a look. Something inside her told her that the right thing to do was to put up with it for the love of God and spare the sister any embarrassment. Only she could not ignore the disturbing noise. Perspiration poured down her in the attempt to pray notwithstanding, but it was useless.

Then Therese hit on the idea of liking this exasperating noise. Instead of trying vainly not to hear it, she devoted herself to listening hard, as if the sound were that of delightful music and her prayer consisted of offering the music to the Lord.

It is wrong to escape anxieties and troubles through vain hopes or through quarreling with those who disturb you. Do not only bear sorrows, but positively love them.

In giving to Abraham the order to sacrifice his son, God gave him the additional happiness of specifying an altar three days' journey away, so that he might enjoy for a long time the idea of giving his most beloved for his Master. He could have placed the wood for the fire on a donkey, but Isaac preferred to carry the wood up the hill himself. Great sacrifices should be borne, not with patience, but with delight.

The heavenly Father Himself, because it was necessary that His Son should die on the cross for the sins of the world, did not sacrifice Him grudgingly: "It pleased the LORD to bruise Him." Adopt this attitude toward whatever disturbs you in life and you will be happy.

DECEMBER 18

*"Therefore whoever confesses Me before men, him I will
also confess before My Father who is in heaven."*
MATTHEW 10:32

*I*n Cambodia a prayer meeting took place in a church. Communist soldiers surrounded it. Some entered, took an image of Jesus from the wall, put it on the threshold and ordered, "Everyone who walks out spits on the image and denies Jesus. If not, he is shot."

What would you have done? Some made their excuses. One had a beloved fiancée, whom he had to marry soon. Another one had an old father to care for. A third one had small children at home. They knew Jesus to be forgiving and full of understanding. He knows that they have acted under duress. So they spat, and saved their lives.

The turn of a sixteen-year-old girl came. She made no excuse. Having guns pointed toward her, and having the alternative of spitting on the image or dying, she knelt, kissed the image, and wiped the spittle from its face. She had loved Jesus. She fell dead over the image of her Bridegroom.

Souls like this girl's are the smile of mankind. Jesus calls Himself "the rose of Sharon, and the lily of the valleys" (Song of Solomon 2:1). He expects His souls to have a heart as pure as the lily. He values such purity.

Flocks of healthy and beautiful sheep come from breeding the right type of lambs. Jesus told Peter, "Feed My lambs." Let us teach our youth such beautiful examples of love even unto death.

"Without shedding of blood there is no remission."
HEBREWS 9:22

*T*he religious Jews face a dilemma. The law of Moses states that sins can be remitted only through the atoning blood of innocent victims. On the other hand, the temple being destroyed, there are no sacrifices anymore in the Jewish religion. The rabbis teach that the daily reading of a portion from Leviticus about the animal sacrifices is accepted by God as if the sacrifices themselves had been brought.

A Christian entered a Jewish shop and told the owner that he should accept Jesus, because the Jews have no more sacrifices. The Jew replied, "You are misinformed. Our reading of the Bible is accepted by God, counting as much as the blood of rams and lambs in times of old."

The Christian said, "All right. Instead of arguing religion with you, I had better buy a few things." He chose a dozen shirts, some shoes, and ties, among other things. Then he asked for an invoice. This was given. He began to read, "So many shirts cost so much, the ties and the shoes so much, the total some $200." He said farewell and left the shop.

The Jew ran after him crying, "Sir, you have forgotten to pay!"

The Christian answered, "Did I not read the invoice?"

"Yes, but you did not pay the money."

To which the Christian said, "Well, I followed the advice of your rabbis that reading the bill is as good as paying."

It is not only Jews who are mistaken in this regard. There are also Christians who believe that saying the Lord's Prayer can take the place of really having God as Father; and calling Jesus a Savior means as much as really being saved by Him.

Look for the reality. Don't be content with formulas.

[Jesus said,] "Love your enemies."
MATTHEW 5:44

*F*ive centuries before Jesus, Sophocles said in *Antigone*, "I am here not for hating, but for loving." The Old Testament, too, taught love toward one's neighbor. Jesus brought love to its greatest height by demonstrating that it should also embrace the enemy.

Ilse Blumenthal-Weiss, a Jew whose husband was gassed and whose son was killed, was in a concentration camp, in which she composed a poem that says, "I cannot hate. They beat me. They trample me under their feet. I cannot hate. They throw stones at me. I cannot hate. I can only weep bitterly."

A high human achievement—to restrain from sentiments of hatred. God gives more: the power to love the enemy.

Love toward the enemy does not mean avoiding the confrontation with evil. Jesus fought against the merchants in the temple and against the Pharisees. Jesus does not mean for us to flatter the enemy, to embrace him. He did not fall around Caiaphas's neck, neither did He offer Himself as his partner in evil deeds.

Love toward the enemy means to understand him better than he understands himself. His hatred blinds him. You can look with unbiased mind upon his position, too. To love the enemy means that, in defending yourself, you will not be obliged to use his methods. To love him means, like Jesus, to take upon yourself his guilt; to consider his sin as being yours and to atone for it by acts of goodness toward him and his victims.

Having the example of Christ before our eyes, we can do this through the power of His Spirit.

"We also glory in tribulations."
ROMANS 5:3

*T*herese of Lisieux was helping with the washing in the convent. A sister opposite her splashed dirty water in her face every time she lifted up a piece of wet clothing from the ledge.

Therese's first instinct was to step back and wipe her face, as a suggestion to her sister that she did wrong. All at once the thought occurred to her, "You're a fool not to take what comes free." So she decided rather to hide her annoyance. She cultivated instead a liking for dirty water. In the end she became so fond of it that she came back at other times for this happy "dip."

Isaiah had predicted the most cruel sufferings for Jesus. It would have seemed normal for Jesus to shun the reading and pondering of this book. On the contrary, it was His favorite. Isaiah is the only author whom Jesus praises—"Well did Isaiah prophesy about you" (Matthew 15:7). Welcome the evils of which you are apprehensive; look difficulties straight in the face. They will not haunt you anymore.

A Soviet Christian was asked, "How could you bear tortures?" He answered, "Since I was converted, I daydreamed of being tortured, knowing that this would be my fate, as another man would have erotic imaginations. When I passed through them, they could not break me anymore."

Whoever embraces the feet of Jesus crucified, embraces also the beam of the cross. Whoever wishes to follow Him has to daily take His cross. Make the cross your joyful expectation. It will become a source of blessing.

Abraham, just when he showed himself ready to make the highest sacrifice, received the blessing from God that in his seed all the nations would be blessed and that his offspring would be like the stars of heaven and the sand of the sea (Genesis 22:17).

DECEMBER 22

"Death spread to all men."
ROMANS 5:12

*I*n St. Lawrence's church in Nuremberg there is a statue called "The woman of the world." She is shown as having a beautiful face and ornamented with jewelry. This is how she looks from one side. From the other side, you see something entirely different: a skeleton on which serpents creep.

St. Francis de Sales advised a Christian, who was a lady at the royal court of France and was obliged to attend parties dressed in beautiful dresses, to escape vanity through spending a few moments before the mirror and imagining how she would look as a skeleton with only a skull instead of a head.

These might not be pleasant thoughts, but nothing is surer than our death. The mortuary is the surest business. It is foolish to try to flee the thought of death.

Jesus knew that He would die, but He could defy death. He said, "Destroy this temple, and in three days I will raise it up" (John 2:19). Paul could also defy death: "If our earthly house, this tent, is destroyed, we have a building from God" (2 Corinthians 5:1).

To receive life eternal is easy. Jesus said in John 5:24, "Most assuredly, I say to you, he who hears My word and believes in Him who sent Me has everlasting life."

Believe in the Lord Jesus now and you will know for sure that death is not your end. It will be the entrance into a glorious life.

$\mathcal{E}$tymologically, compassion means to suffer with our fellow man. Rich men and men in high position, as well as middle-class men, must learn to see how the world looks from below. They feast at Christmas but have not caught its meaning.

Jesus came to earth to experience what it is like when heaven disappoints: when one is hungry and it does not rain manna; when one's only shelter is a stable though he is not an ox; when one is crucified and people under the cross are gambling; when one cries to God and gets no response.

Could men of the middle and upper classes not try the same experience? Why should they not go hungry for a few weeks, as their brethren do without any guilt in Mali or Bangladesh?

Jesus says that a thief can enter heaven, but according to some a black person or a badly dressed man cannot enter a rich man's garden. The thief can play with the angels, but the poor child cannot play with the child of the rich. The dog can lie on the sofa with his mistress, but the servant who has worked the whole day to tidy the garden and the maid with the swollen feet who stood the whole day in the kitchen are not invited to sit down.

I know there are many arguments against such an excessively mild behavior with the poor. It might do them harm. The question is not what arguments the rich and the middle classes have, but how these things look from below, for the sixty percent of mankind who are starving or at least badly fed.

Jesus teaches us not to give to poor men kept at the right distance, but to call the poor, the maimed, the lame, the blind, the most disgusting persons into our homes when we have a feast (Luke 14:13). He called you, a wretched sinner, to come to heaven.

DECEMBER 24

"I labor in birth again until Christ is formed in you."
GALATIANS 4:19

*J*esus surely was not born on December 25. The cold is very piercing during the nights in December near Jerusalem. It was not the custom of the Jewish shepherds to watch their flocks in the fields so late.

The Bible does not tell us the date when Jesus became man. The 25th of December was a holiday and an occasion of a carnival in the Roman Empire in honor of the sun. The Christians took advantage of this occasion, when the persecuting authorities had greater difficulty detecting them, to celebrate the birth of Jesus— but not only His physical birth that had happened at a certain date in history. They also celebrated the daily miracle of Jesus' birth in the souls of those who had accepted Him as Savior.

Jesus was born in a stable and put in a manger. It was wrong that the shepherds, who each had at least a hut, and the wise men, who might have had comfortable houses, allowed the newborn King to remain in a manger on the hay. They should have taken him into their homes. Jesus' place is not in a manger. The less so is it on a cross. He is not happy to stay in heaven either. The place He longs for is in our hearts. That is where He wants to live.

The moment He is born there and I become for Him a Mary— that is the real Christmas. He said that He wished to have a mother for Himself. "Whoever does the will of My Father in heaven is My...mother" (Matthew 12:50).

Celebrate Christmas in this sense.

DECEMBER 25

*I*n the Hebrew original, this prophecy about the coming of the Savior continues as follows: "Unto us a Son is given; and the government shall be upon His shoulder: and His name shall be called Wonderful, Counselor, heroic God (*El Ghibor*) . . ."

It was surely a heroic decision to leave heaven and the world of angels, having decided for Himself to be born in a stable, to be in danger of death from early childhood, to live an entire life of sorrow that would end in crucifixion, for the salvation of mankind who would show no gratitude for this sacrifice. Our Lord knew that ultimately good would triumph because of this sacrifice, so He made it.

Christmas is the memorial of the birth of a heroic God.

The main feature of His followers is heroism. Shallowness and lukewarmness do not belong to Christianity.

A renowned preacher, whose father had been a drunkard and his mother a pious woman, was taught by the latter from early childhood a particular spiritual exercise. He would put on the floor a wine glass, playing cards, dice, pornographic magazines, some money, his own picture, and would trample on it all, shouting, "No! No!" And again, "No! No!" Then he would say to himself, "I belong to a heroic God, and I will always say 'No!' to any temptation to sin."

Let us commemorate the Nativity of a divine hero, forsaking the comfortable ways and making the decision that all heroes in history have made: "To win or to perish, but never to yield."

DECEMBER 26

"If anyone desires to come after Me, let him deny himself."
MATTHEW 16:24

A boy of twelve was asked what he wished to become. He answered, "A missionary in Africa."

"Why?"

"Because then I will be able to hunt lions."

Many of us have the same mentality. We wish to become good Christians. Why? In order to have a better piece of heaven.

The right motive for being a good Christian is to be able to bear a heavier beam of the cross of Christ. The man who is born again wishes to be a better Christian so that in the future, when he passes through sorrows, his first question should not be, "How can I escape?" but, "How can I be useful to the kingdom of God in this new situation?"

We have no sufferings accidentally. They are all foreordained by a loving God. The ship with the apostles passed through a tempest (Matthew 8:23–27). The Lord wished to teach them how to cope with a storm. They would have to face many.

He will awake in time if you are in danger of perishing. Until then, suffer silently and work and fight valiantly. It is for this that you were called to be a Christian, not only to enjoy heaven.

Missionaries are not sent to Africa for the thrill of lion hunting.

"You shall be witnesses to Me...to the end of the earth."
ACTS 1:8

*P*ope Gregory, the Great, received this honored title, even though he was a small man, because of one persistent merit. It was he who, in 596, began the mission among the Anglo-Saxons.

The Christianized Anglo-Saxons became a blessing to the whole world. Boniface, an Englishman, Christianized the Germans. Willibrord, also English, converted the Flemish people; Patrick won the Irish to Christ. The creation of the British Empire gave the Anglo-Saxons the possibility of spreading Christianity to Asia, Africa, and Australia.

Anglo-Saxons brought the evangelical faith to the United States. Even now, 60 percent of all missionaries and 80 percent of all mission finances come from the United States.

To keep Christianity alive in the Anglo-Saxon world is of utter strategic importance. Missionaries must go to the farthest shores, but let us not forget that Christianity is decaying in the Anglo-Saxon world. Only 3 percent of the population of the British Isles goes to church. In America seven out of ten teenagers never cross the threshold of church. Seventy percent of the population is unchurched.

Let us pray for the churches in the Anglo-Saxon world.

"'When I bow down in the temple of Rimmon, may the
LORD please pardon your servant in this thing.' Then
[Elisha] said to him, 'Go in peace.'"
2 KINGS 5:18,19

A Jewish legend says that Moses overheard a shepherd boy praying, "God, if You would appear to me, I would give You wool, milk, and meat for free. If You have some sheep, I would lead them to pasture, without asking for any pay. I would comb Your hair, wash Your robe, and kiss Your hand."

Moses was shocked and shouted to the boy to stop it because the prayer was blasphemous.

Then God appeared to Moses and admonished him for what he had done. God told Moses that he had found pleasure in this naive prayer of the boy, more than in the sophisticated prayers of the know-it-alls.

Be wise in handling the false and primitive religious views of others. For someone who only goes to church, never witnessing for Christ to others, the church-going might be the Christianity of a shy person. A wrong belief in one of the many cults must not be interpreted as wickedness. It can be a transit from worldliness to the knowledge of God. The person gropes in darkness, but he might grope for the right thing. Give him some advice delicately, but do not destroy the little light he has.

As a principle, be stingy in giving advice in religious matters. Ask yourself earnestly how much advice you are ready to take. This should be the dosage of advice imparted by you to others.

"I pleaded with the Lord three times that [the messenger of Satan] might depart from me. And He said to me, 'My grace is sufficient for you.'"

2 CORINTHIANS 12:8,9

*T*wo days remain until the end of the year. We remember the many blessings we received this year, but also the fact that so many desires of the heart and prayers have remained unanswered.

A saint was renowned for having his prayers on behalf of others answered. He was asked, "If this is the case, why then don't you pray that your infirmity should be removed?" He was blind.

He answered, "Submission to the will of God is preferable to the satisfaction of my personal pleasure at being able to see."

Be thankful for answered prayer and accept the will of God for the cases in which you have been refused. He knows best what you need.

Unanswered prayers may have been prayers uttered in ignorance, not knowing the harm that their fulfillment would occasion. A time might come when you will thank God that they have not been fulfilled.

Monica was sad that her prayer for her son, Augustine, was not answered. She had prayed that he would remain with her. He led a wicked life, inclined toward all kinds of occult teachings, and forsook his mother, though she had prayed to the contrary.

Augustine went to Milan, where he met Bishop Ambrose. This led to his conversion. He later became one of the greatest teachers the Christian church has ever had.

"He became poor, that you through His
poverty might become rich."
2 CORINTHIANS 8:9

Recapitulating what we have done this year, we remember our many sins. They have many causes. One of them might be that we do not have the right spiritual teacher.

Beware of religious teachers who have a great following. It is possible they are frauds. If they would tell the full truth, their audience would diminish.

Jesus had thousands around Him when He multiplied bread or healed. His teachings, however, were not accepted by the crowd.

Would the crowd flock to your teacher? Would you follow him if he practiced and taught poverty according to the word of the Master, "Blessed are you poor" (Luke 6:20)?

A saint was offered some money. He refused with the words, "I have the money necessary for today's good."

"The money you have will not last long," he was told. "Take and you will have for the following days."

He replied, "Guarantee me that I will live longer than my few coins will suffice me, and I will accept your money."

Seek the teacher who will tell you not to worry about the many things you lack, but to be content with the few things you have. Jesus, though He was rich, for your sakes became poor (2 Corinthians 8:9).

The verb "to have" does not exist in Hebrew. Only God is the Possessor of all things. You can possess the Possessor of all things. Seek the teacher who will teach you not only how to be content, but how to be jubilant about having God.

DECEMBER 31

"Sufficient for the day is its own troubles."
MATTHEW 6:34

*T*he year has passed. Let all the troubles, sins, and quarrels of the past year pass with it. For our sins there is forgiveness in the blood of Christ. Next year will bring its own troubles. No need to bring into it the trouble of the year that is no more. The quarrels have lost their importance.

A couple, prompted by love, had married. They sat at the table and hugged each other. Suddenly she became afraid. "Did you see?" she exclaimed. "A mouse ran by and entered into the hole there to the right."

He calmed her. "It can do nothing to you. I saw it. A little thing. It entered into the hole to the left."

She insisted that it was the right hole. He used his authority as a husband to impress upon her that he was correct; it must have been in the other hole. They divorced because of this question.

After seven years of separation, friends succeeded in making peace between them. They remarried and sat in the same room at the table. She said, "How stupid we have been to quarrel about a mouse that entered into that hole to the right."

He shouted, "You're starting again?" They divorced the second time. It was forever. Are all our quarrels really less ridiculous than this?

Now another year has gone by. With a year we have come nearer to our appointment with God. What will all our worries and our conflicts that we considered so important count for on the day of His judgment?

Let us examine earnestly what has been amiss during the past year, and start the new year with confidence. We will have in the new year: God, the Savior, the Spirit, the protecting angel. We can be confident.

DAILY SCRIPTURE LIST

Genesis 1:1	*January 13*
Genesis 1:2	*June 21*
Genesis 1:28	*July 31*
Genesis 2:3	*July 29*
Genesis 2:7	*December 1*
Genesis 2:9	*November 10*
Genesis 2:15	*January 24*
Genesis 3:5	*February 6*
Genesis 3:9	*February 9*
Genesis 5:22	*December 9*
Genesis 6:2	*January 7*
Genesis 12:1	*January 30*
Genesis 16:2	*October 16*
Genesis 17:1	*November 12*
Genesis 21:15,19	*February 23*
Genesis 22:2	*March 15*
Genesis 41:29	*May 30*
Exodus 4:10	*April 5, December 10*
Exodus 20:2	*May 11*
Exodus 20:4	*August 18*
Exodus 20:5	*April 24*
Exodus 20:8	*April 21*
Exodus 20:13	*September 11*
Numbers 19:14	*June 30*
Numbers 22:28	*January 5*
Numbers 31:28	*April 23*
Deuteronomy 5:17	*May 13*
Deuteronomy 28:7	*January 15*

Ezekiel 33:8	*June 17*
Ezekiel 34:25	*July 28*
Daniel 5:15	*June 1*
Daniel 10:21	*October 31*
Daniel 11:35	*August 8, November 2*
Joel 2:1,2	*April 18*
Jonah 4:6	*May 16*
Habakkuk 2:4	*August 2*
Habakkuk 2:20	*January 3, August 12*
Zechariah 4:6	*April 17*
Malachi 2:5	*September 12*
Matthew 1:2	*August 19*
Matthew 1:20	*May 5*
Matthew 3:13	*June 15*
Matthew 3:15	*June 20, June 23*
Matthew 3:16	*June 24*
Matthew 5:3	*February 11*
Matthew 5:5	*July 30*
Matthew 5:9	*November 9*
Matthew 5:17	*November 22*
Matthew 5:44	*March 17, December 20*
Matthew 5:47	*August 25*
Matthew 6:6	*June 7*
Matthew 6:9	*February 14*
Matthew 6:12	*March 10*
Matthew 6:14	*January 27*
Matthew 6:24	*June 19*
Matthew 6:26,28	*February 15*
Matthew 6:34	*January 28, December 31*
Matthew 7:1	*March 11*
Matthew 7:7	*July 2*
Matthew 8:4	*July 9*
Matthew 8:23	*November 6*
Matthew 10:16	*July 20*
Matthew 10:29	*February 7*

Matthew 10:32	*December 18*
Matthew 10:41	*July 7*
Matthew 11:1	*November 4*
Matthew 13:4	*January 8*
Matthew 13:30	*February 27*
Matthew 14:30	*January 18*
Matthew 16:21	*October 27*
Matthew 16:24	*December 26*
Matthew 16:26	*August 10*
Matthew 17:20	*March 16*
Matthew 19:6	*April 12*
Matthew 19:14	*October 2, November 30*
Matthew 19:21	*August 3*
Matthew 19:26	*July 3*
Matthew 20:28	*March 27*
Matthew 21:18	*July 4*
Matthew 21:22	*September 17*
Matthew 22:37	*November 5*
Matthew 22:39	*January 31*
Matthew 23:13	*October 24*
Matthew 24:9	*July 21*
Matthew 24:10	*November 11*
Matthew 24:13	*September 26*
Matthew 25:6	*May 19*
Matthew 25:10	*November 19*
Matthew 25:34,41	*March 24*
Matthew 26:22	*February 18*
Matthew 26:24	*December 16*
Matthew 26:26	*October 11*
Matthew 26:30	*October 10*
Matthew 26:41	*March 1*
Matthew 27:18	*September 20*
Matthew 27:32	*March 7*
Matthew 27:46	*August 26*
Matthew 27:49	*May 23*

Matthew 28:17	*May 27*
Matthew 28:19	*February 3*
Mark 1:10	*September 1*
Mark 2:25,26	*March 22*
Mark 3:28	*March 5*
Mark 6:6	*July 27*
Mark 8:1,8	*March 6*
Mark 11:23	*June 8*
Mark 12:31	*April 11*
Mark 16:15	*June 5*
Luke 1:28	*January 4*
Luke 1:38	*August 13*
Luke 1:48	*March 9*
Luke 1:52	*July 26*
Luke 3:11	*May 1*
Luke 5:5	*June 9*
Luke 6:27	*June 6*
Luke 6:30	*July 5*
Luke 6:35	*May 24, October 14*
Luke 6:36	*December 12*
Luke 6:37	*January 11*
Luke 7:6	*October 7*
Luke 9:23	*August 20, November 18*
Luke 9:31	*August 14*
Luke 10:42	*June 12*
Luke 11:1	*June 11, November 24*
Luke 11:2	*November 8*
Luke 12:20	*October 12*
Luke 12:33	*November 29*
Luke 14:10	*August 11*
Luke 15:2	*August 21*
Luke 15:11	*June 3*
Luke 15:20	*September 28*
Luke 16:10	*April 4*
Luke 16:20	*March 25*

1 Corinthians 12:4	*August 24*
1 Corinthians 13:4,5	*May 22*
1 Corinthians 13:7	*February 1*
1 Corinthians 13:13	*April 15*
1 Corinthians 15:55	*April 22, October 26*
2 Corinthians 3:3	*May 7*
2 Corinthians 3:6	*July 20*
2 Corinthians 3:18	*July 11*
2 Corinthians 5:16	*June 29*
2 Corinthians 5:17	*November 7*
2 Corinthians 6:17	*February 28*
2 Corinthians 8:9	*December 30*
2 Corinthians 9:7	*November 21*
2 Corinthians 12:8,9	*December 29*
Galatians 1:2	*June 2*
Galatians 1:15,16	*November 27*
Galatians 2:5	*April 9*
Galatians 2:20	*April 14, October 28*
Galatians 3:8	*April 29*
Galatians 4:7	*June 4*
Galatians 4:19	*December 24*
Galatians 5:17	*October 29*
Galatians 5:19	*December 3*
Galatians 5:22,23	*February 2, April 26*
Galatians 6:1	*September 7*
Galatians 6:5	*June 16*
Ephesians 3:17	*February 29*
Ephesians 4:10	*December 14*
Ephesians 4:14	*May 3*
Ephesians 4:24	*May 15*
Ephesians 4:26	*April 27*
Ephesians 4:31	*October 8*
Ephesians 5:2	*October 22*
Ephesians 5:18	*February 10, April 8*
Ephesians 5:30	*December 4*

Ephesians 6:10	*May 28*
Philippians 2:2	*December 13*
Philippians 2:3	*June 28*
Philippians 2:7	*January 12, December 23*
Philippians 2:8	*August 27*
Philippians 2:9	*April 2*
Philippians 2:10	*September 25*
Philippians 2:14	*April 16*
Philippians 3:8	*December 5*
Philippians 3:13	*September 3*
Philippians 3:14	*September 21*
Philippians 4:8	*May 26*
Colossians 3:1	*October 1*
Colossians 3:4	*June 10*
1 Thessalonians 2:6	*October 13*
1 Thessalonians 5:2	*July 19*
2 Thessalonians 3:8	*May 17*
1 Timothy 1:17	*May 9*
1 Timothy 2:1,2	*April 7*
1 Timothy 3:3	*April 1*
1 Timothy 6:5	*February 26*
1 Timothy 6:10	*September 4*
1 Timothy 6:20	*October 18, October 21*
2 Timothy 2:24	*January 25*
2 Timothy 3:14	*September 24*
2 Timothy 3:16	*April 19*
Titus 2:7	*July 18*
Hebrews 1:1	*December 11*
Hebrews 2:15	*September 19*
Hebrews 4:3	*May 12*
Hebrews 9:22	*December 19*
Hebrews 9:27	*February 24*
Hebrews 10:26	*January 6*
Hebrews 11:13	*July 13*
Hebrews 11:34	*March 3*

*T*he Voice of the Martyrs has many books, videos, brochures, and other products to help you learn more about the persecuted church. In the U.S., to request a resource catalog, order materials, or receive our free monthly newsletter, call (800) 747-0085 or write to:

> The Voice of the Martyrs, Inc.
> P.O. Box 443
> Bartlesville, OK 74005-0443
> Website: www.persecution.com

If you are in Canada, the United Kingdom, Australia, New Zealand, or South Africa, contact:

> The Voice of the Martyrs
> P.O. Box 117
> Port Credit
> Mississauga, Ontario L5G 4L5
> Canada

> Release International
> P.O. Box 54
> Orpington BR5 9RT
> United Kingdom

> Voice of the Martyrs
> P.O. Box 250
> Lawson NSW 2783
> Australia

> Voice of the Martyrs
> P.O. Box 5482
> Papanui, Christchurch 8542
> New Zealand

> Christian Mission International
> P.O. Box 7157
> 1417 Primrose Hill
> South Africa

ABOUT THE AUTHOR

 PASTOR RICHARD WURMBRAND (1909–2001) was an evangelical minister who endured fourteen years of Communist imprisonment and torture in his homeland of Romania. Few names are better known in Romania, where he is one of the most widely recognized Christian leaders, authors, and educators.

In 1945, when the Communists seized Romania and attempted to control the churches for their purposes, Richard Wurmbrand immediately began an effective, vigorous "underground" ministry to his enslaved people as well as the invading Russian soldiers. He was arrested in 1948, along with his wife, Sabina. His wife was a slave-laborer for three years on the Danube Canal. Richard Wurmbrand spent three years in solitary confinement, seeing no one but his Communist torturers. He was then transferred to a group cell, where the torture continued for five more years.

Due to his international stature as a Christian leader, diplomats of foreign embassies asked the Communist government about his safety and were informed that he had fled Romania. Secret police, posing as released fellow-prisoners, told his wife of attending his burial in the prison cemetery. His family in Romania and his friends abroad were told to forget him because he was dead.

After eight-and-a-half years in prison, he was released and immediately resumed his work with the Underground Church. A couple of years later, in 1959, he was re-arrested and sentenced to twenty-five years in prison.

Pastor Wurmbrand was released in a general amnesty in 1964, and again continued his underground ministry. Realizing the great danger of a third imprisonment, Christians in Norway negotiated with the Communist authorities for his release from Romania. The Communist government had begun "selling" their political prisoners. The "going price" for a prisoner was $1,900; the price for Wurmbrand was $10,000.

In May 1966, he testified before the U.S. Senate's Internal Security Subcommittee and stripped to the waist to show the scars of eighteen deep torture wounds covering his torso. His story was carried across the world in newspapers throughout the U.S., Europe, and Asia. Wurmbrand was warned in September 1966 that the Communist regime of Romania planned to assassinate him; yet he was not silent in the face of this death threat.

Founder of the Christian mission The Voice of the Martyrs, he and his wife traveled throughout the world establishing a network of over thirty offices that provide relief to the families of imprisoned Christians in Islamic nations, Communist Vietnam, China, and other countries where Christians are persecuted for their faith. His message has been, "Hate the evil systems, but love your persecutors. Love their souls, and try to win them for Christ."

Pastor Wurmbrand authored numerous books, which have been translated into over sixty languages throughout the world. Christian leaders have called him the "Voice of the Underground Church" and "the Iron Curtain Paul."